Post-Foundational Political Thought

Taking on the Political

Series Editors: Benjamin Arditi and Jeremy Valentine

International Advisory Editors:
Michael Dillon and Michael J. Shapiro

Post-Foundational Political Thought

Political Difference in Nancy, Lefort, Badiou and Laclau

Oliver Marchart

Edinburgh University Press

© Oliver Marchart, 2007

Edinburgh University Press Ltd
22 George Square, Edinburgh

Typeset in 11 on 13 Sabon by
Iolaire Typesetting, Newtonmore and
printed and bound in Great Britain by
Biddles Ltd, King's Lynn, Norfolk

A CIP record for this book is
available from the British Library

ISBN 978 0 7486 2497 3 (hardback)
ISBN 978 0 7486 2498 0 (paperback)

The right of Oliver Marchart to be
identified as author of this work
has been asserted in accordance with
the Copyright, Designs and Patents Act 1988.

Contents

Expanded Contents List

Introduction:
On the Absent Ground of the Social

> The controversy over the concept of the political is of a more serious nature than yet another family quarrel among paradigms; it is about the relevance or irrelevance of political philosophy to our times.
>
> Agnes Heller (1991: 336)

The following study on post-foundational political thought navigates around a curious difference, which has assumed some currency in recent continental and Anglo-American political thought: the difference between *politics* and *the political*, or, in French, between *la politique* and *le politique*, or again, in German, between *Politik* and *das Politische*. As is well known, a distinctive notion of the political was developed first in the German-speaking world, where it was Carl Schmitt who famously – infamously for some – sought to differentiate the political from other domains of the social, including the domain of politics in the narrow sense (see Chapter 2). In 2001, the notion of the 'political', as explicitly differentiated from 'politics', has even been institutionally canonized, with Pierre Rosanvallon taking up a prestigious chair for the 'modern and contemporary history of the political' at the Collège de France (see Rosanvallon 2003). In the German-speaking world, the two most important historical dictionaries take account of the difference between *Politik* and *das Politische* (Sellin 1978; Vollrath 1989), and in the English-speaking world a strong notion of the political as differentiated from the 'weak' notion of politics has become a sort of household concept for those quarters of Anglo-American political theory that are receptive to continental thought (Beardsworth 1996; Dillon 1996; Stavrakakis 1999; Arditi and Valentine 1999; Williams 2000).

Here the trade route first and foremost leads back to post-war France. It leads in particular to a constellation of theory which, for lack of a better name, could be described as 'Heideggerianism of the Left'.[1] In the present investigation this notion does not cover the group of theorists who were Heidegger's direct pupils, the 'first-generation' Heideggerians like Herbert Marcuse and Hannah Arendt, but rather those theorists in France who, with the help of Heidegger, tried to achieve two things: first, to go beyond scientism and its remnants in what was the most advanced theoretical paradigm of their time, structuralism; and second, based on an awareness of the dubious if not despicable political inclinations of Heidegger himself, to re-work and direct his thought into a more progressive direction. What evolved was a particular leftist version not only of 'post-structuralism' (a term that reduces the genealogy of left Heidegger-ianism to the scientific paradigm of structuralism) but of *post-foun-dationalism*, if by the latter we understand a constant interrogation of metaphysical figures of foundation – such as totality, universality, essence, and ground. Post-foundationalism, as will be shown in Chapter 1, must not be confused with *anti*-foundationalism or a vulgar and today somewhat out-dated 'anything goes' postmodern-ism, since a post-foundational approach does not attempt to erase completely such figures of the ground, but to weaken their ontological status.[2] The ontological weakening of ground does not lead to the assumption of the total absence of all grounds, but rather to the assumption of the impossibility of a *final* ground, which is something completely different as it implies an increased awareness of, on the one hand, contingency and, on the other, the political as the moment of partial and always, in the last instance, unsuccessful grounding.

One should not be surprised that in most 'family-members' of the post-foundational constellation, that is, in the otherwise rather diverse theories of the Heideggerian Left, one can find formulae or figures of contingency that appertain to what could be called the post-foundational tropology of groundlessness. In most cases we discover, for instance, a radicalized notion of the *event* as something one encounters and which cannot be subsumed under the logic of foundation: rather, *event* denotes the dislocating and disruptive moment in which foundations crumble. *Freedom* and *historicity* will now be 'founded' precisely on the premise of the absence of a final foundation. Such endless play between ground and abyss also sug-gests accepting the necessity of *decision* (premised upon ontological undecidability) and being aware of *division*, *discord*, and *antagonism*, as every decision – since it cannot be based on a stable ground, nor will it be taken in the solitary vacuum of complete groundlessness – will always be confronted with competing claims and forces. It should be obvious that these figures of contingency, which can be traced back conceptually to Heidegger's work, have thoroughly political implications, and it is one of the aims of the present investigation to bring to the fore these implications in order to allow for a 'grounding' of post-foundational thought *as political* (Chapter 7).

Yet in no way do I wish to deny that from different starting-points one can arrive at very similar conclusions. Pragmatism, for instance, can serve as a starting point for an anti-foundationalist stance, as proved by Richard Rorty's work (whose post-analytic philosophy nevertheless went through the experience of Heidegger and continental thought; see Rorty 1979, 1989). And just let us think of the perhaps more unlikely example of conservative scepticism and of a position like Michael Oakeshott's, which can easily be described as non-foundationalist and may help us to illustrate the difference between a post- or non-foundational stance on the one hand and a radical anti-foundationalist stance on the other. Oakeshott's famous dictum to the effect that in political activity 'men sail a boundless and bottomless sea: there is no harbour for shelter nor floor for anchorage, neither starting-place nor appointed destination' (1991: 60) is directed against attempts at grounding politics. For this purpose, it employs the whole arsenal of non-foundationalist *topoi*: the 'bottomless' abyss serves as figure for a ground which is absent and cannot be laid or fixed to any anchorage point beyond the bounds of the sea. Politics has to accept the fact that it is an open-ended process with neither a clear beginning nor a determined end or destination. As it is grounded *on nothing*, one has to come to terms with precisely the abyss which is its ground: 'that politics are *nur für die Schwindelfreie*, that should depress only those who have lost their nerve' (60). Yet Oakeshott, and this is the point not to be missed, is not an *anti*-foundationalist, since, while the sea is boundless and bottomless, it is still structured: it is not, in other words, a *tabula rasa* but the structured terrain on which we move and where we encounter chances as well as obstacles ('the sea is both friend and enemy', 60). Political activity – unfoundable as it is – does not take place in a vacuum, but is always enfolded in sedimented layers of traditions which, conversely, are ungrounded, flexible and changeable for their part. At no point do we encounter a solid anchorage for our activities, yet no voluntarism follows from this, as we never sail on a sea without waves.

Heideggerians of the Left may arrive at different conclusions, since from their perspective traditions are mainly power-ridden structures by which many-faceted forms of exclusion and subordination are perpetuated. We can conclude that from the absence of ground no necessary political consequence follows (for otherwise it would in fact be feasible to ground a particular political worldview – something which was excluded *ex hypothesi*). Therefore, to elaborate an explicitly leftist version of post-foundational thought is in itself a political decision (see Chapter 7). Yet what distinguishes the left Heideggerians vis-à-vis conservative sceptics like Oakeshott is not only the fact that they are on the Left, but also the fact that they, to a significant extent, build their theories upon the Heideggerian legacy. This becomes clear from the figures of contingency or groundlessness mentioned above and discussed in Chapter 1, but it also is apparent from their employment of the *political difference*: the difference between 'politics' and 'the political'. So how is this difference constructed and what role does it play in post-foundational social and political thought?

Although the theoretical differentiation between 'politics' and 'the political' occurs for the first time in German political thought with Carl Schmitt, the habit of differentiating between these two concepts started in French thought as early as 1957, with the publication of Paul Ricœur's essay 'The Political Paradox' (see Chapter 2), then leading to Jean-Luc Nancy and Philippe Lacoue-Labarthe's work (Chapter 3), which in turn motivated other theoreticians like Claude Lefort (Chapter 4) and Alain Badiou (Chapter 5) to reformulate their own theory in terms of the political difference. Of course, in these theories there is a range of usages of the notion of the political – e.g. as logic or specific rationality, as public sphere, or as event which escapes signification altogether – which are held together not by an overall framework but by their shared 'relation' towards an absent ground. As figures of contingency, they come close to what the earlier Heidegger called 'fomally indicating concepts' ('*formal anzeigende Begriffe*', 1983: 428–31): in circling around the abyss of contingency and groundlessness, they provide a tropological terrain for indicating 'formally' what cannot be represented directly. One aim of the present investigation consists in mapping this terrain, or rather the theoretical constellations framing the notion of the political as distinguished from politics. From our perspective it is not enough, though, to enumerate, nominalistically, the diverse usages of the notion of the political. There is something more to it. This is where what I call the 'grounding question'[3] of post-foundational political thought has to set in: we not only have to describe the development of the concept of the political, we also have to interrogate the latter's very differentiation from politics (respectively from the social). Why does politics, as a single concept, prove to be insufficient at a certain point and therefore has to be supplemented by a further term?

It is my conviction that the political difference is the outcome of a problem or deadlock of conventional political and social theory. As far as the conceptual innovation of the political, and, in particular, the *difference* between the new concept of the political and the conventional concept of politics is concerned, political difference seems to indicate the crisis of the foundationalist paradigm (represented scientifically by such diverse species as economic determinism, behaviourism, positivism, sociologism, and so on). What emerged in the fissures of foundationalism was the new horizon of post-foundational thought, through which it became possible to come to terms with the experience of what Lefort calls the 'dissolution of the markers of certainty' and with the impossibility for (foundationalist) theories to posit a particular marker of certainty as positive ground of the social. With regard to current political theory, the present investigation seeks to substantiate the thesis that the conceptual difference between politics and the political, *as difference*, assumes the role of an indicator or symptom of society's absent ground. *As difference*, this difference presents nothing other than a paradigmatic split in the traditional idea of politics, where a new term (the political) had to be introduced in order to point at society's 'ontological' dimension, the dimension of the institution of society, while politics was kept as the term for the 'ontic' practices of conventional politics (the plural, particular and, eventually, unsuccessful attempts at grounding society).

Thus, for post-foundationalist theories in which this difference is employed, the latter acquires the status of a founding difference that has to be conceived as *negativity*, by which the social (in the sense of society) is prevented from closure and from becoming identical with itself. To indicate this impossibility of final closure, the former concept of 'politics' becomes internally split between politics *eo ipso* (certain forms of action, the political sub-system, etc.) and something that always escapes the efforts of political or social domestication: the political. What comes to block access to the 'pure' moment of the political (unmediated, that is, by the strategic movements of politics or by the sedimentations of the social) is, however, the *differential* nature of the political difference – implying the constant deferral of any stabilization, either on the side of politics or on the side of the political. Seen from the perspective of another theoretical trajectory, the political difference could also be explained, in a Spinozian–Lacanian sense, as the indicator of an absent cause or structural cause (a 'lost cause'), which is only present in its effects: something whose 'existence' we have to assume because of the failures and gaps within political and social signification. As in philosophical thought, where we can only infer the onto-ontological difference from the incompletion of the ontic, in the discourse of political theory we can only infer the politico-political difference (and therefore 'the political' as the moment whose full actualization is always postponed and yet always achieved partially) from the impossibility of society, which is the same as the impossibility of providing an ultimate definition of politics.

Seen from this angle, it is obvious that the distinction between politics and the political parallels what is called in philosophy the ontological difference. This allusion to the ontological difference is not accidental, for it says something about the status of those theories. What unites all theories to be investigated is that they see themselves forced to leave the comfortable realm of positivism, behaviourism, economism, and so on, and to develop a quasi-transcendental distinction, which is not perceivable from the realm of science but only from the realm of philosophy. One could say that – from the observer position of philosophy – the ontological difference plays itself out as a radical incompatibility, an unbridgeable gap between concepts like the social, politics, policy, polity, and police on the one side and the political as event or radical antagonism on the other. The problem is, of course, that the political difference is nothing we can describe with empiricist instruments. It therefore cannot be an object of political science, it can only be 'the object' of a political theory that dares to take a philosophical point of view – without however lapsing into an unpolitical philosophism. This kind of 'philosophical' point of observation is characterized precisely by its ability to differentiate with respect to the very status of undecidability (to its quasi-transcendental status or condition, as opposed to 'empirical' decisions taken in particular contexts), that is to say, to the *necessary* status of contingency. Conversely, one must accept that, behind the aforementioned family resemblances of left Heideggerianism, there is no unifying or underlying principle; rather, there is a lack (the absence of an ultimate ground of society), which generates versions of the political difference and produces a need to draw that line between politics and the political in the first place. In most, if not all cases we can observe a need to demarcate one's own position vis-à-vis a merely positivist, sociologist, empiricist, historicist or economistic understanding of political science.

It should be underlined that the emergence of the ontological difference in political thought proves much less spectacular than it may appear at first glance, as soon as one realizes that it defines the structure of most post-foundationalist theories – and in particular, of course, those of left Heideggerian provenance. As soon as we accept that society cannot be grounded, and never will be, in a solid foundation, essence, or centre, precisely that impossibility of foundation acquires a role which must be called (quasi-)transcendental with respect to particular attempts at founding society. Thus, the notion of foundation is split into a purely negative foundation on the one hand (the impossibility of a final ground), and the possibility of 'contingent foundations' on the other, to use a term coined by Judith Butler (1992) – that is, a plurality of hegemonic moves that seek to ground society without ever being entirely able to do so. Every foundation will therefore be a partial foundation within a field of competing foundational attempts. It is in the light of our post-foundational condition that an explanation can be given to the peculiar fact that what is called in philosophy the ontological difference is mirrored conceptually in the field of today's political theory in the form of the difference between the concept of politics and the concept of the political.

Hence, the different predicates given to the political by theorists as diverse as Schmitt, Ricœur, Wolin, Mouffe, Nancy, Badiou, Rancière and others are of secondary nature when compared to what they share: these theorists see the necessity to *split the notion of politics from within* (and, as it was mentioned above, in a way completely dissimilar to merely 'ontical' distinctions like those between politics, policy, and polity, for instance). By splitting politics from within, something essential is released. On the one hand, politics – at the ontic level – remains a specific discursive regime, a particular social system, a certain form of action; while on the other hand – at the ontological level – the political assumes the role of something which is of an entirely different nature: the *principle* of autonomy of politics, or the *moment* of institution of society. As differentiated from politics, the notion of the political cannot be assimilated to social differences, to repetition, tradition, sedimentation, or bureaucracy. Like other figures of contingency and groundlessness, such as the event, antagonism, truth, the real, or freedom, the political dwells, as it were, on society's non-ground, which makes itself felt in the differential play of the political difference. But society's absent ground is not 'merely' absent. It (re-)appears and is supplemented by the moment which we may call, with reference to J. G. A. Pocock's 'Machiavellian moment' (1975), the *moment of the political.*

So, in a nutshell, what occurs within the moment of the political, and what can be excavated out of the work of many post-foundational political theorists as an 'underlying logic', is the following double-folded movement. On the one hand, the political, as the instituting moment of society, functions as a supplementary ground to the groundless stature of society, yet on the other hand this supplementary ground withdraws in the very 'moment' in which it institutes the social. As a result, society will always be in search for an ultimate ground, while the maximum that can be achieved will be a fleeting and contingent *grounding* by way of politics – a plurality of partial grounds. This is how the dif-ferential character of the political difference is to be understood: the political (located, as it were, on the 'ontological' side of Being-as-ground) will never be able fully to live up to its function as Ground – and yet it has to be actualized in the form of an always concrete *politics* that necessarily fails to deliver what it has promised. But politics and the political, the moment of ground and the moment of the actualization of this ground, will never meet because of the unbridgeable chasm of the difference between these terms, which in itself is but the signature of our post-foundational condition.

This book is devoted to an interrogation of this 'Machiavellian moment' of the political and of the conceptual constellation within which the political arises right at the heart of the traditional concepts of politics and of the social. Yet in a second step, this book pursues a more ambitious objective, which is to determine the very theoretical or philosophical *status* of a political thought that does not hesitate to engage fully with all the consequences following from the 'invention' of the political difference. At this initial stage of the argument we can only indicate our suspicion that none of the political post-foundationalists discussed in this book is aware of these radical consequences. While some, like Badiou, explicitly assign the political difference only a particular lot in their theoretical architecture (in Badiou politics is only one out of four 'truth procedures', including 'love', 'art', and 'science'), others tend to underrate the radical implications entailed by their employment of the political difference. For, once it is assumed that the political acts as a grounding supplement to *all* social relations, it will not be possible to restrain its effects – and even the effects of its absence – to the traditional field of politics. All dimensions of society (including the fields of 'love', 'art', and 'science') will consequently be subjected to the constant play of grounding/ungrounding as it is conceptually captured by the political difference.

If this is agreed upon, the trading area of post-foundational political thought must be significantly expanded. It is not only that it will include the entire field of the social and of social relations as its 'object domain', it will also have to claim a status of primacy vis-à-vis all other disciplines. For if the political ontology implicit in the politico-ontological difference is concerned with the quasi-transcendental conditions of grounding/ungrounding of all social being (and all being, in this sense, is social), then it cannot any longer have the status of a regional ontology. It will turn into a general ontology which, given our post-foundational premises, will necessarily be haunted by the spectre of its own eventual impossibility, of the impossibility of what traditionally is called a 'first philosophy'. Yet such ultimate impossibility of a first philosophy, in the sense of a foundational discourse, does not absolve us from the task of philo-sophically reflecting upon the very dimension of grounding – even as no philosophy will ever find, or found, an ultimate ground. And yet the necessity of something of the order of a first philosophy survives in the exigency of our post-foundational condition – a condition in which the quest for grounds is not abandoned (like in the case of a simple-minded *anti*-foundationalism), but is accepted as a both im-possible and indispensable enterprise. It is within the medium of such reflection on the grounding/ungrounding dimension of all social being that post-foundational political thought unfolds.

Acknowledgements

The arguments presented in this book have profited greatly by comments by Ernesto Laclau, Chantal Mouffe, Yannis Stavrakakis, Urs Stäheli, Simon Critchley, Etienne Balibar, the series editors, Benjamin Arditi and Jeremy Valentine, and the two anonymous readers for Edinburgh University Press. Special thanks go to Kari Palonen for providing access to his immensely valuable studies into the conceptual history of 'the political', and to Shu-fen Lin, who was there at the 'moment of decision' when the topic was chosen, and from the initial stage onwards accompanied the work with her encouragement. Some of the material presented in Chapters 4 and 5 was previously published in *Acta Philosophica* XXI/2 (2000) and *Polygraph* 17 (2005).

Notes

1. The notion of the Heideggerian Left (*la gauche heideggérienne*) is taken from Dominique Janicaud and his monumental study on the reception of Heidegger's thought in France (2001: 291–300). The expression 'left Heideggerianism' has also been used, in a more critical sense, by Richard Wolin (2001), to describe Herbert Marcuse's position vis-à-vis his teacher Heidegger.
2. For a different post-foundational way of approaching such 'weak ontology' in political theory, and in particular with regard to the respective work of George Kateb, Charles Taylor, Judith Butler and William Connolly, see White (2000).
3. I differentiate, pace Heidegger (1994), between the 'guiding question' as to the notion, in our case, of the political (the question that characterizes most of the theories discussed, from Schmitt to Ricœur and onwards), and the 'grounding question' as to the very nature of the difference between politics and the political *as difference*. Yet it should be noted that the transition from the guiding question to the grounding question is not a gradual undertaking but requires what Heidegger calls a *leap*, the instantiation of 'another beginning'.

Chapter 1
The Contours of 'Left Heideggerianism': Post-Foundationalism and Necessary Contingency

> The dissolution of the myth of foundation does not dissolve the phantom of its own absence.
>
> Ernesto Laclau (1989: 81)

1.1 Anti-Foundationalism and Post-Foundationalism

In the present chapter I seek to substantiate our main thesis – according to which the political difference must be understood as symptomatically pointing at the crumbling grounds of foundationalism – by analyzing its elements step by step, starting with an account of the notion of post-foundationalism itself and of the quasi-transcendental argument by which post-foundational thought proceeds. We will then examine the Heideggerian roots of post-foundationalism (around the four concepts of event, moment, freedom, and difference), which will put us in a better position to detect the commonalities between the Heideggerians of the Left discussed in Chapters 3–6. I will then proceed to show how the ontological difference is implicated in the radical notion of contingency, which lies at the (negative) 'core' of current post-foundational thinking.

The term foundationalism can be used to define – from the viewpoint of social and political theory – those theories which assume that society and/or politics are 'grounded on principles that are (1) undeniable and immune to revision and (2) located outside society and politics' (Herzog 1985: 20). In most cases of political and social foundationalism, a principle is sought which is to ground politics from without. It is from this transcendent ground that the functioning of politics is claimed to be derived. If we think of economic determinism, for example, it first provides a set of principles (the economic 'laws') which are presented as the essence of politics (what politics is 'really' about) and, secondly, it locates this ground (the economic 'base') outside of, or beyond, the immediate realm of politics, the latter being thus turned into a 'merely superstructural' affair.

This short reflection on modern foundationalism may provide the starting point for developing some of the criteria for what could be rightfully called a *post*-foundational constellation. To do so, however, a much more complicated argument is needed than simply to invert foundationalism into anti-foundationalism. It is often said that the problem with the foundationalist debate is the dualistic way in which it was formulated, 'that it has been left in the strong foundationist terms of a choice between an ultimate foundation and none at all (the one-or-none thesis)' (Fairlamb 1994: 12–13). And indeed, insofar as the anti-foundationalist view is premised on the negation of, or simple opposition to, the foundationalist view, it obviously shares the same horizon with foundationalism. The conclusion to be drawn from this, however, is not the one used by foundationalists for launching their standard attack on anti-foundationalism: 'Don't you see', foundationalists ask anti-foundationalists, 'that by necessity you have to make use of foundationalism in developing anti-foundationalism? Are you not yourself thereby attesting to the fact that by denouncing all foundations you are erecting a new final foundation – a kind of "anti-foundation"? Don't you therefore have to agree that it is impossible eventually to surmount foundationalism?'

Such a critique might be valid with respect to very crude forms of anti-foundationalism, but I suspect that, to some degree, it represents a caricature even of 'actually existing' anti-foundationalisms (like Feyerabend's), let alone of post-foundationalisms. The 'anything goes' variants of anti-foundationalism and postmodernism come in rather conveniently as a bug-bear, even as fewer and fewer theorists, if any, actually hold such views. Thus, one cannot but suspect that the framing of the discussion in dualistic terms – where anti-foundationalists are merely negating or inverting foundationalist premises – is part of the strategy of foundationalists rather than being the strategy of post-foundationalists. It has been remarked that, in the debate, the negative label of 'antiness' is assigned from the standpoint of foundationalism, which implies that the 'terrain of the debate, by means of a political act, privileges the *meaning* assigned to foundation that is invoked by the primary term of the dichotomy' (Doucet 1999: 293–4). Framing the ongoing debate in terms of the divide between foundationalism and anti-foundationalism favours foundationalism and thus is upheld and deliberately instrumentalized by foundationalists.

While certainly correct as an assessment of the foundationalism/ anti-foundationalism debate, this cannot be the whole story. For questions have to be addressed as to where the power of foundationalism to frame the debate according to its own terms (positing itself in the first position and denouncing everything else as derived of and parasitic upon itself) comes from. The foundationalist strategy seems to work for one reason: the paradigm of foundationalism is in fact hegemonic to a large degree. Its dominance allowed foundationalism to frame the discussion in its own terms. Conversely, in order to enter the debate and engage foundationalism, *anti*-foundationalism necessarily had to enter foundationalist territory while claiming to stand entirely outside the foundationalist paradigm. But if launching an anti-foundationalist attack on foundationalism seems to give an advantage to the latter's position as first term – if not strengthening it – what options are left?

1.2 The 'Quasi-Transcendental Turn'

The answer – which can be traced back to Heidegger, as we will see – is, of course, the following: instead of an outright attack on foundationalism or 'metaphysics', what should be attempted is the subversion of the very terrain on which foundationalism operates, a subversion of foundationalist premises – and not their denial. (For if it is not possible entirely to step out of that discourse – due to its hegemonic status – it follows that non-foundationalist discourse will always have to work to some degree on foundationalist terrain.) Such a deconstruction of foundationalism is something quite different from its simple inversion. The standard foundationalist attack on post-foundationalism (misreading it as anti-foundationalism) therefore misses the mark. For Gayatri Spivak, for instance, deconstruction is not even *non*-foundationalist – let alone *anti*-foundationalist. Rather, as 'a repeated staging of attention on the construction of foundations presupposed as self-evident', it offers 'a perpetually rehearsed critique of the European ethico-political universal' (1993: 153).

Judith Butler makes a similar point to the effect that the notion of foundations is something we cannot easily get rid of. Rather, the theorist should direct his/her attention to what is excluded by the erection of foundations. Thus, Butler contends that

> the point is not to do away with foundations, or even to champion a position which goes under the name of antifoundationalism: Both of these positions belong together as different versions of foundationalism and the sceptical problematic it engenders. Rather, the task is to interrogate what the theoretical move that establishes foundations *authorizes*, and what precisely it excludes or forecloses. (1992: 7)

The notion of contingent foundations, proposed by Butler as an alternative framing of the debate, could best be described as an ontological weakening of the status of foundation without doing away with foundations entirely. It is on its account, that what came to be called post-foundationalism should not be confused with anti-foundationalism.[1] What distinguishes the former from the latter is that it does not assume the absence of *any* ground; what it assumes is the absence of *an ultimate* ground, since it is only on the basis of such absence that grounds, in the plural, are possible. The problem is therefore posed not in terms of *no* foundations (the logic of all-or-nothing), but in terms of *contingent* foundations. Hence, post-foundationalism does not stop after having assumed the absence of a final ground and so it does not turn into anti-foundationalist nihilism, existentialism or pluralism, all of which would assume the absence of *any* ground and would result in complete meaninglessness, absolute freedom or total autonomy. Nor does it turn into a sort of post-modern pluralism for which all meta-narratives have equally melted into air, for what is still accepted by post-foundationalism is the necessity for *some* grounds.

What becomes problematic as a result is not the existence of foundations (in the plural) but their ontological status – which is seen now as necessarily contingent. This shift in the analysis from the 'actually existing' foundations to their status – that is to say, to their conditions of possibility – can be described as a quasi-transcendental move. Although implicitly present in Spivak's notion of a 'perpetually rehearsed critique' in the previous quotation as well as in Butler's notion of 'interrogation', this quasi-transcendental turn is made explicit by Ernesto Laclau who, starting from the post-foundational premise that 'the crisis of essentialist universalism as a self-asserted ground has led our attention to the contingent *grounds* (in the plural) of its emergence and to the complex process of construction', comes to the conclusion that '[t]his operation is, *sensu stricto, transcendental*: it involves a retreat from an object to its conditions of possibility' (1994: 2).

Yet the questioning of grounds – as a quasi-transcendentalist enterprise – does not only lead to a better understanding of the empirical context through which certain grounds become dominant, for those conditions of possibility of any contingent foundation should not be confused with 'empirical' conditions. What is hence at stake in post-foundationalist thought is the status attributed to foundations, whereby the primordial (or ontological) absence of an ultimate ground is itself the condition of possibility of grounds as present – that is, in their objectivity or empirical 'existence' as ontic beings. In other words: the pluralization of grounds and of identities within the field of the social is the result of a radical impossibility, a radical gap between the ontic and the ontological, which has to be posited in order to account for plurality in the ontic realm.

Why does it make sense to introduce the differentiation between the ontic and the ontological even if some proponents of anti- or post-foundationalism from the pragmatists camp, like Oakeshott and Rorty, but even post-structuralists like Rancière, consider this difference redundant? The answer is that, if one has to accept *both* a plurality of contingent foundations which 'empirically' – if always only temporarily – ground the social *and* the impossibility of a final ground for that plurality, it follows that this impossibility cannot be of the same order as the empirical foundations themselves.

In order to substantiate this claim, it is advisable to consult once again the *locus classicus* of post-structuralism, Derrida's essay 'Structure, Sign and Play in the Discourse of the Human Sciences' (in Derrida 1978). There Derrida famously argues against the structuralist conception of a centered structure which is, in his eyes, 'in fact the concept of a play based on a fundamental ground, a play constituted on the basis of a fundamental immobility and a reassuring certitude, which itself is beyond the reach of play' (279). This concept belongs to an era of the West (to the foundationalist paradigm, as we would say), whose matrix is the metaphysical determination of Being as presence in all its senses, some of which Derrida enumerates: '*eidos, arché, telos, energeia, ousia* (essence, existence, substance, subject) *alétheia*, transcendentality, consciousness, God, man' (279–80). This matrix has suffered dislocations, a moment of 'rupture' which 'is not first and foremost a moment of philosophical or scientific discourse', but also 'a moment which is political, economic, technical, and so forth' (282). The rupture 'is no doubt part of the totality of an era, our own', and it is indicated by the proper names of Nietzsche, Freud and Heidegger even as the event itself 'has always already begun to proclaim itself and begun to *work*' (280).

Thus we encounter in Derrida a two-sided account of the event of rupture within foundationalism: on the one hand, that rupture is described both as part of the totality of our own era – something like the current paradigm-shift within foundationalism – and, on the other, as a 'moment' which has *always already* been there. Here the possibility is announced of describing a paradigm-shift without, in a historicist way, restricting the moments of emergence of such events to our own time. The result is that, on the one hand, post-foundationalism is a new 'paradigm' which can be described as 'disruption' of foundationalism from within through the realization of contingency, a notion which will be elaborated upon later. Here, a continuous movement of generalization of the latter's logic can be detected in the history of (political) thought, in particular through a process of conceptual temporalization and politicization which, as we will see in the next chapter, commenced in the late eighteenth century (the period Koselleck and German *Begriffsgeschichte* refer to as '*Sattelzeit*'), expanding and disturbing the foundationalist paradigm from within. On the other hand, to name this event '*moment*' – even a moment which has always already been there (potentially, I would add) – rather than seeing in it an exclusively contemporary development (let alone a continuous unfolding of 'critique' or an 'evolutionary' superseding of one paradigm by another) hints at a different possibility: what if the post-foundationalist moment – which essentially consists in the realization of contingency as necessary – has in fact been actualized 'before' post-foundationalism, in particular, in terms of political thought, in the work of Machiavelli – who could be anachronistically added to Nietzsche, Freud and Heidegger? I will return to this question at the end of the present chapter, although it is in fact related to the problem of quasi-transcendentalism.

For now, let us return to the problem of why the quasi-transcendental impossibility of a final ground cannot be of the same order as the plurality of empirical foundations. There is one solution given to this problem – Derrida calls it the 'classical hypothesis' – which assumes that a field like society, for instance, cannot be totalized because of its empirical infinity and the empirical limitations of the 'totalizer': the subject. According to this solution, the plurality cannot be grounded because it will always prove to be 'too plural' for anybody to ground. Derrida shows that this solution is not the only one, for ungroundability can also be determined from the concept of the standpoint of play. The nature of the field excludes totalization because the field 'is in effect that of *play*, say, because instead of being an inexhaustible field, as in the classical hypothesis, instead of being too large, there is something missing from it: a center which arrests and grounds the play of substitutions' (1978: 289).

It is not because of empirical reasons that systems cannot be grounded, but because of the fact that a ground or center is lacking – not by chance but by principle (a lack which in turn leads to an endless supplementary play of substitutions). While the 'classical hypothesis' conceives of the impossibility of totalization or grounding in an empirical way, the 'post-classical' hypothesis conceives of it in a quasi-transcendental way. The ultimate grounding of a system is not impossible because the latter is too plural and our capacities are limited, but because there is something of a different order, something lacking, which makes pluralization itself possible by making *impossible* the *final* achievement of a totality. Consequently, the 'post-classical hypothesis' assumes that the ontological status of this impossibility of an ultimate ground must be stronger than the status of any of the multiple and contingent foundations established through processes of grounding. Why is that so?

A claim to the impossibility of an ultimate ground: of *the* 'ground', implies claiming something which is of necessity true for all empirical foundations, for if it were otherwise – if not all foundations were blocked from becoming 'ground' – one would have to assume the possibility for *some* foundations to become 'ground'. In this case, the status of the impossibility of an ultimate ground would be weak: it would be a residual, or only partial, impossibility, which does not hold for all foundational attempts. It might hold for some but not for others. Thereby the possibility of a positive, singular ground is not ruled out – but this was the assumption from which we started (pragmatist anti-foundationalists like Rorty included). Thus we can only do two things: either we give up our starting point and return to a foundationalist stance, or we bear the consequences and take the final step of accepting that the impossibility of becoming 'ground' must hold for *all* contingent foundations – if one wants to remain anti-foundationalist – and so its status is stronger than the status of each of those plural foundations: the impossibility of ground is a *necessary* impossibility. It describes the necessary absence of an ultimate ground. An absence which, as must be noted, is a productive absence, and not merely negative. What can be called the 'absent' ground is in no way an 'anti'-ground. To trace this argument back to its theoretical origin, we must now turn to Martin Heidegger.

1.3 Heidegger: *Event, Moment, Freedom, Dif-ference*

In claiming that the ground remains present in its absence, we underline the fact that the ground's absence does not imply that the process of grounding comes to a halt. On the contrary, the ground remains, to some extent, 'operative' *as* ground only on the basis of its very absence, which is why the absence of the ground must not be envisaged as 'total' cancellation, as 'mere' absence. This argument owes so much to Martin Heidegger that it would not be exaggerated to regard Heidegger as one of the main 'founders' of post-foundationalism. For Heidegger, the absence of the ground is in the nature of an abyss, that is to say, of a ground *without* ground, of a bottomless ground. So grounding still occurs – the 'function' of the ground as ground does not disappear completely. However, it occurs only to the extent that it passes through an 'a-byss' which *is* the ground: The ground grounds as a-byss ('Der Grund gründet als *Ab-grund*', 1994: 29). And as the ground, for Heidegger, is necessarily abyssal, the a-byss remains present in the ground as the latter's 'essencing' (*Wesung*) or holding sway.

It is essential to understand that the place of the absent ground (or abyss) does not remain empty in the ordinary or commonsensical understanding of emptiness; Heidegger talks about an extraordinary and originary way of remaining empty or un-filled/un-fulfilled, which amounts to an extraordinary opening (1994: 379). Precisely by remaining empty – by always deferring its own 'fulfilment' – it permits an opening, disclosure and *Lichtung* (379). For this reason, we should not perceive abyss in any way as a mere antithesis of ground; since in the former, something of the nature of the latter always remains. Instead, Heidegger claims: 'Der *Ab*-grund ist Ab-*grund*' (379).

Here, Heidegger relates both abyss and ground in a figure so typical for his thought: the chiasm or *chiasmus* defined by Jean-François Mattéi, who investigated 220 different cases of this figure in Heidegger's work, as 'the figure of the reversal of a proposition whose members are contained within both the initial proposition and the inverted one and produce a distinctive pattern of crossed overlapping' (Mattéi 1995: 41). 'Der *Ab*-grund ist Ab-*grund*' is a chiasm which is supposed to mean: the ground is a-byss, and the a-byss is ground. By underscoring, on the one hand, the 'Ab' in *Ab*-grund, and, on the other, the 'grund' in Ab-*grund*, Heidegger stresses the fact that two dimensions have to be differentiated in some way but, at one and the same time, *cannot* be differentiated neatly, as they are ceaselessly crossing over into each other. It is because of the inseparable intertwining between ground and abyss that the ground can be recognized as abyss and yet keeps something of its own nature as ground. What the figure of the chiasm allows Heidegger to do is to express *both* the intricate relation or reversibility of both terms *and* their non-identity.

So in a certain way the 'absent ground' we referred to when talking about today's post-foundationalism still functions or 'operates' as ground – even as Heideggerians might prefer not to talk about function or operation but to take recourse to the verbalized form 'grounding'. Yet the ground grounds only on the very basis of its abyssal character: that is to say, only via its very own absence, via what we might call its absencing or 'de-grounding'. The a-byss is the never-ending deferral and withdrawal of ground, a withdrawal which belongs to the very nature of the latter and cannot be separated from it. This implies, and herein Heidegger indeed proves to be one of the 'founders' of post-foundationalism, that, if the grounding operates only by way of a constant withdrawal or 'hesitance' (*Zögerung*) of ground, then the moment of a definite and final foundation will never come. Instead, for Heidegger, what is revealed or disclosed is precisely the withdrawal of ground. It is that withdrawal – and not a firm ground – which shows itself and opens itself up in the form of an originary clearing or *Lichtung* (1994: 379–80). It is the clearance of the *event* (*Ereignis*) – arguably the most important notion of the later Heidegger – in which the truth of 'beyng' (which resides in the withdrawal of ground) is unveiled.[2]

By way of recapitulating the previous section on Heidegger's idea of ground, it must be stressed once more that the most important aspect for an investigation of post-foundationalism lies in the fact that the retreat of ground does not imply the latter's final disappearance, since we are not engaged in a purely 'logical' argumental step of simple negation of ground.[3] Heidegger deconstructs ground by showing how at the very heart of it we encounter an abyss. Ground and a-byss remain intimately intertwined. Therefore ground, as the dimension of grounding/degrounding, does not disappear – as it may in crude forms of anti-foundationalism – but is put under erasure (Heidegger 1996: 367). As in the case of Sein, which Heidegger also occasionally puts under erasure, one of the reasons for this 'Durchstreichung' or cancellation is found in the post-foundational aim of not eradicating the dimension of ground completely but problematizing its status as *fundamentum inconcussum* or separate, definable entity (which would confuse the level of ground or 'beyng' with the ontic level of beings).

There are at least four (quasi-)concepts developed by Heidegger in connection with the idea of the absence, withdrawal, retreat or 'staying-away' (*Weg-bleiben*) of ground, or, as we would put it in more contemporary parlance, of an ultimate foundation. Those concepts will prove to be central to our purposes. They include *event*, *moment*, *freedom*, and *difference* in its radical sense as *Unter-Schied*. All these conceptual approaches circle around the problematic outlined above as the problematic of grounding/degrounding in a nearly tautological fashion. Heidegger's strategy is conceptually to encircle what escapes any direct definition or proof (i.e. that which cannot be grounded by thought, since the attempt to ground it would mean to fall prey to metaphysics once more).

(1) *Event.* The verbalization of nouns so typical of Heidegger's discourse prevents us from reifying an unfolding 'process' into a mere object, it keeps us, in other words, from presenting the play of grounding/degrounding – which, we will see, is also the play of *Seyn* (beyng) that happens between the ontological level of *Sein* (Being) and the ontic level of *Seiendes* (beings) – as if it were leading to a final and firm ground. Hence the main Heideggerian terms (his *Leitworte*) are not intended to point to a substantive and stable essence, but rather to a never-ending *process*. Accordingly, the a-byss (i.e. the absence of ground) 'presences' in the ground in the form of a never-ending 'happening' which is the happening of the appropriative event. While

event (*Ereignis*) is often phrased as a noun, it must always be understood in the verbal sense of *Er-eignung* or of one of its verbal synonyms, *Geschehen*, that is to say, it must be understood in a processual sense, as *Wesung* or *essencing of the ground*. So we can say that grounding/degrounding unfolds and 'essences' in the event or happen-*ing*. Employed by Heidegger as *singulare tantum*, event names the most general dimension of beyng: Beyng 'essences' (*west*) as the event (1994: 260), whereby the truth of beyng is unconcealed. Therefore the event must not be confused with ontic occurrences, since it is nothing but their grounding dimension or their condition of possibility.

(2) *Moment*. The time–space which originates from the event and which also is the very time–space of the a-byss ('Der Abgrund als der Zeit–Raum', 1994: 29) is described by Heidegger as '*Augenblicks-Stätte*', as the site of a 'momentary glance' (*Augenblick* or *kairos*). In short, the time–space of the event has the character of a 'moment' in the sense of *Augenblick*. Seen under the aspect of grounding, the ground/abyss is located in that 'moment' of the in-between ('das *Zwischen*') in which the event happens (and which is also the location of man, who is 'enowned' by the event). However, this moment in the sense of *Augenblick* must not be conflated with the temporal phenomenon of a 'point' in time, of a punctual 'now' within linear time, as it refers to the originary temporality of the event (it is only after the fact, after something has emerged in the event, that it can be reconstructed into a linear chronological succession of historical occurrences). To envisage the moment in terms of originary temporality indicates that it is not a category referring to the ontic level, the level of beings. Rather, it points to the much more fundamental level of beyng, that is, the level of ground/abyss, so that in Heideggerian terms the moment can be defined as the instance in which the very groundlessness of the ground is actualized in the happening of the event of ground-*ing*. This is the reason why, from the perspective of today's social post-foundationalism, the category of 'moment' could prove highly productive, and it is also the way in which the notion of 'the moment of the political' or the radicalized notion of the 'Machiavellian moment' should be understood in our own investigation.[4] From that radical perspective, the category 'moment' refers to those instances in which the abyssal character of the social – the contingency of its very own foundations – surfaces and is reactivated or 'enacted' by theoretical and political practice.

(3) *Freedom*. While beings are grounded by ground (through a processual movement of *grounding*), ground itself cannot be grounded anymore. The a-byss discovered at the bottom of ground leads Heidegger to the most radical notion of freedom. There is freedom because there is no ground of the ground, and vice versa. Thus, at the 'bottom' of the a-byss, at the ground without ground, we discover freedom: freedom is the ground's ground (1996: 174). In this most radical understanding, freedom is the condition of every grounding and the very origin of ground (165). Once more, it names the abyssal character of ground at the level of *beyng* (Seyn), which 'grounds' beings in a movement of excess and withdrawal but cannot itself be grounded. Perceived from another angle, Heidegger holds that grounding is the originary relation of freedom to ground. Freedom as the movement of grounding proceeds by *giving* ground and, at the same time, *taking* and withholding it. In other words, freedom grounds *and* un-grounds. Without that originary relation between freedom and ground, grounding would not be feasible at all. And it is because of *Dasein*'s 'thrownness' and finitude that freedom, for *Dasein*, is '*Freiheit zum Grunde*': freedom *to* (the) ground. One could venture to claim that what is prefigured in that Heideggerian argument is a form of positive freedom (freedom *to*), whose very condition is the 'negativity', 'emptiness' or bottomlessness of the ground on which it is based. And we will see that, in post-foundational political thought, freedom, understood in this radical sense, will remain a core concept.

(4) *Dif-ference*. Finally, one can approach the question of ground from the perspective of the ontico-ontological difference. It would not be exaggerated to claim that Heidegger's whole enterprise culminates in his effort to deconstruct the ontological difference in all its metaphysical variants. For our own investigation of the difference between politics and the political, his reflection on the nature of *dif-ference* will prove to be the most important aspect of Heidegger's deconstruction of foundationalism.

1.4 The 'Grounding Question' regarding the Ontological Difference

So how does Heidegger proceed regarding the question of difference? First, he perceives in the ontological difference – i.e. the difference between the ontic level of beings and the ontological level of being –

the 'guiding question' (*Leitfrage*) of all occidental metaphysics. This guiding question was always the question concerning the very being-ness (*Seiendheit*) of beings, which then was found in being conceived as the ground – a stable anchor or substance – of all ontic beings. Metaphysics is and always has been the quest for such ground, which can assume different names: logos, idea, cause, substance, objectivity, subjectivity, will, or, in more theological terms, the supreme being or God. While metaphysics, in Heidegger's view, always employed the difference between being and beings in its diverse forms, that difference never came into view *as difference*. Yet for Heidegger, that 'Unter-Schied' or *dif-ference* – that is, the difference *as* difference (1957b: 37) – is the very matter of thinking, 'die Sache des Denkens', which imposes itself upon thinking. Thinking, then, is required to pass from the metaphysical 'guiding question' to the 'grounding question' (*Grundfrage*). To ask the grounding question is to think through the problem of grounding under conditions of an abyssal ground and, at the same time, to rethink the metaphysical versions of the ontological difference from the perspective of difference qua difference. The latter now is understood, as Rudolphe Gasché remarks, as a *radical* or more originary and fundamental difference, which (un-)grounds all other forms of difference: 'As the "ground" of all difference based on relation and distinction, difference *as* difference not only is in a position of anteriority to difference, but also differs in nature from the vulgar concept of difference' (1994: 92).

In order to be able to distinguish the foundational concept of being from the more originary play *between* being and beings (the happening of their difference *as* difference), Heidegger resorts to the more archaic spelling '*Seyn*' ('beyng'). Beyng now designates neither the ontological nor the ontic side of the difference but, rather, the event of *differencing* itself. So we have to be careful not to think difference as distinction, for this would mean that what is different between ontological being and ontic being was simply added to the difference, whereby the latter becomes objectified as one more being. Rather, the 'grounding question' circles around beyng itself, whereby the latter is nothing but the very happening (the unconcealment) of the difference between beings and being *as difference*. A *dif-ference* which is un-concealed in the *event*, where the latter is defined as the contempor-aneity of beyng and beings.

A further aspect of the ontological difference is of importance: the fact, namely, that the play of beyng (as the play of the difference between being and beings) can never be accessed in its 'pure' state, nor can the ontological level of being be stripped bare of the historic specificity of the latter's manifestation – which is, again, ontic. So, while beyng has to be thought of in all its 'autonomy', that is to say, without recourse to any ontic being, paradoxically, it is impossible to talk about beyng without some such recourse: 'on the one hand, the truth of beyng must be thought from itself and not . . . from beings; but, on the other hand, the truth of beyng must be sheltered in beings and to this extent still thought – if differently – within a certain purview of beings' (Sallis 2001: 187). Framed in terms of the less pastoral vocabulary of contemporary post-foundationalism, the argument could be rephrased as follows: The *ontological* level cannot be accessed immediately, for this would require envisaging it as solid ground (as being). If it is to fulfill its function of *grounding*, however, the ground, as we have seen, is simultaneously an a-byss. Since there is no ground of beyng, the ontological level is irremediably separated from the ontic level. And it is precisely because we cannot access the ontological level *directly* that – if we want to approach it at all – we will have necessarily to pass through the ontic level, in order to 'wave' at something which will always escape our grasp because of the irremediable gap between the ontological and the ontic, beingness and beings, the ground and what is grounded.

There can be no doubt that it is impossible to discuss post-foundational thought without taking into account the Heideggerian legacy. As Reiner Schürmann puts it in his classic study of being and acting in Heidegger: 'With that event [the event of appropriation] discovered at the core of every phenomenon, "the foundations crumble," it is *grundstürzend*.' And this has very real consequences for theory and politics, for it 'frustrates the very desire for an unshakable ground of theory and action' (1990: 155). This *post*-foundational movement of Heidegger's thought – which is 'fundamental' without being foundational (see also O'Neill 1993) – doesn't completely dispose of a *fundamental dimension* beyond the level of mere ontic occurrences (that is to say, he doesn't turn into a positivist – which is only another species in the family of foundationalists anyway).

But how to describe Heidegger's theoretical stance? I submit that Heidegger's approach is best described as quasi-transcendentalist. While Heidegger was of course reluctant to locate himself within the trajectory of Kantian transcendentalism, David Kolb is certainly right when claiming: 'Heidegger abandons the search for grounds. But emphasizing his distance from foundationalism may obscure how near he remains to the transcendental search for conditions of possibility' (1986: 173). As Heidegger has exemplified with his own reading of Kant, the transcendentalist form of reasoning can in fact be understood as an *ontological* form of reasoning 'in disguise'. Seen from this vantage point, a transcendental argument does not necessarily aim at the epistemological conditions of understanding, but could also seek to develop the ontological conditions of being – and this is exactly the 'ontological' way in which we will use transcendentalist vocabulary in the following lines of argument.

The question remains, however, as to where to locate those non-foundationalist conditions of possibility within the Heideggerian framework. And, although we should not mistake beyng for simply the 'transcendental condition' of beings, it is still feasible to define beyng as 'condition of possibility, as that by which the very space of the circulation between beings and beingness is first opened' (Sallis 2001: 185). Yet, as Derrida has argued on numerous occasions, a transcendentalism of this sort will always and by necessity remain a *quasi*-transcendentalism, where one aspect which the '*quasi*' indicates is that ground and abyss, conditions of possibility and conditions of impossibility, are inseparably interwoven, and the other aspect indicated by the '*quasi*' is that all transcendental conditions will always emerge out of particular *empirico-historical* conjunctures.

1.5 Contingency

Via this short excursion into Heidegger's version of the argument, I hope to have substantiated theoretically the claim that only the assumption of a ground which is present *in its absence* leads (a) to the possibility of contingent foundations in the plural and (b) to a proceduralization of that positive 'ground as pure presence' into a process of *grounding* as presencing/absencing. But again, to combine (a) with (b) and to speak about plural and procedural *groundings* presupposes the assumption that a singular, present ground is impossible. The impossibility of such a ground is the necessary condition of possibility for grounds in the plural – in the same way that the contingency appertaining to '*contingent* foundations' is a necessary contingency.

Understood in this way, 'contingency' becomes the operational term whose function is to indicate precisely this necessary impossibility of a final ground. By putting the concept of contingency under scrutiny, we now turn toward one of the key-terms – if not *the* key-term – of current post-foundational and post-structuralist theories. Like the prefix 'post' (in 'postmodernity', 'post-structuralism', 'post-Marxism', etc.), contingency has become a sign of our age, part of our intellectual horizon and the key operational term within the theoretical paradigm of post-foundationalism: 'Postmodernity is the condition of contingency which has come to be known as beyond repair'. This 'beyond repair' of which Zygmunt Bauman (1996: 51) speaks can be understood – apart from its more pessimistic overtones – as just another way of conceding the *necessity* of contingency for our age: the 'Age of Contingency' (Bauman). What is 'beyond repair', though, is both our age – which has to come to terms with its very own contingency – *and* the idea of an ultimate foundational ground; or, to put it differently, it is that ground itself which is terminally 'out of order' – 'out of joint' (Derrida 1997).

Today, it is frequently assumed that the phenomenon of contingency has spread into more and more realms of society and that it is experienced as the absence of a necessary foundation for truth, faith, or politics. However, even as the horizon of the experience of contingency was significantly expanded in modernity, contingency is anything but a modern invention. As the experience of the paradoxical, it has been available to earlier periods even as its effects were restricted to certain discourses. According to Niklas Luhmann (1996: 62–3), the experience of the paradoxical in early European thought hinted at the idea that, in terms of values, an ultimate ground cannot be attained. Early European thought encountered its own paradoxical foundations only in residual discourses like mysticism, theology, rhetorics, and philosophy, but the paradoxes of (self-)foundation were not allowed to affect the untouchable normative groundwork of society as such. Yet, precisely because the potentially paradoxical nature of ground could become perceivable at any time, it had to be kept at bay through classification and norms.

So it is not the case, if we are to follow Luhmann in this respect, that an idea of the impossibility of ultimate foundations was not present at all in 'premodern' European culture and only was invented in 'modernity'. Rather, this idea has always been there, if only in certain discourses, and it was not until the end of the eighteenth century that – according to Koselleck and *Begriffsgeschichte* – this paradoxical logic spread across more and more discourses and became generalized in society through the increasing temporalization and politicization of concepts. Formally, as Luhmann puts it, one can say 'that all connections are now described as *contingent*. They are *temporally* contingent in that they are no longer determined by the past, by an immutable Nature, by social origin; they are *objectively* contingent in that they could always be different; and they are *socially* contingent in that they no longer depend on consensus (keyword: "democracy")' (64). This dissolution of stable normative foundations – which may be traced back to the hypothetical moment when the (reflexive) realization of contingency became generalized – leads to a situation in which competing value-claims cannot have recourse to a higher principle any longer. We find ourselves on Max Weber's battlefield of warring gods. Any decision for or against any of those value-claims must be contingent by its very nature, that is, by necessity.

There is certainly nothing in this to contradict a historical genealogy of the increasing awareness of contingency and the increasing discursive availability of post-foundational motives for society's self-description. Such a genealogy would retrace the shifting borders between the foundational and the anti- or post-foundational paradigm, both within different discourses (or 'social systems') and across discourses. In order to be successful, however, a genealogy of this kind implies the avoidance of at least two impasses:

For one part, one should not fall into the (anti-foundationalist) trap of simply inverting the Hegelian idea of a teleological progress towards an increasing awareness of necessity into its exact opposite: the idea of a teleological progress towards an increasing awareness of contingency. Such a tendency can be observed in modernization theories, and it is, ironically again, Luhmannian systems theory which comes close to this idea by linking the generalization of contingency to a process of societal 'evolution', wherein the ever-increasing differentiation and autonomization of social sub-systems seems to work with the inevitability of a natural law.

The second impasse is a certain historicism or nominalism regarding the notion of contingency. Here contingency is described as a signifier whose historical changes in application (its attachments to varying signifieds) are described in meticulous detail. Even where it locates itself within the anti-foundationalist paradigm, like the versions of conceptual history discussed in the next chapter, an approach of this kind overlooks something which indeed *is* perceivable for a theorist like Luhmann: what the signifier 'contingency' points at is not (or not merely) a specific signified. Rather, it is an event. The event of crisis namely, that is to say, of a certain dislocation in the process of signification itself. It indicates the moment where signification breaks down and the groundlessness of signification – and, ergo, of society as the (impossible) totality of all signification – is experienced.

As Luhmann knows well, such a breakdown of signification (or 'observation' in Luhmann) can be experienced in the form of a paradox. And, for systems theory, a paradox emerges where the conditions of possibility of an operation are, simultaneously, its conditions of impossibility. The point made by deconstruction, however, is that paradox, as a name for these quasi-transcendental conditions of (im)possibility, is not only a regrettable incident which can occur in certain situations but must not in others. Rather, the paradoxical coincidence of the conditions of possibility and conditions of impossibility appertains to all systems and all signification. For signification to be possible at all, the breakdown of signification is not only one possible outcome but a necessary precondition. Here we encounter 'the necessity of defining the transcendental condition of possibility as also being a condition of impossibility' (Derrida, 1996: 82). What is necessary, as Derrida puts it, is the simultaneity, if not identicalness, of the conditions of possibility and conditions of impossibility of every significatory identity, and therefore the necessity of contingency. Thus signification is contingent *by necessity*, and this once more attests to the status of contingency as quasi-transcendental. This is a move away from the weak (logical) notion of the contingent as that which could be otherwise to the much stronger (quasi-transcendental) notion of necessary contingency. They are distinguished from one another by their relation to necessity, as follows.

In the weak notion, which is also the traditional one, contingency refers to those identities (or 'beings') which are neither impossible nor necessary – so that they 'could be otherwise'. What is not ruled out on this account is the possibility of ontic identities whose existence is not contingent but which, theoretically at least, could be necessary. By contrast, or by radicalization, the strong notion of contingency implies that being neither impossible nor necessary is itself necessary for *all* identity. What is ruled out here is the possibility of any identity which is not contingent. The strong notion of contingency thus ties the possibility of identity as such, inseparably, to the impossibility of its full (= non-contingent) achievement, thereby affirming the paradoxical or aporetical necessity of that tie between possibility and impossibility. In this sense, contingency can be used – and this in fact is the preferred usage of contingency in our own investigation – as an operational term indicating the necessary impossibility, in scientific terms, of systemic closure or, in ontological terms, of the full being-ness of beings or ground.[5]

This leads us to a second meaning of the 'quasi' in the deconstructive usage of the idea of the quasi-transcendental. The first meaning, to recapitulate, resides in a sort of double movement which indicates the necessity both to uphold transcendental questioning – a strengthening of the philosophical view vis-à-vis the purely empirical approach – and to weaken it from within, by defining the condition of possibility of something as that thing's simultaneous condition of impossibility. (The crucial point not to be missed here lies in the fact that the traditional notion of possibility can only be weakened by *strengthening*, that is, by rendering *necessary its link to impossibility*. It is this link which, in Derrida's words, cannot be annulled.) Yet the 'quasi' can indicate one more aspect of the relationship between transcendentality and empiricity – understood here in the sense of *historicality*. In a 'reflexive' move with respect to the status of the quasi-transcendental theory itself, the 'quasi' can indicate this theory's radically historical and contextual conditions of emergence, as opposed to the necessarily 'supra'-historical status of its quasi-transcendental claim. For even the aporetical transcendental conditions of (im)possibility – as conditions for signification or identity as such – must claim supra-historical or supra-contextual validity. It might sound outlandish to claim the supra-historical status of something after just having discarded any form of historical teleology and History with a capital H. But one should consider the alternative, for it would be even more absurd to concede that a fully closed and totalized signifying system might not be possible today, but nevertheless to insist that it has been possible in the past or could be possible at different times and in different contexts. If this were the case, the necessary link between possibility and impossibility would be severed (and we would have the ordinary traditional concept of contingency).

But on the other hand both the experience of crisis (of the absence of 'ground') and the realization of that crisis as necessary contingency are always historically and contextually located and locatable. The *terms of realization* of those quasi-transcendental conditions are historical and contextual: only under specific historical conditions can one encounter society's necessary contingency and groundlessness, and only from within a specific context, that is, from the ontic observer position of a specific discourse can one realize that absence in terms available within the specific discourse. 'Contingency' as a concept is simply the name given to the absent ground from the viewpoint of theoretical discourse and on the basis of the traditional vocabulary and conceptual stock available within theory and metaphysics. So there is not the slightest incoherence in the claim that the status of contingency is supra-historical (this is why it is transcendental), while both the experience of contingency and its reflective realization are subject to certain historico-empirical conditions (that is why it is *quasi*-transcendental in the second sense of 'quasi').

This is where the abovementioned idea of 'moment' becomes productive. Even for an evolutionist such as Luhmann, the encounter between contingency and the paradox has always been possible historically, even if it has only been effectively realized in certain systems or discourses (such as mysticism or rhetorics). If the encounter with contingency was always possible even as it was not always actualized, then it must depend on specific circumstances for contingency to be realized. It must depend on what we can call the historical *constellation* whether or not that 'moment' of contingency will arise and is realized from the viewpoint and within the language of those discourses in which it is encountered. That moment of the encounter with contingency can be called – from the viewpoint of political theory – the *moment of the political* (Pocock 1975, Palonen 1998).

To conclude: if in the first section of this chapter, the section on foundationalism, it was claimed that the quasi-transcendental conditions of (im)possibility should not be confused with empirical conditions of possibility, now this claim is supplemented by arguing in turn that the realization of the quasi-transcendental move itself has empirical conditions of possibility. After first having discovered a radical gap between the empirical and the transcendental, we now discover a 'circle': the historical is itself the (ever-changing) condition for the transcendental to emerge. This acknowledgement of historicality is what the 'quasi' is supposed to give evidence of: the always specific constellation which allows for the emergence of the post-foundationalist moment, that is to say, for the realization of the transcendental necessity of contingency and the impossibility of a final ground. This enabling constellation is itself radically historical, 'empirical', and part of the ontic realm – which is to say that the realization of contingency *as necessary* is the *non-necessary* outcome of empirical conditions. Only within a particular historical conjuncture has it become possible to question the foundationalist horizon and to develop a post-foundational counter-concept of contingency and groundlessness.

1.6 Moment and Constellation

An approach like the one outlined above obviously has consequences for any inquiry into the history of post-foundationalist political thought – in particular, into that of which the difference between politics and the political has become a conceptual trace: the absence of an ultimate ground of society. Such an approach will search for the moment of the political *within* the historical continuum of political theories as it is described by conceptual history, for instance, but this does not release us from the necessity of ascribing a quasi-transcendental status to that moment *as moment* – for, insofar as it marks the encounter with what we call the quasi-transcendental conditions of all identity, that moment must be located, strictly speaking, *outside* the historical continuum. This certainly has consequences: instead of seeing in post-foundationalism a completely new 'invention' of our modern or post-modern times, one must insist that radical contingency, i.e. necessary contingency, has always been there in the form of a 'moment' realized by certain specific discourses. However, even as the transcendental status of the radical notion of contingency cannot be captured in its radicality by a historicist and nominalistic description, this in no way implies that conceptual history is redundant. For the 'external' moment, in turn, is only realizable *within* a certain historical constellation. And, since it can always only be perceived and realized from *within* the historical continuum, one will have to describe the constellation (in particular, the theoretical constellation, but also its connection to non-theoretical discourses and social systems), in which the moment emerges within an always specific conceptual light, that is to say, under different 'names': as event, as freedom, or as antagonism.

Therefore, it is important to analyze and portray the anti- or post-foundationalist struggle against (or within) the foundationalist paradigm as well as its slow but steady enlargement into a new paradigm of its own, a new horizon of intelligibility, which can be described in historical terms as a trench war where only gradually the post-foundationalist paradigm has gained ground. Within such an account it might always be subject to interpretation whether a certain author actually did formulate the radical notion of contingency rather than some version of the traditional, non-radical notion – and one can argue for Machiavelli being historically the first who might have touched on a coherent version of the radical notion of contingency in his conception of political autonomy; it might even be argued that the notion of contingency in all its radicalness is only perceivable retrospectively from our own historical viewpoint. And yet, being a historical product does not affect the very *status* of the concept as a quasi-transcendental term – as a term for the conditions of (im)possibility of all significatory systems, identities or 'beings'. Thus, a radical distinction must be made between contingency as necessary and contingency as not necessary. No historical or contextual shades and grades are possible with respect to that difference: either contingency is ontologically necessary or it is not (to assume it is only 'a bit' necessary or 'not quite' necessary and still call it 'necessary contingency' would be ludicrous, because it means collapsing it into the ontic which would imply denying the very difference one wants to define). Therefore, as to the quasi-transcendental conditions of all identity, the question is not so much whether or not contingency is 'there' in earlier periods, but rather how the *encounter* with contingency, for example in the form of paradoxes, of fortune, of freedom, of antagonism, of 'democracy', is realized and accounted for or how it is dismissed and disavowed.

It is therefore essential to supplement the discourse of the historian – or 'historical materialist' – with the discourse of the philosopher, for the quasi-transcendental dimension is best describable through the conceptual tools provided by philosophical discourse. What cannot be encompassed by a merely historicist view – which is defined through restriction to the ontic level of the historical concurrencies of a given term – is the source or ground/abyss of those quasi-terms. For what is given in the moment of the political is not only a crisis within a specific discourse (which leads to conceptual change only), but the encounter with the crisis or breakdown of discursive signification as such – in political terms, the encounter with society's abyss or absent ground. And it is the realization of the groundlessness of the social as the entirety of the discursive, rather than just the realization of the groundlessness of any particular discourse, which has come to define the emerging post-foundationalist constellation. What came to be called *modernity* consists, to a significant degree, in the very generalization of the moment of the political as the moment of groundlessness and contingency: it is the crisis of the foundationalist horizon, which starts expanding into a new horizon right from the gaps and fissures within the old foundations. Before some of the left Heideggerian elements of this constellation are explored in Chapters 3–6 in a 'synchronic' fashion, as it were, I will try to present 'diachronically' some historical cornerstones of the concept of the political vis-à-vis the concept of politics in the following chapter.

Notes

1. Hereby it should be clarified that the prefix 'post' in post-foundationalism does not refer to the latest moment of a temporal sequence, but, by showing a distance from both foundationalism *and* anti-foundationalism, it serves as an indicator of their problematic dichotomic relation. For a discussion of 'post-isms' see also Derrida (1990).

2. Heidegger resorts to this archaic spelling (*Seyn* in German) in order to differentiate the evental aspect of *Seyn*-as-difference from the ontological level of being or *Sein*.

3. It should be mentioned that, for Heidegger as for Derrida, there is nothing 'nihilistic' to this absence of ground. The 'negativity' of the ground does not imply an absence of *any* ground (*Grundlosigkeit*), nor can it be reduced to a logical *negation* of ground. Rather, what it implies is an *affirmation*: the affirmation, namely, of the ground as a distant and deferred one. It is true, however, that, while it would not be proper to talk about negativity or negation, there is a more primordial *Nicht* or nothing involved in the abyss/ground chiasm which belongs to beyng and the appropriative event as such.

4. For an extensive discussion of the Heideggerian concept of *Augenblick* as the 'time of the Political' see also Peg Birmingham (1991).

5. The same point as to the necessity of contingency – and the

inversion of this relation – has been made by another Heideg-gerian of the Left, Giorgio Agamben: 'The world is now and forever necessarily contingent or contingently necessary' (1993: 39), which again implies a notion of being which 'is not con-tingent; it is necessarily contingent. Nor is it necessary; it is contingently necessary' (104).

Chapter 2
Politics and the Political:
Genealogy of a Conceptual Difference

With the collapse of certainties, with the deterioration of their foundations and the effacement of their horizons, it became possible – even necessary and urgent – to resume the question of what had been called 'the essence of the political'.

> Philippe Lacoue-Labarthe and Jean-Luc Nancy (1997: 144)

2.1 The Political Paradox

Politics, as Paul Ricœur once remarked, 'only exists in great moments, in "crises", in the climactic and turning points of history' (1965: 255). In 1956, troops of the Warsaw pact states invaded Hungary and cracked down on the Hungarian revolution. This event had heavily dislocating effects on Western political thought – no matter whether Marxist or not. As a reaction, Paul Ricœur published one of his best-known essays, 'The Political Paradox', in which he seeks to come to terms philosophically with the exigency of the Hungarian events (1965). Counter to state-Marxism, his aim is to think what he perceives as the double originality of politics: a specifically political rationality and a specifically political evil. In order to work his way towards this double specificity he has to disentangle the rationality of politics from the sphere of economic rationality, to which it was reduced by Marxism. In other words, the Hungarian events did not lead to a generalized skepticism on Ricœur's part regarding the 'over-politicization' of society; quite to the contrary, he wanted to restore the lost specificity and relative autonomy to politics. In order to achieve his goal he was forced to introduce a distinction between the political and politics, that is, between *le politique*, most often translated into English as *polity*, and *la politique*. Ricœur thus presents his 'political paradox' in the form of, in our terminology, the political difference: 'This autonomy of the political [*du politique*] appears to me to draw on two contrasting traits. On the one hand, the political [*le politique*] realizes a human relation that cannot be reduced to the conflicts between classes . . . On the other hand, politics [*la politique*] develops specific evils, which are precisely political evils, evils of political power; these evils are not reducible to others, particularly not to economic alienation' (1964: 261, my translation).

It is noticeable that in this paragraph Ricœur employs the term 'the political' (*le politique*) twice: *both* for indicating the relations of 'living together' beyond class conflict, which are opposed to a trait of power (named politics: *la politique*), *and* for referring to a specific autonomy, which encompasses both traits: the trait of 'living together' and the trait of 'power'. The autonomy of the political thus consists of the double features both of the political and of politics. Fred Dall-mayr, who is most perceptive regarding the French politico-political difference in the Anglo-American world, speaks about a subtle choice of terminology that is rich in theoretical implications – the choice, namely, that consists in 'the distinction between politics seen as polity (*le politique*) and politics viewed as policy-making or decision making (*la politique*), or between a broadly shared political framework or public space, on the one hand, and the pursuit of partisan strategies or programs, on the other' (1993b: 178). So the main distinction achieved by Ricœur's enterprise is between an ideal sphere of the political (the polity embodying rational concord), defined by a specific rationality, and the sphere of power (politics); yet both of them contribute to the autonomy of the political (*autonomie du politique*). Communism tried to subordinate political happiness and justice to a policy of economic redistribution (which leads into a specifically political evil on the level of politics), instead of respecting the autonomy of the political as a sphere in its own right.

The later Ricœur will retain the assumption of a 'two-sided nature' of the political even as he increasingly understands rationality as an aspect of the juridical. The political is rational since the state is governed by a constitution, it ensures a geographical unity of jur-isdiction, and it links the history and tradition of the community to its future, thus ensuring intergenerational integration. When Ricœur speaks about this form of rationality, he sometimes refers to it as the *reasonable* that has been accumulated through history. On the other hand, however, 'rationality has its other side: the residue of founding violence' (1998: 98), whose trace is left within the community, for 'there is probably no state that was not born out of violence, whether by conquest, usurpation, forced marriage, or the wartime exploits of some great assembler of territories' (98). Despite all rationality, a residual violence within the state always remains, incorporated, as it were, by the authority which is granted the capacity of decision. And it is from these violent traces that fresh outbreaks of violence may emerge, which are inscribed in the very structure of the political.

It is important to realize that Ricœur is not, in a naïve fashion, denouncing the level of 'mere' strategy and power; nor does he propose to free the political, as the realm of the just and rational organization of living together, from such power-politics. While Ricœur insists on a specific rationality of the political (and of the state), he also insists on the inevitability of the struggle for political domination and power. Rather than being separable, the political and politics stand in a paradoxical relation, whose elucidation is the task of political philosophy. Or, to put it the other way around, Ricœur's famous 'political paradox' consists in the mutually contradictory and yet inseparable relation between *le* and *la politique*. The political paradox is constituted as paradox precisely because the conflicting relation of the two terms – the 'contrast between permanence and flux, between rational idea and contingency, between theoretical concept and practical implementation' (Dallmayr 1993b: 183–4) – is inseparable: 'For Ricœur, the core of the political paradox resides precisely in this interlacing of ideality and reality, of polity and policy, of reason and power' (187). Leaving aside, for reasons of space, the philosophical implications of Ricœur's argument, I would like to stress the mere fact that Ricœur's differentiation between *politics* and *the political* has its ultimate aim in the proof of the autonomy and specificity of the political vis-à-vis other social domains such as the economic.

Therein we find one of the main topoi of a non-foundational idea of the political: its aim is to carve out the specificity of the political realm and to defend its autonomy versus other domains of the social and society at large, not by falling back upon a ground or essence of the political domain (a substantive definition of, for instance, the good life), but by employing a paradoxical formulation, which avoids or rejects the question of ground. Ricœur's claim in 'The Political Paradox' that a specific political rationality can only be defined if it is opposed to 'economico-social rationality' is one of the earliest French formulations of the topos of an opposition between political and economic rationality, which is framed in the terminology of the political difference between *la politique* and *le politique*. As a motive of contraposition between the autonomous political domain and other domains of the social, Ricœur shares that claim with thinkers largely outside the French context, such as Hannah Arendt or Sheldon Wolin, and with early German predecessors like Carl Schmitt. Yet it seems that the way 'the political' is understood differs between the followers of Arendt and the followers of Schmitt. While the 'Arendtians' see in the political a space of freedom and public deliberation, the Schmittians see in it a space of power, conflict and antagonism. It is as if the split Ricœur detected at the core of the political – the split between the 'rationality' of a polity (*le politique*) and the strategic and conflictual struggles of politics (*la politique*) – also described, in a very broad sense, two schools of thought or paradigms within political theory, where one group of theorists tends to stress the first and another group the second aspect of the political. I will call the first theoretical trajectory the Arendtian trait of the political and the second the Schmittian trait of the political. While in the first one, to put it somewhat schematically, the emphasis lies on the *associative* moment of political action, in the second the emphasis lies on the *dissociative* moment.

2.2 The *Associative* Political: the Arendtian Trait

Hannah Arendt herself – who is famous for her frequent nominalization of the adjective 'political' – does not consistently differentiate between 'politics' and 'the political' or *die Politik* and *das Politische*. However, the German philosopher Ernst Vollrath – who places himself within the Arendtian tradition – credits Arendt with the achievement of having found or invented the political difference: 'What Arendt had discovered might be called, in contradistinction to the Heideggerian "ontological difference", "the political difference", that is, the difference between politically authentic politics and politically perverted politics, that is, apolitical politics as political apolitics' (1995: 48). There is nothing surprising to this allegiance. The way in which Arendt is indebted to Heidegger's post-foundationalism has been presented in detail by Dana R. Villa (1996). Although it would be difficult to place Arendt herself in the constellation of left Heideggerianism – not because she is not a Heideggerian, but because she does not really seem to be a leftist in the usual sense of the term – she is certainly to be credited with the politicization of Heidegger's thought.[1]

If we want to follow Vollrath's hint further, we will have to consider two aspects of the political difference. First, the introduction of the political difference splits the concept of politics into a *political* form of politics (often nominalized by Arendt as 'the political') and an *a-political* form of politics. This implies that the meaning of what is 'really political' has to be extracted from the concept of politics: one has to find a necessary criterion – and according to Vollrath only a 'pure concept of the political' can serve as criterion. Arendt's whole philosophical enterprise is devoted to the quest for this pure concept of the political mentioned by her in a letter to Jaspers: 'The occidental philosophy never has had a pure concept of the political [*einen reinen Begriff des Politischen*] and never could have one since by necessity philosophy has spoken of Man in singular, and has simply neglected the fact of plurality' (quoted in Vollrath 1995: 47). A concept of the political has to be wrested from politics. So, in the second place, the 'pure concept' of the political has to be wrested from politics on the premise of its potential subordination to the social, that is, to bureaucratic, economic or instrumental forms of rationality. The invention of the political difference takes place against the background of society encroaching upon both the private and the political. I will return to this aspect in the discussion of what I call the neutralization thesis of the political. For now, let us underline that, in order to develop a 'pure concept' of the political in Arendt's sense, one has to insist on the very autonomy of the political. By taking up Arendt's ideas and connecting them to Ricœur's, Vollrath (1987: 20) develops the 'non-deducible quality or modality' of the political by 'autonomizing' it from other domains of the social. The measure which allows him to assess the authentically political character or rationality of politics is found by Vollrath in the 'associative moment, politically speaking, the communicative qua communal moment that lies at the bottom of this concept' of the political (27).

What is stressed by all Arendtians is this *associative* aspect (the aspect of *acting in concert* or *acting together*) versus the *dissociative* aspect of the political stressed within the Schmittian tradition. While

Vollrath's work remains mostly unknown in the Anglo-Saxon world, one of the most prominent of the Arendtian or 'quasi'-Arendtian theorists who employ the political difference is certainly Sheldon Wolin.[2] His definition of the political (presented in extenso in his *Politics and Vision*, 1960) is rather typical for the associative paradigm:

> I shall take the *political* to be an expression of the idea that a free society composed of diversities can nonetheless enjoy moments of commonality when, through public deliberations, collective power is used to promote or protect the well-being of the collectivity. *Politics* refers to the legitimized and public contestation, primarily by organized and unequal social powers, over access to the resources available to the public authorities of the collectivity. Politics is continuous, ceaseless, and endless. In contrast, the political is episodic, rare. (1996: 31)

While Wolin is definitely to be located within the associative trajectory, he does not go as far as Arendt in separating the political from the social. While he is, like Arendt, sceptical of the level of material interests, as Jane Mansbridge (1996: 49) has observed, he stopped short of excluding them from the public realm, objecting only to placing them at the centre of the political association. So Wolin, like Ricœur, sought to integrate politics as the struggle for competitive advantage with the political as a space of commonality, rather than insisting on an unbridgeable divide. He also gives the notion of the political a more egalitarian or democratic (that is, less elitist) spin by insisting on the urgency of creating a culture of commonality and incorporating the political in the everyday lives of countless people. The necessity of retaining the political difference, however, prevails precisely because Wolin, just like Arendt, is deeply concerned about the effects of an inauthentic, that is, bureaucratized, politics in the way it is practiced within the political system. The authentically political, on the other hand, is characterized by a certain 'political-ness' which includes the care and responsibility for our common and collective life.

Now it should be apparent, and Wolin's case should have clarified it, that what we called 'associative' – the associative trait of the political – is not meant to indicate merely the phenomenon of political collectivity (all politics is collective), but the way in which the collective is established. This is where the main difference lies: seen from an

Arendtian angle, people in their plurality *freely associate* within the public realm, motivated, as Wolin would have it, by their care for the common. Seen from a Schmittian angle, though, a collectivity is established through an external antagonism vis-à-vis an enemy or constitutive outside, that is, by way of *dissociation*. Within both trajectories, the respective concept of the political was created in order to account for either the associative or the dissociative dimension. Each dimension serves, within its respective trajectory, as the specific criterion that allows for the *autonomy* of the political to be established vis-à-vis society and the social-plus-economic.

2.3 The *Dissociative* Political: the Schmittian Trait

It has become a commonplace to trace back the 'invention' of the notion of the political to Carl Schmitt's seminal 1932 book on *The Concept of the Political*. What he tries to find there is a specific criterion which would guarantee the autonomy of the political against different social domains – and, as is well known, he locates the *specificity* of the political in the particular distinction between friend and enemy (Schmitt 1996: 26). This criterion is not derived from any other and therefore corresponds to the respective distinction of other domains, like the distinction between good and evil in the moral sphere, beautiful and ugly in the aesthetic sphere, profitable and unprofitable in the economic sphere. However, Schmitt takes care to stress the fact that the political, in contradistinction to other spheres, must not be understood as a *domain*: 'it is independent, not in the sense of a distinct new domain, but in that it can neither be based on any one antithesis or any combination of other antitheses, nor can it be traced to these' (26). The fact that the political does not have to draw on other distinctions attests to its 'inherently objective nature and autonomy' (27). While the quality of autonomy must in principle be granted to other distinctions too, the political is in a privileged position by being the 'strongest and most intense of the distinctions and categorizations' (27). Thus, not only a relative autonomy but also a certain *primacy* has to be granted to the political.[3] This primacy is derived from any social grouping's most extreme case or case of emergency, war, in which the friend/enemy distinction overrides all other distinctions. What serves as the constitutive political principle of a given community (of any *association*) is a *dissociative* operation: antagonism.[4]

As a distinction which can potentially occur in all social domains, the political in Schmitt is emancipated from the political domain in the narrow sense, in particular in the sense of the state – which is indicated in Schmitt by his differentiation between 'politics' and the adjective 'political'. As Benjamin Arditi comments: 'This distinction between the noun "politics" and the adjective "political" is not fortuitous. It provides an initial – although by no means unproblematic – tool to develop a de-territorialised conception of the political which includes but exceeds the bounds of the formal sphere of politics. The advantage of this concept of the political is that it does not tie political phenomena to a particular institutional setting, and allows us to think the political as a mobile and ubiquitous field' (1995: 13). While the difference between 'politics' and 'the political' is implicitly present throughout Schmitt's work, an explicit conceptualization of the difference occurs only at a later stage of his theory: in the preface to the 1972 Italian edition of his *Concept of the Political*.

For Schmitt, the political preferably delineates the *outer* borders of political unities: it defines the relation between states. But the historical moment in which *internal* antagonisms started to spread, thus folding the statal or outward friend/enemy distinction into the inner sphere of a given unity, necessitated a renewed reflection on the nature of politics. So a new phase of reflection for political thought started when a diversity of new political subjects emerged – a process which called into question the classic political monopoly of the state. Schmitt makes it explicit in his Italian 1972 preface how this historical process necessitates, on the theoretical and conceptual level, an enlargement of the notion of 'politics' previously attributed to the state:

> From this followed a new degree of reflection for theoretical thought. Now one could distinguish 'politics' from 'political'. The new protagonists become the core of the entire complex of problems called 'political'. Here lies the beginning and thrust of every attempt to recognize the many new subjects of the political, which become active in political reality, in the politics of the state or nonstate, and which bring about new kinds of friend-enemy groupings. (quoted in Schwab 1996: 12–13)

Every political actor, statal or non-statal, has to submit to the criterion of the political. Politics then becomes a residual term for the institutional sphere of the state. Yet there is another way of coming to terms with *internal* political disturbances, a way hinted at by Schmitt in his German preface of 1963: the possibility of *police*. Politics-as-*police* is what characterizes the early modern European state which had managed to come to terms with the trauma of religious wars and to achieve internal order and security. In this (largely ideal–typical) Hobbesian state of a fully erected *Leviathan*, the political indeed is a matter only of the external politics between states, while internal politics turns into a question of policing an already established order, that is, into a question of '*Polizei*' (Schmitt 1963: 10–11).

As soon as the friend/enemy criterion is no longer applicable, we automatically lose all politics in the radical sense and thus are left with the mere policing of disturbances such as rivalries, intrigues or rebellions. In the most extreme case we are left with what Schmitt calls '*Politesse*' – which is something like a 'polite', that is, 'gamelike', way of politics: '*petite politique*' – so that there are three modulations of the political: external politics, internal poltics, and '*Politesse*' (120). In the case of '*Politesse*', enmity may be sublimated to a refined or conventionalized form of rivalry, so that the friend/enemy distinction can be reactivated. Yet Schmitt makes it very clear that in game-theoretical approaches to politics such reactivation is not possible any more: the friend/enemy relation completely disappears in the process of rational calculation (121). On the other hand, the political can be reactivated by a figure like the modern revolutionary, who, again, turns police into politics while abhorring any form of '*Politesse*'. This might illustrate how the political as antagonism or logic of antag-onization serves as a catalyst for politics, police and '*Politesse*'.

The work of Chantal Mouffe, to which we will return in Chapter 6, stresses the aspect of the political as antagonism in a way which, from a position on the Left, enters into a critical dialogue with Schmitt.[5] In a move reminiscent of Schmitt, Mouffe defines the political as the disruptive moment of antagonism, while seeing in politics the prac-tices and institutions through which a certain order is organized. Among others, the German theorists Oskar Negt and Alexander Kluge also tried to make Schmitt productive for the discourse of the Left. From the viewpoint of our investigation, their approach is relevant because it employs the political difference in a neo-Schmittian way: politics is understood as the essential notion of institutionally defined 'object domains' ('*Sachbereiche*', 1993: 45). Such domains are only partially political, since 'the political' describes, as with Schmitt, the degree of intensity of an association or dissociation

(91). However, and this is what defines all Schmittian approaches of the Left, these theorists insist that political antagonism is only to be judged positively if it is *internal* to a political unity. Thus the totalizing tendencies of Schmitt's own approach are counteracted. The same point is made by Slavoj Žižek, who holds that, '[i]n contrast to Schmitt, a leftist position should insist on the unconditional primacy of the inherent antagonism of the political' (1999b: 29).

2.4 Neutralization, Colonization and Sublimation of the Political

Both the Arendtian and the Schmittian trajectory share what can be called the neutralization or sublimation thesis. According to this thesis, the political becomes increasingly neutralized or colonized by the social (Schmitt, Arendt) or sublimated into non-political domains (Wolin). The primacy of the political is not a triumphant but an endangered primacy – always in danger of becoming entirely closed up in the 'iron cage' of bureaucratized, technologized, and depoliticized society.

Schmitt, in his 1929 essay entitled 'The Age of Neutralizations and Depoliticizations', based his argument on the supposition that technology has assumed the role of a central sphere of thought in the twentieth century. It is the last in a series of spheres of thought which always, at a given historical stage, prove to be central. Centrality here means that the problems of other spheres tend to be solved in terms of the central sphere: in the sixteenth century this was theology, in the seventeenth century it was scientific rationality, in the eighteenth century, moralism and humanism, and in the nineteenth century it was economism. What is important from the viewpoint of the political is that the decisive friend/enemy disputes are fought in terms of the central sphere; this in turn leads to a shift towards a new, supposedly neutral sphere. For instance, after the religious struggles of the sixteenth century, Europeans sought a neutral sphere in the field of science, where problems are resolved without conflict. As a consequence, the former central sphere was decentered and in turn became neutralized.

> Europeans always have wandered from a conflictual to a neutral sphere, and always the newly won neutral sphere has become immediately another arena of struggle, once again necessitating the search for a

new neutral sphere. Scientific thinking was also unable to achieve peace. The religious wars evolved into the still cultural yet economically determined national wars of the 19th century and finally into economic wars. (Schmitt 1993: 138)

The neutral sphere, precisely because it is neutral, serves as an imaginary ground for the rest of society. So it has become today's widespread belief that 'the absolute and ultimate neutral ground has been found in technology, since apparently there is nothing more neutral' (138). The neutrality of every ground, however, is an illusion: it only displaces and occludes political antagonism. Hence the movement from one central sphere to another can be described retrospectively as a movement of (failing) depoliticization, and today people 'believe subconsciously that the absolute depoliticization sought after four centuries can be found here [in technology] and that universal peace begins here' (141). Technology serves today as the ultimate neutral, that is, supposedly depoliticized, ground – a ground beyond the friend/enemy distinction. The age of neutralization and depoliticization of which the title of the essay speaks is our age of a technological 'non-political politics' (Freund 1995: 29).

Left neo-Schmittians like Chantal Mouffe also perceive an increasing neutralization of the political: 'When we look at the current state of democratic politics through a Schmittian lens, we realize how much the process of neutralization and depoliticization, already noticed by Schmitt, has progressed. Does not one of the most fashionable discourses nowadays proclaim the "end of politics?"' (1999: 2). What has taken the place of the political in liberal–democratic capitalism, according to Mouffe, is a 'post-political' politics of consensus which goes under the name of 'deliberative democracy'. The dimension of antagonism is thus erased from political theory (but not from political practice, as the irruptions of fundamentalism and of right-wing and racist politics, i.e. of a clearly antagonistic politics, prove). What Mouffe proposes instead for democracy is an agonistic model of a 'conflictual consensus' that seeks to come to terms with the political rather than disavowing it.

It was said that, within the Arendtian framework, accounts of the political difference are constructed around the larger distinction between the political and *the social*. While in the Arendtian tradition, the political is defined as the space for public deliberation and commonality, the social bears, from the political point of view, rather negative characteristics, which lead Pitkin to describe Arendt's theory about the increasing colonization of the political by the social as 'the attack of the Blob'. According to the Arendtian 'colonization thesis', the social constantly encroaches upon the political. As Pitkin observes: 'In *The Human Condition*, society is variously said to "absorb", "embrace", and "devour" people or other entities; to "emerge", "rise", "grow", and "let loose" growth; to "enter", "intrude" on, and "conquer" realms or spheres; to "constitute" and "control", "transform" and "pervert"; to "impose" rules on people, "demand" certain conduct from them, "exclude" or "refuse to admit" other conduct or people; and to "try to cheat" people' (Pitkin 1998: 3–4). This is precisely what Pitkin poignantly calls the 'attack of the Blob', without however fully realizing that Arendt's polemic against society and in favor of the political is premised upon her anti-foundational stance, for which 'society' is nothing but a figure of foundation. Politics or, for that matter, the political cannot be grounded in anything outside itself, that is, outside the *in-between* space of those who assemble in order to act. This is why, for instance, the notion of *truth* in the eyes of Arendt (1968) is to be excluded from the political realm because it serves as a potential ground which would eventually bring public action and deliberation to a halt. The same goes for categories of the social which plays for her an entirely foundational role: every bureaucratic or managerial societal logic fulfils exactly the same function as a ground which eventually renders true politics, which must remain groundless, redundant.

It should also be mentioned that a variation on the colonization thesis is presented in Sheldon Wolin's quasi-Arendtian work – a variation which can be called the 'sublimation thesis' (see also Pateman 1989 and Pitkin 1972). In his *Politics of Vision*, Wolin argues that the nineteenth century witnessed what he calls an 'attack on the political' in favor of society: 'The abolition of the political was proclaimed by almost every important thinker, and most projects for a future society excluded political activity from the routine of daily life' (1960: 414). While an anti-political impulse has its roots in the beginnings of political thought, the modern anti-politicism is specific in that it offers particular substitutes and is directed 'at the sublimation rather than at the elimination of the political' (414). The 'community' and the 'organization' become substitute 'love objects' and the political is sublimated in a double move: on the one hand the political proper, as the care for what is general to a society, becomes increasingly bureaucratized and discredited, on the other hand, more and more social spheres (in particular the sphere of corporate and other organizations) become 'politicized', albeit in a deficient way, so that '[w]hat has been denied to the political order has been assimilated to the organizational order' (418). Thus, rather than completely disappearing, the political association is reduced 'to the level of other associations at the same time that the latter have been elevated to the level of the political order and endowed with many of its character-istics and values' (430–1). This process has two sources: First, pluralists, sociologists and advocates of small groups and commu-nities have championed a view of society consisting of separate little islands. Second, the politicalness of the political order has been reduced by a seeming politicization of these groups or entities (e.g. business leaders are designated as 'statesmen' of their corporation). Such assimilation of political conceptions to non-political situations amounts to what one could call a 'placebo'-politicalness. Here the political is not truly political because of the restricted nature of the constituency. Political concepts have meaning only in reference to a general order, and this cannot be substituted by multiple and frag-mentary constituencies.

Today, in post-foundational social theory, the idea that the political is in danger of being colonized (which does not exclude the constant possibility of its return) in one or the other way is shared by most, if not all, left Heideggerians. For instance, the thesis of the 'retreat of the political', proposed (as we will see in Chapter 3) by Jean-Luc Nancy and Philippe Lacoue-Labarthe, is clearly to be situated within the Arendtian trajectory and presents a highly sophisticated version of the sublimation thesis. For Nancy and Lacoue-Labarthe, as for Arendt, 'this retreat/withdrawal/closure takes the form of the "general im-pregnation" of the economic/techno-social into the political, effacing it as "a dimension of a specific alterity", namely the site, space or opening of disclosedness of the unique and singular' (Yar 2000: 25).

The neutralization or colonization thesis – the idea that the political is increasingly colonized by the forces of society – is of course logically premised upon the recognition of the autonomy of the political. In other words, the claim as to the heteronomization of the political presupposes that the political has been largely autonomized – for otherwise its autonomy could not be under threat. As a matter of fact, the main aim of theories within the Arendtian and the Schmittian trajectory seems to lie in claiming the autonomy of the political. Such a claim might sound paradoxical, as the autonomy of the political is itself only a result of the fact that society has lost its capacity to fulfil its role as a ground: the political has become autonomous precisely because it cannot be grounded anymore by any other social sphere nor by society as a whole. On the contrary, by stressing the autonomy of the political we might arrive at a point where the conditions are turned upside down, and the political itself now emerges as the *instituting* function of society: now it is the political which is the instance that grounds *and ungrounds* the social. So, for instance, in the Arendtian trajectory, Claude Lefort (see Chapter 4) will call the political the moment by which the symbolic form of society is instituted, while for Ernesto Laclau (see Chapter 6), to some extent from within the Schmittian trajectory, the political is both the disruptive moment of the dislocation of the social and the founding moment of the social's institution vis-à-vis a radical outside. Before presenting the respective theories of left Heideggerian post-foundationalists in detail, a short diachronic account should be given of the historical emergence of the concept of the political.

2.5 The Conceptual Difference: a Diachronic View

The purpose of the following sections is to delineate the historical process by which the concept of the political came to be 'emancipated', carved out of the polis-family of words, and eventually distinguished from the concept of politics. To recapitulate, in what we call the 'moment of the political' in the present study, one has to distinguish three elements: first, the political is supposed to indicate the name for the specificity of politics: the specific quality, rationality or criterion of politics. Second, if the specific criterion is to be independent of and irreducible to other criteria, politics must be autonomous with respect to other domains or spheres of the social. The term 'the political' now indicates the autonomous quality of politics vis-à-vis morality, the economic, and so on. And third, at a certain point – that is, when the ungrounded nature of the social becomes apparent – the political assumes primacy over the social and now indicates the very moment of institution/destitution of society. In order to indicate all three elements of the 'political moment', it proved to be necessary to differentiate between the 'pure' concept of the political on the one hand and politics (which, as a social sub-system, belongs to the sphere of society) on the other hand.

So if the moment of the political is in actual fact threefold, then what had to come together historically in order for the notion of the political to emerge is a clear awareness of both the *specificity* of politics and the *autonomy* of politics, an awareness which in turn, and at a specific point, leads to the assumption of the *primacy* of the political. How should we envisage this process historically? In order to approach the historical emergence of what we call specificity, autonomy and primacy it is perhaps helpful to return to the classic essay by Giovanni Sartori, *What is Politics?*, from 1973. In this essay Sartori describes the historical autonomization process of politics vis-à-vis other social spheres as follows:

> When we speak about the autonomy of politics, the concept of autonomy should not be understood in an absolute but rather in a relative sense. Moreover, four theses can be posited with respect to this notion: (1) that politics is *different*; (2) that it is *independent* - i.e., that it adheres to its own laws; (3) that it is *self-sufficient* - i.e., autarchic in the sense that it is sufficient for explaining itself; (4) that it is a *first cause*, generating not only itself, but given its causal supremacy, everything else. (1973: 11)

As Sartori notes that the second thesis of independence and the third thesis of self-sufficiency often go together, one could feel justified in rejoining them, thereby arriving at a triple thesis with respect to the autonomization process of politics: politics is now posited, in our own words, as specific (by being different from other spheres), autonomous (which means independent and autarchic), and as a 'first cause', that is to say, as being prior to anything social. Let us consider the matter step by step. To assume that politics is different amounts to insisting on its specificity with respect to other social spheres like morality, economy and religion. As Sartori remarks, 'the notion of politics applies to everything, and therefore to nothing in particular, as long as the realms of ethics, economics, politics, and society remain united and are not embodied in structural differentiations – that is, in structures and institutions which can be qualified as political in that they are different from those which are declared economic, religious, or social' (6). It is apparent for Sartori that, in the history of political thought, the first 'hard and fast separation' of politics from other spheres of action occurred with Machiavelli. It was there that 'politics established itself as being different from morality and religion' (11).

Yet the specificity of politics is, as Sartori realizes, a necessary but by no means sufficient condition for its autonomy. In the 'Machiavellian moment' something additional had to be posited: 'Machiavelli not only declares the difference of politics from ethics, but also arrives at a clear-cut affirmation of its autonomy' (11). Things political had been juridicized by Roman and theologized by Christian thought so that, until Machiavelli, political discourse was 'jointly and indissolubly ethicopolitical' (10), that is to say, political questions were indissolubly intertwined with and subsumed under moral, religious and juridical issues, such as questions concerning the good regime or the well ordered or just society. Under historical conditions of the ethicopolitical, it did not make much sense to speak about 'politics' outside the ambit of ethical, moral and religious discourse. Only with Machiavelli does it come about that politics 'attains a distinctive identity and "autonomy"' (11); it is both specific and autonomous. This newly achieved autonomy is captured by Sartori in the following thesis, which condenses the Machiavellian revolution into a single tautological statement: 'Politics is politics' (11). Politics is politics by virtue of being differentiated from other areas or activities and by virtue of following its very own autonomous rules and laws. Yet the most extreme form of the autonomy of politics was not, for Sartori, conceptualized by Machiavelli but by Hobbes, whose 'panpoliticism' assumes the 'absolute independence and self-sufficiency of politics', a 'pure' politics which is 'all-pervasing and all-causing': 'If the prince of Machiavelli governs according to the rules of politics, the leviathan of Hobbes governs by creating these rules and by establishing what politics is' (12).

This most extreme form of the autonomy of politics is also the point, if we were to follow Sartori, at which something of the order of the priority or supremacy of politics is theorized for the first time, albeit in causal terms. Sartori is able to make this rather strong claim for the supremacy of the political in Hobbes, since he restricts the moment of politics to the originary fiat by which order – the order of the Leviathan – is established. He thereby misses what is more important, the fact, namely, that such order is only established in Hobbes for a single reason: to do away with politics altogether. The covenant sanctions the end of politics, not the beginning. Thus, Hobbes is only one in the series of political thinkers who eventually sacrifice the moment of the political, if we take this expression as referring to the moment of strategy. In the case of Machiavelli, however, politics is not, as in Hobbes, a question of all or nothing (the ungrounded state of nature or the Leviathan), but a question of strategically approaching a situation which always remains ungroundable (at the ontological level), but which is also always partially grounded (at the ontic level). Political theory, in the words of Ernesto Laclau, was, to a large extent, 'an effort to circumvent this strategic moment and to limit the effects that it could have over the process of social reproduction' (1996b: 66).

If the history of political thought is also a history of the oblivion of the political (construed as strategic play with contingency or, as Machiavelli would have it, with *fortuna*), it was only at certain points, in certain 'moments', and here, in particular, in the Machiavellian moment, that strategic calculation was made the source of substantive values (rather than the other way around). Yet these moments played a marginal role in Western political thought. So the assumption of the primacy of politics was actually prepared by Machiavelli but eventually achieved much later: this occurred, as we will see, in the nineteenth century, was given a theoretical and conceptual basis in German thought of the first decades of the twentieth century, taken up in post-war French thought, and eventually lead to the spread of the idea of the political difference, which is the topic of our study.

Still, from a retrospective point of view, the Machiavellian separation was a decisive step, but, according to Sartori, only the first one. Something additional had to happen historically and here it seems that Sartori has captured the historical preconditions of emergence which eventually allowed for a conception of the political (and for the primacy of the political) – if only at the most general level. These preconditions consist of the historical separation between the sphere of politics and the sphere of society. In other words, if politics was to 'emancipate' itself fully, the idea of an autonomous society had to be established first. The premises for this kind of an invention of society did not exist before the end of the eighteenth century; and the invention took place via the detour of the autonomization of economics (Sartori 1973: 15). In the nineteenth century, the birth of the discipline which Comte called 'sociology' marked the point where society was granted not only the status of autonomy (vis-à-vis the state) but also that of primacy: for Comte, the political system was nothing but an outgrowth of the social system. Theoretically, the pan-sociologism of Comte thus constitutes the reverse side of what Sartori takes to be Hobbes' pan-politicism: 'We thus come full circle: the pan-politicism of Hobbes is turned upside down and reversed into the pan-sociologism, or the "sociocracy", of Comte' (16). Leaving aside the previous question of whether or not the qualification of pan-politicism holds for Hobbes, we find that Sartori describes here the paradigmatic opposition between society and the political which still echoes in current post-foundational debates about the political. Where Sartori is certainly right is in his claim that only after the invention of a totalizing notion of society, a strong – that is, autonomous – concept of politics and eventually of the political can gain wider influence (precisely because 'the political' assumes the role of counteracting sociologist or foundationalist conceptions of society). In modern theories of the political there is a highly conflictual relation between these terms – as is illustrated by the manifold claims to the neutralization, colonization or sublimation of the political by the social.

2.6 The Politicization of Concepts and the Concept of the Political

What escapes Sartori, of course, is the concept of the political as differentiated from politics. When he speaks about the autonomization process of politics, he speaks about a structural and institutional differentiation *within* the realm of society. As long as politics is taken to be merely one more social sphere – differentiated from other social spheres – the political in the strong sense does not come into play. The concept of the political which is in a position actually to claim *primacy* and not only autonomy affects the question of the ontological *nature* of society and can only be discussed by reflecting on society's (absent) ground, not by describing society's structural or institutional differentiation. Nevertheless, Sartori's general observations as to the increasing autonomization of the modern concept of politics can be substantiated by research in the field of conceptual history. As Reinhart Koselleck and his German *Begriffsgeschichte*-school have shown, the process of a slow but constant 'dissolution of the markers of certainty' (Lefort) was itself accompanied by an increasing politicization of concepts.

According to Koselleck, between 1750 and 1850 – in the period Koselleck calls *Sattelzeit* – a major *horizon shift* in the meaning of social concepts occurred: old words acquired new meaning. While from our present-day perspective the older meaning of concepts became unusual, sometimes obscure even, their new meaning is more or less immediately accessible for us. In other words, what emerges during that process is the modern meaning of many terms, so that, for Koselleck, this conceptual *Sattelzeit* marks the beginning of modernity.

Koselleck (1972) detects four related criteria shared by all reconceptualizations of that time. First, a *democratization* of concepts occurs, which implies that the field of application of political language is enlarged and becomes available to wider sections of the population. Before the watershed at the middle of the eighteenth century, political terminology remained a privilege of the aristocracy, of jurists and scholars, but now a public sphere emerges, the section of *literati* within the population grows, an intensive form of reading (the same few books being read again and again) is replaced by an extensive reading of newspapers, journals, and the like. Second, a *temporalization* of categories occurs, which undermines the idea of an eternal stability or repeatability and, instead, captures processual meanings and experiences. The temporalization of previously static concepts into *Bewegungsbegriffe* – concepts of movement such as *progress* or *history* – from there on enables us to describe social phenomena as processes rather than stable equilibria. Third, and as a consequence, what could be somewhat awkwardly translated as the 'ideologizability' ('*Ideologisierbarkeit*') of concepts becomes ever more important. In the very moment in which, in our words, society's static ground is undermined and can no longer guarantee the more or less identical reproduction of the social structure, concepts are freed to assume more abstract meanings. They are elevated to the form of 'collective singulars' ('*Kollektivsingulare*') such as *history as such* (singularized and, thus, abstracted from concrete histories) or *freedom as such* (abstracted from concrete corporate freedoms of earlier times). And fourth, the *politicization* of concepts leads to an increasing importance of polemical and mutually opposing concepts ('revolutionary' vs 'reactionary'), by which increasingly large sectors of the population are mobilized. Thus, many concepts become entrenched in relations of conflictuality, if not antagonism.

It is highly interesting that all four criteria seem to catch, at a phenomenological level, the effects of an increasing politicization process that reaches far beyond the fourth criterion of conflictual politicization. *Democratization* and *ideologization* are as much political criteria or phenomena as politicization proper, and one could add *historicization* – which lies behind Koselleck's notion of temporalization – to this series of genuinely political phenomena. All of these phenomena – taken together as well as independently – indicate a single large historical process of politicization, and in the final instance point at the contingency that lies at the ground of all concepts. Not only that the meaning of concepts is redefined (something which, of course, occurs throughout history), but the supposedly stable ground of conceptuality itself crumbles. Concepts are now redefined *in praxe* as *Bewegungsbegriffe*.

Of course, the same holds for the concept of politics, and today's differentiation between politics and the political will only be the eventual outcome of these conceptual innovations. Koselleck's general observations regarding the time of what he calls *Sattelzeit* are supported, in the case of 'politics', by Kari Palonen (1993), who observes that in the course of this horizon shift the conventional quasi-Aristotelian conception of 'politics' as discipline – as a static sphere or sector – disappears and gives way to a conception of politics as activity. The transmutation in the use of politics in the plural into politics in the singular can be understood as indicating the autonomization of the concept. A further sign for the temporalization which occurred during Kosellek's *Sattelzeit* is the introduction, in English, of neologisms such as *politicking* and *politicization*, which clearly transport a processual, performative meaning, thereby turning politics into a *Bewegungsbegriff*. For Palonen, the temporalization of politics into an activity (into what Palonen calls an 'action concept') replaces the older notion of politics as a social sphere differentiated from other social areas. As Palonen perceptively argues, '(t)he phenomenon of politics, however, is poorly suited to the spatial metaphors of thinking in spheres. If there is some central idea in the understanding of politics after the horizon shift, it is no longer the *locus* of politics, but rather the quality of politics as an activity' (1999a). Thus we can witness – at least in German and, to a lesser degree, French sources – a growing awareness of politics as an activity or practice, which becomes a commonplace in the second half of the nineteenth century, even while British sources display a subordination of political activity to the metaphorical arsenal of economic activity.

It is in the continental sources – first of all, German sources, in contrast to the French and English sources – that Palonen detects the characteristics of what we would call, within the framework of our inquiry, the experience of the event of the political and of the political as event. There we can find 'important conceptualizations of politics in terms of a sudden change, of a dramatic break, of an extraordinary moment or of passing opportunities' (1999a: n.p.). Nietzsche's idea of *große Politik* can already be interpreted, in Palonen's view, as something which is supposed to create a rupture in normal politics. Later, the neologism *Politisierung* is used by the German expressionist writers Ludwig Rubiner und Kurt Hiller in order to criticize routine politics. The notion of *kairos* as an extraordinary occasion becomes important with Helmuth Plessner. But, most famously, it is in Carl Schmitt's notion of *Ausnahmezustand* – 'the state of exception' – in his *Political Theology* and in Walter Benjamin's notion of *Jetztzeit*, understood as an interruption of the chronological order of things, that characteristics of the event were framed in terms of political discourse. In France, a similar movement occurred after World War II only, and in the Anglo-American world – if we leave aside the special case of Hannah Arendt – it was even later, and mainly through the reception of French post-structuralism, that a similar concept of the political as *event* was theorized.

One can thus observe that, as a rule, in British and Anglophone political thought a radical notion of the political – as being located on an entirely different ontological level than polity, politics, policies, and the like – occurred later than in continental political thought. The process of radicalization of the ordinary notion of politics seemed to shift from German debates in the early years of the twentieth century to post-World War II France, and only during the last years spilled over from French thought into the Anglo-American debates (again, with the more 'continental' thinker Arendt and her followers as an exception to the rule) (Palonen 1999a). One of the reasons for such uneven development – apart from different philosophical inclinations in the respective cultures of the time – could be found, as Palonen submits, in the fact that 'the British discussion is related to the daily practice of *politicking*, while the German and partly the post-World War II French debate, rather, refers to *politicization*, to opening *Spielräume* for politicking outside the normal polity' (ibid.). In other words, the British discussion remained largely within the range of a notion of politics understood as an activity restricted to the political field. Conversely, a view of this kind effectively rules out the possibility of developing a more radical notion of the political (be it as all-encompassing permanent *dimension* of all social life or as the moment or event of grounding/ungrounding society as such).

2.7 The Crisis of the Social – or Why Conceptual Nominalism is Not Enough

What could be the immediate event that eventually triggered the coining of a pure concept of the political, first in Germany and then France? This question seems to demand a rather speculative answer, yet Palonen proposes at least one possible approach to the problem by reverting to an observation by Hannah Arendt: 'The twenties in Germany had much in common with the forties and fifties in France. What happened in Germany after the First World War was the breakdown of a tradition – a breakdown that had to be recognized as an accomplished fact, a political reality, a point of no return – and that is what happened in France twenty-five years later' (Palonen 1989: 82). Seen from this angle, it was the constellation of *crisis* which constituted a certain parallel in the intellectual field between post-World War I Germany and post-World War II France. The crisis presented itself in the form of a breakdown of tradition, a dislocation of the sediments of the social. In short: the experience of contingency and the ungrounded nature of society was something one had to come to terms with, which served as the 'reality-background' for a re-conceptualization of politics as 'the political', and this stands at the end of a conceptual development which began in Koselleck's *Sattelzeit*.

Of course, it is not a new thesis that political philosophy is a phenomenon of crisis. For Sheldon Wolin, 'most of the great statements of political philosophy have been put forward in times of crisis; that is, when political phenomena are less effectively integrating institutional forms' (1960: 8). Yet the hypothesis that conceptual innovation is triggered by, or at least connected to, social crisis becomes plausible indeed if we assume that 'a crisis' is nothing other than the result of a growing non-correspondence between an old conceptual paradigm and its changing institutional or social context (where competing counter-hegemonic paradigms seek to take the old paradigm's place). From this vantage point, it is against the background of a paradigmatic crisis that conceptual innovation occurs, in response to the old paradigm's decreasing capability to provide a model or horizon of intelligibility/plausibility in a new situation. Thus, what the conceptual innovation of 'the political', and, in particular, the difference between the new concept of the political and the conventional concept of politics are about is to point, as we hold, to the crisis of the foundationalist paradigm (represented by such diverse directions of thought as economic determinism, behaviourism, positivism, sociologism). This paradigm came to be internally rearticulated as foundational theories were increasingly confronted with the impossibility of positing uncontested 'markers of certainty' as a positive ground of the social. With regard to recent *political theory*, the hypothesis was put forward by us that the conceptual difference between politics and the political assumes the role of an indicator or 'symptom' of society's absent ground. This difference represents nothing other than a split in the traditional idea of politics, where a new term (the political) had to be introduced in order to point at the 'ontological' dimension, the dimension of institution/destitution of society, while 'politics' was kept as a term for the 'ontic' practices of conventional politics: the particular and, eventually, always unsuccessful attempts at grounding society.

So, at the end of the conceptual politicization process, as described by Koselleck and *Begriffsgeschichte*, not only did certain concepts become 'political' (temporalized, democratized, historicized), but the political roots of all concepts became visible. At the end of the politicization of concepts stands the concept of the political. What had occurred, together with the politicization of concepts, was the dislocation of the foundationalist horizon. Now, as the horizon change comes full circle, that is, after a process of continuous autonomization, the political itself (the political as that which cannot be confined within the limits of the domain of politics) becomes the new horizon. We now perceive the very constitution of society and the social through the political looking-glass.

This is precisely the reason why a *conceptual historical* investigation into the concept of the political must not be satisfied with a purely nominalistic approach to its object, since the logic of 'conceptualization' or of 'language' itself cannot be separated from politics. After the horizon shift, we all stand within a political horizon, and therefore must be aware of the fact that not only political discourse but *language as such* functions politically. One could not put this more bluntly than J. G. A. Pocock, who – in a truly chiasmatic formulation – conceives of 'politics itself as a language-system and language itself as a political system' (1973: 28). Similarly, James Farr argues that a political theory of conceptual change 'must take its point of departure from the political constitution of language and the linguistic constitution of politics'. Which implies that 'its premises must acknowledge that in acting politically actors do things for strategic and partisan purposes in and through language; and that they can do such things because the concepts in language partly constitute political beliefs, actions, and practices. Consequently, political change and conceptual change must be understood as one complex and interrelated process' (1989: 32).

What is the implication of all this? Isn't it apparent that the invention of a 'pure' concept of the *political* is itself premised upon the historical process of the politicization of *concepts*? In other words, doesn't the temporalization of concepts go hand in hand with the growing awareness of groundlessness and contingency? And if we eventually come to think of the difference between politics and the political *as (temporal) difference*, that is to say, *as a process of oscillation and dislocation which renders impossible any static ground*, then, isn't that difference just another way of indicating and thinking about contingency? If this is so, if the political difference is just another (paradoxical) form of speaking about the groundlessness on which we stand, then the consequence would be that it becomes impossible for us to approach the concept of the political in a purely nominalistic fashion (which would simply be *anti-*, not *post-*foundational), as one concept among many within the polis-family of words. It is not an object – or concept – among others to be analyzed but, rather, it is the very name of the horizon of constitution of any object – including the constitution of our own position as conceptual historians or political theorists. The difference of politics vis-à-vis the political, therefore, must be read as a sign of temporalization that keeps open and possible processes of politicization which otherwise – that is, in a society that imagines itself as based on a firm and stable ground – could not be envisaged. This *radical difference* – which, accordingly is nothing but the conceptual symptom of the temporal dislocation involved in the unfixable process of grounding/ungrounding – must not be confused with the level of 'ordinary' or ontic differences between concepts and, hence, is not visible for a die-hard nominalist.[6] We will have to change perspective and return to those trajectories of philosophical thinking where *radical difference* and *contingency* are thought of in a non-nominalistic and thus *post-*foundational way. This is what we did in the present chapter and will take up in Chapter 7; in the subsequent chapters I will analyze the post-Heideggerian constellation of political postfoundationalism, whose key points are indicated by the proper names: Nancy, Lefort, Badiou, and Laclau.

Notes

1. For an extensive discussion of Arendt's political position as a non-leftist but radical Heideggerian see Marchart (2005). It must be mentioned, however, that the Arendtian political difference is presented by Vollrath in a rather schematic and not quite Heidggerian way, since the difference comes close to being reified into a distinction.

2. To hold that Wolin is to be placed within the Arendtian trajectory does not imply claiming that he remained entirely uncritical towards Arendt. See for instance Wolin (1990: 183), where he holds against Arendt's rigid separation between the political and society: 'The problem of the political is not to clear a space from which society is to be kept out, but it is rather to ground power in commonality while reverencing diversity – not simply respecting difference.'

3. Although Schmitt himself does not make this point, one could argue that the primacy of the political can be assumed because the political amounts to the 'secret truth' of other distinctions, if by the political we understand not a distinction among many but the *very principle of distinction as such*, that is, *antagonism*.

4. 'Dissociation' is, of course, an operation which has *both an associative and a dissociative* side: 'The distinction of friend and enemy denotes the utmost degree of intensity of a union or separation, of an association or dissociation' (Schmitt 1996: 26).

5. Benjamin Arditi's proposal of democratically 'up-dating' Schmitt also relies on Ernesto Laclau and Chantal Mouffe's work (see again Chapter 6). It rests on two basic assumptions: 'First, the political is an excess that escapes domestication, and therefore prevents the total closure of an order, i.e. the institution of "the real and perfect *status civilis*". Alternatively, the presence of conflict can be seen as the mark of a constitutive lack that both prompts the state to pursue the idea of order and prevents its ultimate realisation. Whether as an excess or a lack, the political signals the permanent deferral of the institution of "order" – of any order – as a full and definitive construction. Secondly, politics and the political are interconnected registers. Barring Schmitt's exceptional case of war, in democratic orders there is a productive interplay between them' (1995: 86–7).

6. In other words, a purely nominalistic version of conceptual history is not able to account for the radical difference between politics and the political. Even where these nominalist theories claim to be anti-foundationalist, they cannot 'secure' the groundlessness of the social, since it is not feasible for a nominalist theory to ascribe a quasi-transcendental status to the 'absent ground' (for a nominalist there is, *ex hypothesi*, only the level of the ontic).

Chapter 3
Retracing the Political Difference: Jean-Luc Nancy

3.1 Philosophy and the Political: the Deconstruction of the Political

Every inquiry into social post-foundationalism and the conceptual difference between politics and the political will have to take into account the work presented and elaborated at the Centre for Philosophical Research on the Political between 1980 and 1984. The Centre, founded by Philippe Lacoue-Labarthe and Jean-Luc Nancy, turned out to be the location for the most intense and influential re-elaboration so far of the notion of the political, or of the difference between politics and the political. The way Claude Lefort and Alain Badiou, for instance, frame their own versions of the political difference (oftentimes in contradistinction to Nancy and Lacoue-Labarthe's version) is certainly influenced by the debates at the Centre. Through the 'comparative' approach we employ across the next chapters it will be possible to acquire a broader understanding of the way in which the political difference unfolds within a diverse and yet related set of theoretical approaches from 'post-structuralism' or 'left Heideggerianism'. These approaches are, in one or the other way, 'contingency theories'; they share a strong notion of the event; they grant a crucial role to division and antagonism; of course, they all deny the possibility of a final ground of the social, and still are 'grounded' on their own variants of something like the ontological difference. The theorists discussed in this and the next chapters represent, as it were, certain 'clans' of left Heideggerianism, and this also determines the way in which the political difference is framed in their work: while Nancy and

Lacoue-Labarthe work from the viewpoint of deconstruction, Claude Lefort's work is deeply influenced by Maurice Merleau-Ponty. Alain Badiou's work can be read as a Lacanian (critical) contribution to the topic. And Ernesto Laclau and Chantal Mouffe, finally, start from a deconstructivist stance (with some Foucaultian elements) but soon come to include Lacanian elements into their theory.

If we now turn to the first, the deconstructivist, family-member, the colloquium on Jacques Derrida's text 'Fins de l'homme' ('Ends of Man'), which took place shortly before the Centre's opening in 1980, is usually considered to be the prelude to, or even the starting point of, Nancy and Lacoue-Labarthe's later work on the political. The question of the political was taken up there in a seminar (Lacoue-Labarthe/Nancy 1981a) where Derrida's work was interrogated as to its relation to the question of the political or politics. Yet the participants went beyond the confines of Derrida's work by inquiring into the very nature of the relation between politics and philosophy as such. This whole problematic was raised in particular in Lacoue-Labarthe's contribution to the seminar, to which a large part of the joint theoretical project of Nancy and Lacoue-Labarthe in the next years came to be devoted, and to which large parts of Nancy's work seem to be devoted until today.

What Lacoue-Labarthe calls for in his intervention is both a *deconstruction* of the political and – what actually goes hand in hand with it – a *rejuvenation* of the question of the political. All this on the basis of what is essential for Lacoue-Labarthe and Nancy: 'the question of the link which indissociably unites the political with the philosophical' (1997: 95). This *deconstruction* of the political (with regard to the philosophical) proceeds by retracing what, from then on, came to be called in Nancy and Lacoue-Labarthe's work the 'retreat of the political'. This means 'that the very *question* of the political retires and gives way to a kind of obviousness of politics or the political – to an "everything is political" ' (97) to which we submit, according to Lacoue-Labarthe, not only in totalitarian states but also in liberal democracies. In the modern age he detects, following Hannah Arendt's diagnosis of totalitarianism, the unconditional domination of the political. The *totalitarian fact* – comprising both the Party State and 'psychological dictatorship' (by which he understands the regime of Western liberal democracies) – accompanies historiographically the end of philosophy or *the completion of the philosophical*. The unconditional domination of the political thus

represents in all its forms the completion of a philosophical programme – be it realized or not. In other words, the philosophical
desire par excellence always consisted in the attempt practically (i.e.
politically) to realize the philosophical programme. The *totalitarian
fact*, in which everything becomes political, is but such realization.

Now, to rejuvenate the political *as question* means engaging in the
reactivation of this political obviousness of the 'everything-is-political',
which is precisely what stands in the way of a real engagement with the
political. To deconstruct the political necessitates that we differentiate
ourselves both from the philosophical and from the philosophical
desire of practical realization. By 'retreat of the political' Lacoue-
Labarthe basically understands a 'gesture of dissociation' with regard
to the philosophical. Yet such dissociation must not search for something like a safe haven, as there is no 'retreat' – in the topographical
sense of a *place* of retreat – outside or beyond the philosophical. For
this reason, the retreat cannot be 'a matter of turning away from the
political and of "moving" to something else' (ibid.: 96). One has to
engage with it within the medium of philosophy via the *deconstruction
of the political*. This of course is an immense work in which, if the
philosophical and the political are essentially intertwined, for Lacoue-
Labarthe the whole of philosophy is implicated.

What was presented at the colloquium on Derrida's 'Ends of Man'
comprised in a nutshell all the central themes one will run up against
time and again in most of Nancy and Lacoue-Labarthe's texts: the
necessary co-belonging of the philosophical and political; the urgency
of a deconstruction of the political and an interrogation of the
problematic of the political based on the historical fact of the latter's
omnipresence. These topics were taken up in November 1980, only a
short time after the colloquium, when the Centre for Philosophical
Research on the Political was opened at the Ecole Normale Supérieure
in Paris. In the introductory statement at the Centre's instauration
Nancy and Lacoue-Labarthe formulated the central question, which
was supposed to be tackled by the institution in the years to come:
'How to question (indeed, can one), today, what must provisionally
be called the *essence of the political*?' (1997: 105).

3.2 The 'Retreat' of the Political

By the 'essence' of the political we must of course not understand an
eternal or immutable Platonic idea of the political. What the authors

call 'essence' reveals itself only as something which is absent, or which *absences/presences* through the movement of its very 'retreat' (or 'withdrawal'). It is thus advisable to begin this chapter by shortly reflecting on the way in which Nancy and Lacoue-Labarthe circumscribe rather than define the notion of retreat. The authors are keen to emphasize that by retreat we should not understand a Hegelian movement of dialectical sublation or *Aufhebung* (the political is far from being sublated in something like the Hegelian state), nor should we see in it a Marxist reduction of the political merely to a matter of superstructure. Instead, the notion is employed in two senses. First, in the sense of the blinding obviousness of 'everything is political'. The political retreats before our very eyes and we are blinded by the fact that we *cannot not* see it – which is precisely what constitutes its retreat. And in its second sense, the retreat constitutes a 're-tracing of the political, re-marking it, by raising the question in a new way' (Lacoue-Labarthe/Nancy 1997: 112). The political does not, in other words, disappear without traces, rather it is re-tracing itself as a question to be posed again. The authors' claim, then, amounts to something other than the simple-minded or commonsensical equation to the effect that 'where everything is political, nothing is political'. This equation does not work out without remainder: there will always be something more than 'nothing', since there will always be the trace of absence or retreat. The retreat in this second sense would thus retrace the contours of the lost specificity of the political and would open opportunities for a reinvention of it's actual conditions (139). So we encounter a double movement, the conceptual aspects of which are associated with the name of Heidegger.

It is Heidegger's notion of *Entzug* or 'withdrawal' which corresponds to his notion of *Seinsverlassenheit* ('abandonment of/by beyng'). For Heidegger, to put it somewhat over-schematically, it is due to our intense concentration on the level of beings that being retreats or withdraws, which leads to our forgetfulness or oblivion of being. But the latter can only fall into oblivion because it has withdrawn already: behind our concentration on beings we not only forget about being, but also about the epochal fact that being is already on retreat. Thus, *Seinsvergessenheit* must not only be understood as the forgetfulness of being but, what is more, as the forgetfulness of *Seinsverlassenheit*, of the retreat of being (so that the *Seinsvergessenheit* of man 'presupposes' the ontological and historical condition of *Seinsverlassenheit*, 1994: 114). Yet it is important to see that, for

Heidegger, even as he speaks about the destinal structure of *Geschick*, we are in no way delivered to an inescapable fate: neither are we compelled to go along with it blindly, nor does it make sense, on the other hand, to rebel against it blindly. Rather, it is important to 'reflect' on what conceals itself by way of its very unconcealment, by way of its 'blinding obviousness' on the level of beings. The obviousness of the level of beings conceals the withdrawal of being, which is hidden precisely within the obviousness (ibid.: 111).

Nancy and Lacoue-Labarthe's project will to a large degree consist in a critical *political reformulation* of these Heideggerian themes. With respect to the difference between politics and the political, this implies that, if Nancy and Lacoue-Labarthe's 'retreat of the political' is modeled upon the Heideggerian ideas of *Seinsverlassenheit* and *Seinsvergessenheit*, then there is reason also to associate, even if they themselves do not explicitly do so, the difference between the political and politics with the ontological difference. Here it is crucial to note that, in Heidegger, the oblivion of being in the last instance is not so much about the forgetfulness of being per se as about the forgetfulness of the ontological difference – the difference between being and beings – *as difference*. To retrace the political as question and to re-engage in such interrogation, as Lacoue-Labarthe and Nancy do, is all the more necessary as, according to Heidegger (1994: 108), the age of *Seinsvergessenheit* is at the same time an age characterized by the absence of all questionability. In this age, there is nothing questionable in the radical sense, there are only 'problems' and 'difficulties' to be overcome by calculative reasoning. In this moment, Nancy and Lacoue-Labarthe set out to answer to Heidegger's injunction that *Seinsverlassenheit* – as '*Politikverlassenheit*' – be recollected in its self-concealing history.

Before we return to some of the quasi-transcendental traits of the retreat of the political as they were excavated by Nancy and Lacoue-Labarthe (here we think in particular of notions such as ground, finitude, relation, community, being-with, and the like), we should therefore dwell for a moment upon the epochal coordinates of the abovementioned 'self-concealing history', within which the retreat of the political unfolds and which were interrogated upon by Nancy and Lacoue-Labarthe. Their proposition that we live in an age in which 'everything is political' is more than an ideological commonplace. Under its domination, they hold, the political becomes *unapparent* – an unapparence 'proportionate to its all powerfulness'

(Lacoue-Labarthe/Nancy 1997: 126) – and acquires the obviousness of an 'it goes without saying'. Nancy and Lacoue-Labarthe take the obvious seriously, since for them it describes our very condition in an 'epoch where the political is completed to the point of excluding every other area of reference' (111). Thus, the political equals what – with recourse to Hannah Arendt – they see as the *totalitarian phenomenon*, as the 'unsurpassable horizon of our time' (126).

What exactly is Nancy and Lacoue-Labarthe's understanding of totalitarianism? In a broad sense, it designates the merging of the political with diverse authoritative discourses, among which the authors count socio-economic, technological, cultural, or psychological discourses. Simultaneously, the political converts itself – given the absence or the spectacularization of public space – into 'technological' forms of management or organization, a process which leads to the effective silencing of genuinely political questions. Liberal democracies, and herein their understanding differs from other theories of totalitarianism, are not excluded by Nancy and Lacoue-Labarthe from the regimes which incur this charge (which would be an unconvincing exception anyway, given the authors' argument as to the *all-encompassing* epochal nature of the 'undivided reign of the political', 1997: 126). The 'new totalitarianism' the authors want to mark out can, in a first step, be determined in economic fashion by three basic traits. First, the victory of the *animal laborans*; second, the 'recovery of "public space" by the social' (129), which implies that communal life is no longer regulated by public or political ends, but according to the necessities of subsistence; and third, the loss of authority and of freedom as related to the transcendence of a foundation. The last point also marks out a difference between the 'new totalitarianism' and 'classical totalitarianism': while the latter incorporated any form of transcendence (they give the example of the reason of history in the case of Stalinism or politics as plastic art in the case of Nazism), the former dissolves any transcendence into all spheres of life, which also dissolves any alterity. As an effect, the retreat appears as the retreat of transcendence or of alterity. What is left, on the other hand, is a situation of immanence, a regime (in the broadest sense of the word) that will later be called by Nancy *immanentism*.

Nancy and Lacoue-Labarthe's argument as to 'the total immanence or the total immanentization of the political in the social' (115) is easily recognizable as what in Chapter 2 was called the *colonization thesis*, which underlies, one way or another, nearly all theories employing the political difference. The sphere of the political, the public, or the city, as it is usually diagnosed, became increasingly colonized by the forces of the social and of society. In Nancy and Lacoue-Labarthe, too, it is the 'eco-socio-techno-cultural' (129) complex taking over the city and leading to the retreat of precisely the 'civility' of the city. It is on the basis of the colonization thesis that the differentiation between politics in the deprived sense (siding, as it were, with the social) and a strong notion of the political will be sustained.

3.3 *La Politique* and *le Politique*

Nancy and Lacoue-Labarthe's introduction of their version of the difference between *la politique* or politics and *le politique* or the political – which was to become crucial for later debates around the political difference – must be understood against the backdrop of their critique of foundationalism in both its 'philosophical' (in the disciplinary sense of the term, including the discipline of political theory) and scientific variants. When they call for a certain vigilance with respect to the scientific reduction of phenomena to positively given empirical facts, they do this because they are suspicious of what one could call the reduction of the phenomenon of the political and its retreat to politics as a distinct sub-domain of the social – a reduction in which we must see nothing other than a metaphysico-technological variation on the reduction of the phenomenon or play of beyng to the level of beings: 'Vigilance is assuredly necessary, today more than ever, as regards those discourses which feign independence from the philosophical and which claim, correspondingly, to treat the political as a distinct and autonomous domain' (Lacoue-Labarthe/Nancy 1997: 109).

Insofar as they insist on approaching the political by way of its retreat only, the authors have to take pains in differentiating it from the positively given domain of politics. Thus, by employing the notion of *the political*, Lacoue-Labarthe and Nancy 'fully intend not to designate *politics*' (110). Examples for the latter would be, for instance, the politics of 'the Chinese Emperors, the Benin kings, of Louis XIV or of German social democracy' (125). In all these cases, politics describes a certain domain or certain forms of action attributed to particular social actors. One can even go a step further and assume that, while the political is nothing which is 'merely in charge of order and administration' (Nancy 1991: xxxvi), politics is a form of technological action and thinking consisting nowadays mainly of institutionalized social *management* and of what Foucault would call *governmental technologies* or police (Nancy 1992: 389). It appertains to the realm of calculation, where all arising problems and difficulties are to be 'resolved' by administrative means, while everything questionable in the radical sense, that is, *questionability as such*, disappears.

This is how the political difference was understood by most commentators on Nancy and Lacoue-Labarthe. Patrice Loraux, for instance, in a debate with Nancy and Lacoue-Labarthe, proposed to define politics in the following way: 'if *the political* is that which is thus aimed at in a retreat, *politics* would be, then, the state of the "everything is political", and *a* politics . . . organisation, bricolage, institution (*a* politics would not be a species of the genre *"politics"*)' (Lacoue-Labarthe/Nancy 1997: 141–2). For Simon Critchley, '*le politique* refers to the essence (a word apparently employed with little deconstructive reticence) of the political – what, before Heidegger, one might have referred to as the philosophical interrogation of politics – whereas *la politique* refers to the facticity or empirical event of politics . . .' (1993: 74). Fred Dallmayr, directing our attention more to the public-space aspect of the political as an arena in which politics and political struggle can occur, refers us to the distinction 'which has become current in recent Continental thought: that between "politics" and "the political", where the former designates partisan strategies and concrete institutional devices and the latter the arena or *"mise en scène"* presupposed by these strategies' (1997: 182). And Christopher Fynsk, paraphrasing Nancy, designates '*le politique* : the site where what it means to *be* in common is open to definition' and '*la politique*: the play of forces and interests engaged in a conflict over the representation and governance of social existence' (1991: x). It turns out that philosophers and political theorists are attentive to Nancy and Lacoue-Labarthe's version of the political difference, because it is this difference, I would claim, upon which the post-foundationalist stance in contemporary political thought in fact hinges: the difference between politics and the political should be read as one of the main 'expressions' (albeit a *non-expressive* expression) of society's and community's absent ground – respectively, of the presence of ground *as absence*. Nancy and Lacoue-Labarthe's thinking of the retreat of the political in terms of the political difference was to be further elaborated by Jean-Luc Nancy in his later work on the question of community, of being-in-common or being-with, of singularity and of freedom, to which we now turn.

3.4 Community and the Political Difference

If we were to wrap up what has been discovered so far concerning the ontological difference and the retreat of the political and 'apply' it to Nancy's thought of community, we might come close Christopher Fynsk's conclusion as to the relation between the ontic and ontological: it serves in Nancy as both *gap and bridge*, not only between politics and the political, but it also marks the *gap and bridge* 'between his thought of community and any existent political philosophy or program' (1991: x). This is why, for instance, Nancy distances himself to some degree from the traditional thought of the Left, according to which, first of all, one would have to develop and work out a more or less detailed political programme. In contraposition to such a stance, Nancy's approach to the question of community, as Fynsk insists, 'is thus to work a term like "community" in such a way that it will come to mark what Heidegger would call the difference between the ontic and the ontological and to oblige us to think from the basis of this difference'(x). In other words, Nancy's questioning of the notion of the political (as differentiated from politics) evolved into a *post-foundational theory of community*, which was laid out in particular in *The Inoperative Community* (1991), in *The Compearance* (1992) and in his *Being Singular Plural* (2000).

What is important to understand, though, is that Nancy's theory (or questioning) of community is *intrinsically* a theory (or questioning) of the political. Thus we can already find in the preface to his *Inoperative Community* what might amount to a definition of the relation between the political and community: 'the political is the place where community as such is brought into play' (Nancy 1991: xxxvii). In the very first pages of the *Inoperative Community* it becomes apparent that community (as being-in-common) is based, or founded, upon the very difference between politics and the political. Without introducing this difference, Nancy would not be in a position to develop his radical notion of community (unless by way of excluding anything political altogether).

Let us trace in more detail the different aspects of community, and let us do so by proceeding on the *via negativa* and by first establishing what community in the radical sense *is not*. In order to arrive at community's 'reverse side', we would just have to imagine a world whose ordering functions were reduced to politics (without any traces of the political). In Nancy's theory, this would amount to *a society without community*. Hence the first of community's antitheses is society, if by society we understand 'the dissociating association of forces, needs, and signs' (1991: 11). However, Nancy immediately issues a warning against any form of social romanticism à la Tönnies. Nancy's philosophy has nothing to do with 'modernization-theory' and does not assume a lost paradise of a communal happy-together that one is supposed to rediscover (which would only amount to just another attempt to realize a supposed essence of community). The community he is looking for is nothing which could be found in reality prior to the advent of society. So there is no point in sentimentally yearning for something which in actual fact never existed. Rather than being historically superseded by society, one could say that community constantly appears *in the wake* of society, as an event (ibid.). Again, we encounter the now familiar topos of colonization of the political (in form of community) by the social (in form of society) – only that, for Nancy, society itself has drawn to a closure, because, like politics, it is everywhere. An 'end' or 'ending' in Nancy and Lacoue-Labarthe (be it the end of philosophy or the closure of the political or the wake of society) is never a *dead-end*, it is always at the same time an opening.

Now, the modern form of regime corresponding to the rule of society is what Nancy terms 'immanentism', by which we have to understand the modern regime of totalitarianism, but in a rather enlarged sense. There are two symmetrical figures of immanentism: what we called the classical form of totalitarianism on the one hand, and the set of disconnected individuals of liberalism on the other. Immanentism is hence defined as 'the general horizon of our time, encompassing both democracies and their fragile juridical parapets' (3). It is located within what would be called, according to our own lexicon, the foundationalist horizon. As far as classical totalitarianism is concerned, Nancy cites the example of 'actually existing communism', in which the main goal was to produce and put into effect socially a supposed essence of community: 'economic ties, technological operations, and political fusion (into a *body* or under a *leader*) represent or rather present, expose, and realize this essence necessarily in themselves' (ibid.). Concerning democratic liberalism, Nancy poignantly argues: 'one cannot make a world with simple atoms. There has to be a *clinamen*' (ibid.). That is to say, there has to be a principle of relation between those atoms which liberalist individualism does not account for. What unites all versions of immanentism is the foundationalist principle of immanence, that is to say, the denial of any transcendence in the sense of a constitutive outside. Instead, immanentism posits an *internal* incarnation of transcendence (what in Lefort, as we will see shortly, would be the party or the body of the leader), which serves as the principle of communal fusion that Nancy calls *communion*.

We thus encounter a twofold characteristic of immanentism: 'work' and communion. When Nancy speaks for instance of totalitarianism as a regime that *ignores* the retreat of community, thus condemning 'the political to management and to power (and to the management of power, and to the power of management)' (1991: xxxix), what corresponds to this is a form of community based on the technologico-metaphysical notion of 'operation', 'work' or 'working' (as opposed to Nancy's idea of an *inoperative* or 'unworked' community). Community nowadays – in the epoch of society – is something to be organized and thus produced. It is a matter for technological planning and management, not for politics proper. Therefore, the result of this operation must not be conflated with community proper either. The other characteristic is what Nancy calls *communion*: community fused into the figure of *the One*, like that of the social body, the fatherland or the Leader, which violently serves as an entirely immanent representation of transcendence. These two characteristics of community in its deficient mode – 'work' and communion – are far from being disconnected, since fusion does not come about as naturally or organically as the organicity of its end product might suggest; rather, it is produced by organizational, that is, by socio-technological means. All our political programmes, Nancy holds, are based on this notion of 'work': 'either as the product of the working community, or else the community itself as work' (xxxix).

What, then, do we have to understand by an *inoperative* community – a community which is not constituted as an organic *œuvre*? Nancy will claim that it is difficult to ascribe any positive content to community in this radical sense: it is nothing but *resistance to immanence*, and in its resistance towards the logic of immanence and communal fusion it is *transcendence*: what from a Lacanian perspective, one would call *extimacy*, in Nancy refers to a state of being ' "posed" in exteriority, according to an exteriority, having to do with an outside *in the very intimacy* of an inside' (xxxvii). Community does not consist – as communion does – in the transcendence of a being immanent to it (in an ontic identity assuming ontological dignity), but, on the contrary, 'in the immanence of "transcendence" – that of finite existence as such' (xxxix). Community is based on the experience of *finitude* which, on the other hand, is ignored by forms of immanentism. It should now be comprehensible why we started our exposition of Nancy's thought on community by elaborating on the concept of immanentism and work, that is, of community's 'antitheses'. This puts us in a position to realize that Nancy himself engages with community via a procedure of 'negation'. Yet one must not mistake this negation as dialectical. What Nancy's thought aims at is not only that which *retreats* within, and from, the foundationalist horizon, but it is the *retreat itself*. As a movement, the retreat does not have a definite location, nor does it own a positive content and can therefore only be re-traced through the interrogation of its very movement.

Such 'inoperative' community can only occupy a strange non-place, which has to do with the fact that existence, as Nancy (2000) does not stop reminding us, is essentially *co*-existence. Being is essentially *being-in-common*. And community does not come about via the immanentization of the *common* (as communal fusion). Rather, it arises in the *in* of *being-in-common*:

> Being *in* common has nothing to do with communion, with fusion into a body, into a unique and ultimate identity that would be no longer exposed. Being *in* common means, to the contrary, *no longer having, in any form, in any empirical or ideal place, such a substantial identity, and sharing this* (narcissistic) '*lack of identity*' which in philosophical parlance is called, since Heidegger, *finitude*. (1991: xxxviii)

Community is based, or founded, on the lack which derives from the impossibility of complete immanence and is defined as 'the infinite lack of infinite identity' (ibid.).[1] Finitude stands in a series of categories through which Nancy seeks to re-trace community: finitude, sharing or com-pearance, and singularity. These categories appear in the following description of the essence of finite being: 'The essence of Being as being-finite is inscribed by finitude a priori as the sharing of singularities' (1991: 28). What do we have to understand by *sharing* of *singularities*? Here we come closer to the nature of the clinamen, of the social relation and of community's basic elements (which are not individuals).

Nancy, however, warns us not to confuse such relation with traditional ideas of the social bond. Sharing or compearance is precisely what happens in the communal *in-between* of singularities, without any form of communion being established. It is a different way of talking about the movement of the *retreat* of community rather than its essence. It seeks to describe the specific phenomenality of finite (and thus communal) beings. To approach what is difficult to illustrate, Nancy employs a specific formulation: 'finitude *co-appears* or *compears* (*com-paraît*) and can only *compear*: in this formulation we would need to hear that finite being always presents itself "together", hence severally; for finitude always presents itself in being-in-common and as this being itself . . .' (ibid.). This form of finite relation as com-pearance is closer to origins than the social bond, which Nancy thinks is established by power relations and thus belongs to the realm of the ontic, while the appearance of the *in-between* of community belongs to an entirely different register:

> It consists in the appearance of the *between* as such: you *and* I (between us) – a formula in which the *and* does not imply juxtaposition, but exposition. What is exposed in compearance is the following, and we must learn to read it in all its possible combinations: 'you (are/and/is) (entirely other than) I' ('*toi [e(s)t] [tout autre que] moi*'). Or again, more simply: *you shares me* ('*toi partage moi*'). (29)

Singularities have, in other words, nothing in common, they 'have no *common being*, but they com-pear [*com-paraîssent*] each time *in* common in the face of the withdrawal of their common being' (1993: 68). It is only through the withdrawal of communion (or immanence, or 'work') that community appears. So how do we have to conceive of the nature of those singularities? We have to think of the finite being as a singular being, which is not the individual. The notion of the singular is used by Nancy in a critical move against the immanent-ism of the individual. The difference lies in the fact that the individual is modeled upon the self-sufficient modern subject which, in its monadic existence, does not rely on other individuals, it does not *relate*, it does not *compear* and it does not *share*. Singularities, on the other hand, are exposed to the in-between through their relation of sharing. They are constituted by 'the sharing that makes them *others*: other for one another, and other, infinitely other for the Subject of their fusion, which is engulfed in the sharing, in the ecstasy of sharing: "communicating" by not "communing"' (1991: 25). Yet the places from where the singular beings 'communicate' are no longer defined as places of fusion, but rather as places of *dislocation*: 'Thus, the communication of sharing would be this very dis-location' (25).

3.5 The Moment of the Political: Event

Singularities are *dislocated*. If they do not occupy a specific social or communal location, as they only arise through and by the act of sharing, if they do not relate to the whole of community (to the communion as the One), but rather to the very *withdrawal* of community as a whole, then one is forced to approach the questions of relation from the angle of division, of connection from the angle of disconnection, of community from the angle of its retreat, and of communion from the angle of its disruption ('what divides us is shared out to us: the withdrawal of being', Nancy 1993: 69). An important aspect of what Nancy and Lacoue-Labarthe call 'retreat' is thus encapsulated in the phenomenon of a disruptive *surprise*, which in turn constitutes the retreat's nature as *moment* and *event*. And one has to add that, as much as this applies to the question of community, it applies to the political, given that 'the question of a disjunction or a disruption' is 'more essential to the political than the political itself' (Lacoue-Labarthe/Nancy 1997: 119). That is to say, the question of *retreat as such* (as always being a question of *relation*, and it could be, as Nancy and Lacoue-Labarthe hold, 'that the retreat is the – theoretical and practical – gesture of relation itself', 140) involves a thinking of *dissociation*. Nancy and Lacoue-Labarthe even go as far as claiming that what unites most interventions given in the series of meetings at the Centre for Philosophical Research on the Political is a thought of relation as constitutive of the break, or of a *deconnection*.

Nancy has elaborated on the *dis-sociating* event-ness of community and the political in a series of writings. As in most post-structuralist and post-Heideggerian conceptions of the event, the latter is 'not the thing that happens (the content or the non-phenomenal substrate) but *the fact that* it happens: to wit, the eventfulness of its event (or, yet again, its event rather than its advent)' (Nancy 1998: 92–3). For Nancy, the closure of metaphysics, i.e. the dislocation of the foundationalist horizon, made it possible to start thinking about the event as such – and therein constitutes but an event of opening itself. If it is not to be an object of machination and calculation, the event can only arise from surprise, 'or it is not an event' (97). It is characterized by a structural unexpectedness, where 'structural' indicates the ontological status of the event as something ineradicably and necessarily unexpected. And it is exactly because of its disturbing and surprising nature that the event creates (or is based on) discord, conflict and rupture: 'There is *discord* between being and being [*étant*]: being is in conflict with the present, given, and registered beingness of being [*étant*]: being is in conflict with being's substantial, founding essentiality' (101).

Once more we stumble across the ontological difference. The event is described by Nancy, pace Heidegger, as the conflict, *Streit*, or *Austrag* between being and the beingness of beings, between the ontic and the ontological (as what previously was described as *play* – which amounts to the same thing, since both *play* and *conflict* are figures of contingency). The event of difference, in other words, is disruptive with respect to all immanence and identity. We can speak – and Nancy does speak – about this moment of disruption as the *moment of the political*, as the *moment*, or the *event*, of being-in-common. Hence, following Nancy, we arrive at a definition of the *moment of the political* as the disruptive event of the 'in-common', where the 'in-common' erupts and disrupts the techno-structural relations of the social and of politics in the deprived sense. Community, then, emerges within the disrupted and dislocated structure of the foundationalist horizon.

For Nancy, another name for the surprising event of the being-in-common of singularity is *freedom* (1993: 78). Freedom is the *event of community*, or, as one should preferably frame it, it is *one of the names* for the event of community and of the political. What this claim entails is the assumption that freedom must be located at the same ontological level as all the other categories by which community was described so far. Freedom, for instance, shares the characteristics of finitude (13), but it also shares the characteristics of singularity. Freedom stands in a relation of reciprocal conditioning with sharing, being-in-common, and singularity, even as sometimes Nancy seems to emphasize one or the other aspect as primordial. Nevertheless, I would hold that all these notions constitute different ways of approaching one thing: the very absence of foundation. Before supporting this claim, however, we should for a moment consider what is added to the argument by Nancy in his *Experience of Freedom*. It is apparent that, more than ever, Nancy enters the lexicon of emancipatory politics with this work by pondering, among other things, on the nature of political space, equality and fraternity.

First, if we grant for a moment that freedom has to be considered yet another name for the groundless nature of community, a name for the ground as absent, then the groundless ground of the social is opened up by/as freedom in the form of political space. This argument is developed by Nancy in a manner reminiscent of Hannah Arendt. Freedom is the space – or spacing – of the political: 'the political does not primarily consist in the composition and dynamic of powers . . . but in the opening of a space. This space is opened by freedom – initial, inaugural, arising – and freedom there presents itself in action' (78). This notion of space stands in clear opposition to what would be a definite location for an immanent incarnation of transcendence (the body of the leader). Freedom cannot be imposed, nor can it be granted by any instance internal or external to the community, but 'it appears as precisely the internal exteriority of the community: existence as the sharing of being' (75). This is also called by Nancy a condition of 'transimmanence', and the 'place' granted to it – 'public or political space' – is nothing but an internal exteriority. As a non-place of this kind, freedom constitutes a space which has no definite location, rather, it is the very space of *dis-location*, the movement of *spacing*. In this enlarged or 'ontological' meaning, one can say that the political is the originary space of freedom, it is the 'spaciosity' of freedom (ibid.). In the same way, the 'public sphere' in the ontic sense should not be confused with *the political as spacing* in the ontological sense. Rather, the latter serves as a condition of possibility for politics and 'public spheres' in the narrow sense.

What these quasi-transcendental 'modes' of freedom – politics and the public sphere – share is that they are defined not in relation to any substantive, positive, empirically given, or measurable content, but in their relation towards something – a figure of closure – that withdraws: immanence, substance, the subject, total community. I will refer to this common reference as the *withdrawal of ground*. It is important to see, however, that through the movement of the withdrawal of ground being is (partially) founded – which is why we are not confronted with a plain and simple form of anti-foundationalism, but with the movement of post-foundational thought: 'Freedom *is* the withdrawal of being, but the withdrawal of being is the nothingness of being, which is the being of freedom. This is why freedom *is not, but it frees being and frees from being*, all of which can be rewritten here as: *freedom withdraws being and gives relation*' (68). In other words: freedom – which has no substance of its own (it 'is not') – grounds (or 'frees') being-as-relation (i.e. being-in-common) by withdrawing being (or the beingness of being in the ontic or 'ontified' sense, that is, ground). Hence, freedom can be said to be the ungrounding ground of sharing, singularity and relation. But of what nature is this ungrounding ground? Obviously it cannot be one more ground: freedom cannot serve as foundation in the strong sense, nor is there any necessity for freedom, on its part, to be founded. Rather, freedom 'is the very thing that prevents itself from being founded' (12), or, put differently, it is the name for groundlessness as the movement of grounding/ungrounding. From this perspective, freedom can be defined as:

> the foundation which by itself does not secure itself as foundation (cause, reason, principle, origin, or authority), but which refers through its essence (or through its withdrawal of essence) to a foundation of itself. This latter foundation would be the securing of every foundation – but it cannot be precisely this on the model of any other foundation, since no other foundation *fundamentally* secures itself as such. The foundation of foundation consequently founds in a mode which is also that of non-securing, but which this time refers clearly to the withdrawal of its own essence and to what we could call the definitive in-dependence of its own dependence. The foundation of foundation therefore founds, in Heideggerian terms, in the mode of the 'abyss': *Abgrund*, which is the *Grund* of every other *Grund*, and which is of course its own *Gründlichkeit* as *Abgründlichkeit*. (83)

Groundlessness, thus, must not be mistaken for the simple absence of all grounds or for the simple opposite of ground in the singular. The abyss does not serve as a new ground – not even in the negative, as a bottomless or groundless 'black hole' – but as the very movement of the *withdrawal* and *retreat* of ground: 'the logic of the retreat is abyssal: in every retreat, that from which one is retreating retraces itself' (Lacoue-Labarthe/Nancy 1997: 149).

We have now arrived at the point where it has become patently clear that, in Nancy as in all post-foundational thought, the withdrawal of ground is not the same thing as the simple absence of ground. Nancy's position is *post*-foundational, not *anti*-foundational. If we still want to think of ground in terms of its absence, it will be an absence which remains *present* as, and through, the movement of withdrawal. And it is under this perspective of the withdrawal of ground that Nancy's main conceptions of freedom, the event, community, sharing (relation), finitude and singularity run together. These quasi-transcendentals of groundlessness serve as what one could call tropes of contingency, that is, approximative attempts, within discourse, at encircling something whose constitutive absence denies any immediate access, but still 'presences' through the movement of its withdrawal. While these notions are located within discourse, the withdrawal itself can only be experienced as an event that disturbs all foundational discourse. The very absence of ground appears or 'materializes' itself only in the form of, or through, an event that might be discursively designated, as in the case of Nancy, as freedom, or sharing, or being-in-common. However, there is a constant struggle in Nancy's work to interrogate from within discourse what can only be thought of as the experience of an event.

The epochal shift towards post-foundationalism in itself constitutes such an event. And it is announced in what Nancy does not stop thinking about: the end, limit and limitation of philosophy in the sense of the end of all foundationalist discourses. Nancy, in the words of his commentator Christopher Fynsk, conceives of the event of philosophy's end as 'the collapse of all foundational discourses and the advent of modernity or postmodernity' (Fynsk 1991: viii). For Nancy, this end or, better still, *ending* of philosophy 'would be *deliverance from foundation* in that it would withdraw existence from the necessity of foundation, but also in that it would be set free from foundation, and given over to unfounded "freedom"' (Nancy 1993: 12). Thinking would then no longer be the search for solid grounds but it would be the exposure to the withdrawal of ground and the interrogation of its retreat.

3.6 The Danger of Philosophism and the Necessity of a 'First Philosophy'

While Nancy's work represents one of the most powerful contemporary theorizations of a post-foundational and left Heideggerian concept of the political and of philosophy, it also exhibits some of the problems and dangers involved in a practice of *thinking* which deliberately wants to shake off all remnants of political philosophy as a discipline. One of the dangers involved in such a purely 'philosophical' approach to *thinking* – even as the latter is based on the philosophical *ending* of philosophy – can be located in what one might call Nancy's tendency towards a certain philosophism. Let us try and elaborate this critique by turning to Nancy's most fundamental theoretical intervention: the small book – which nevertheless counts as his magnum opus – entitled *Being Singular Plural*.

What Nancy openly declares to do with this book – although he concedes that it is not his ambition, but an exigency of the thing itself and of history – is to revamp 'the whole of "first philosophy" by giving the "singular plural" of Being as its foundation' (2000: xvi). By 'first philosophy' one has to understand ontology, the science not of this or that particular species of beings, but of being in general. Yet being in general can no longer be conceived of as a universal, all-encompassing, homogeneous category. It is internally shattered, dispersed into a primordial plurality of beings, a plurality that cannot be derived from any deeper origin. Plurality is primary; it is the unsurpassable precondition of all being: '*The plurality of beings is at the foundation [fondement] of Being*. A single being is a contradiction in terms. Such a being, which would be its own foundation, origin, and intimacy, would be incapable of *Being*, in every sense that this expression can have here' (12).

Nancy insists so much on Being as the plurality of always singular instances of being because this plurality is inscribed into the very differential structure of Being. Nancy's ontology is an ontology of the *between*-beings and of being-*together* or being-*with*. The latter term was introduced by Heidegger, who nonetheless did not develop it in a sufficient fashion. If Nancy's project consists in restarting first philosophy as an ontology of singular–plural Being, then the place from which first philosophy must be restarted is Heideggerian fundamental ontology, but 'with a thorough resolve that *starts from the plural singular of origins, from being-with*' (26). In other words, if 'the "with" is at the heart of Being' (30), we have to reverse the order of ontological exposition in philosophy: *Mitsein* ontologically precedes *Dasein*. The *between*, the *with* and the *together* are all irreducible aspects of being – which therefore can only be thought of as *being singular plural*.

The danger of philosophism emerges as soon as the political implications of this claim – on the level of politics as well as on the level of the political – become neglected. Certainly, for Nancy, his more recent ontology of being-with has to be understood in the light of his previous notion of the retreat of the political, which does not signify the disappearance of the political but the disappearance of the 'ontological presuppositions of the politico-philosophical order'(37) (for instance in the substantial sense of community or, generally speaking, in a foundationalist sense). Yet, while his Heideggerian criticism of the politico-philosophical order of foundationalist metaphysics (of 'philosophy' in the traditional sense) – and of its implementation by self-styled philosopher–kings in form of a 'philosophical politics' – is certainly justified, Nancy tends to throw out with the metaphysical bathwater all the resources of political philosophy as a discipline. It is true that political philosophy more often than not has served as a means of depoliticization, a convenient tool for legitimating the establishment of a 'well-ordered' society – and we will return to the problem in the concluding chapter. However, Nancy's philosophism seems to lure him into the opposite trap. When claiming that 'philosophical politics regularly proceeds according to the surreptitious appeal to a metaphysics of the one-origin', that it is 'a politics of exclusivity and the correlative exclusion – of a class, of an order, of a "community" – the point of which is to end up with a "people", in the "base" sense of the term' (24), he might score a couple of valid points, but this does not devaluate political philosophy as a name for the intellectual attempt to understand and describe the impossibility and, simultaneously, necessity of drawing lines of exclusion in order to create *some* order, *some* community, *some* people, *some* foundation. Since Nancy tends to emphasize the dislocating moment of the political (the political in its retreat), what he seeks to downplay is the instituting moment of the political, which is usually counted as political philosophy's ownmost affair. As a result, Nancy's only recourse is 'philosophy itself', which is why '[p]hilosophy needs to recommence, to restart itself from itself against itself, against political philosophy and philosophical politics' (25).

That such philosophism – the attempt to think being-with from within philosophy alone while at the same time denouncing the whole of *political* philosophy – is not a feasible strategy will become apparent as soon as we investigate somewhat closer into Nancy's founding categories. As Nancy makes it sufficiently clear, it is the 'with' which constitutes Being (which is always already being-with) and not the other way around, and we therefore have to think the 'being-with' as such. Accordingly, 'the "city" is not primarily a form of political institution; it is primarily being-with *as such*' (31). The philosophism of this statement lies in the vain attempt to grasp something like a 'being-with *as such*', irrespective of the city in its *political* rather than its philosophical sense. The fact that in the city being is *shared* in the form of being-with does not explain the logic behind this sharing *within the city*. In other words, the category of the 'with' in its purely philosophical mode cannot explain why the city is kept together as a city and what keeps it together. The same problem occurs with Nancy's notion of the 'we'. Since Being is being-with, one cannot speak of it any more in the third person, but 'Being could not speak of itself except in this unique manner: "we are". The truth of the *ego sum* is the *nos sumus . . .*' (33). But who is this 'we', and where does it come from, if not from a homogenizing construction out of the dispersed plurality of beings? Nancy seems to think that one can have a singularly plural 'we'. But such a 'singularly plural' identity would neither be an 'I' nor would it be a 'we', it would quite simply be a severe case of personality disorder, a case of psychosis, where no stabilization of meaning can be constructed and no identity can be forged out of the pure dispersal of elements.

Nancy's problems with explaining the logic behind this *instituting* aspect of the political have to do with his adherence to the associational trait of the political. If we start, as Hannah Arendt does, in a fashion comparable to Nancy, from the primacy of plurality, we run the risk of portraying the world in an all too peaceful way – no wonder Nancy resorts to the quasi-Christian metaphor of mutual sharing – and of underestimating the constitutive role of conflict and antagonism. While Nancy touches on these categories, what he refers to as division and '*Streit*' not only remains under-theorized, but also is in constant danger of being 'philosophized', that is to say, of being emptied of all *politics* and turned into a purely philosophical matter for *thinking*. What is captured well by Nancy is the disrupting aspect of the 'retreat of the political', yet the *instituting* moment of the political, which always has to be instantiated within a certain 'ontic' politics, is captured by Nancy to a much lesser degree. Yet if we do not want to fall into the trap of anti-foundationalism, we will always need *some* foundation, and this implies that the play of the ontological difference has to be temporarily halted and that the retreat has to be stopped (even if it will be impossible to stop it once and for all).

If this is the case, though, plurality cannot reign unhindered. From a more dissociational view on the political, it could thus be argued that an entirely plural universe would be fully empty, not only of politics but of the political as well. It would come close to a universe of unconnected monads, and it is not for nothing that Nancy positions his own ontology within the tradition of Leibniz's monadology (39). Such pluralism, as a dissociationalist might argue, just replaces the metaphysical essentialism of the centre with an essentialism of the elements, the foundationalism of the ground with the foundationalism of *no ground*, i.e. the anti-foundationalism of a pure dispersal of grounds. What cannot by thought of in that case is the necessity of establishing links between these elements in order to achieve *some* order and *some* ground. (Nancy's mere announcement of the necessity for some sort of clinamen does not provide us with the theoretical means to understand the very logic of *linking*.) And, since this can only be done by way of a process of exclusion (of other possible orders and other grounds), a moment of antagonism enters the picture. If, on the other hand, the 'plurality' of the world is considered to be a given fact, this antagonistic and instituting moment of the political is denigrated, and a pacified and depoliticized notion of the political takes over.

Nancy's philosophism very much contributes to such a depoliticized notion of the political as he shrinks back from what appears to me as the only reasonable consequence to be drawn from his ontology of being-with: to define and rearticulate it as a *political* ontology.[2] Nancy himself hesitates because of his averseness to regional philosophical disciplines and regional ontologies – an averseness resulting from his aim to develop a new first philosophy, not reducible to any regional ontology. The fact, however, that there is no being-with 'as such' (or there can only be a being-with 'as such' from the perspective of philosophism) does not devaluate Nancy's project of ontology as a first philosophy. Given the grounding role of the political, such a first philosophy makes sense, but it makes sense only as a political ontology. So we must not only reverse the usual order of exposition in philosophy, we also have to reverse the order of 'disciplines', for only an ontology that is a *political* ontology can explain the nature of the 'with' without falling into one form of philosophism or the other. While Nancy sees clearly that '[e]ach time, Being as such is Being as the Being of *a* being' (46), he is not prepared to agree that, as a consequence, one would have to claim that ontology as such is only ontology as the ontology of *a particular ontic realm*; and that, vice versa, it can only be an 'ontic ontology', not an ontology 'as such'. Yet if it is supposed to retain its status as ontology, as the science of being in general, thus also retaining the status of a first philosophy, then it will be caught in this double bind – which is precisely the double bind of the ontological difference as political difference: ontology must aspire to be an ontology of all being and yet, in doing so, it can only proceed from a particular, 'ontic' region. Every *prima philosophia* is always and can only be a *philosophia secunda*, and nevertheless will have to claim the impossible status of a first philosophy.[3] This impossible, and yet necessary, role of a post-foundational *prima philosophia* can today, as will be elaborated upon in the concluding chapter, only be claimed by the hitherto marginalized sub-discipline of *philosophia politica*.

This claim, since it is a regional ontology that takes over the (eventually impossible) task of representing ontology as a first philosophy, is precisely this: a claim. It cannot be derived from any deeper underlying ground, for then the 'first philosophy' in question would have given up its own grounding status. To raise this claim, hence, is a political move in itself. A first philosophy has to be *made* first: a decision has to be taken as to the ground or starting point; an ontic discipline comes to fill out that impossible role of 'fundamental ontology'; plurality has to be reduced, which in turn will produce some sort of exclusion and antagonism. The work of Claude Lefort, to which we now turn, will pave the way for this argument, which will be discussed extensively in the concluding chapter.

Notes

1. Conversely, it is impossible to separate the fate of community and the fate of the political. A thinking of community as essence and immanence necessarily leads to a closure of the political because it assigns to community a *common being*, whereas community is about being *in* common and thus resists absorption into a common substance.

2. It could be argued that Nancy does present us with a *social* ontology and not with an 'ontological ontology', an ontology pure and simple. But even if we granted this point, this ontology,

by virtue of being a *social* ontology, would still adhere too much to the modern subordination of the political to the social, while a post-foundational approach that has to account for the very process of (contingent and temporary) *founding*, and thus, for the *institution* of the social, will have to start from the obverse assumption of the primacy of the political over the social (we will return to this in our chapter on Laclau).

3. '*Secunda philosophia*', to be sure, should not be understood in the Aristotelian sense of physics, but in the sense of a *prima philosophia* which will constitutively be *less* than a *prima philosophia*, not seizing to claim its status.

Chapter 4
The Machiavellian Moment Re-Theorized: Claude Lefort

4.1 Thinking, Philosophy, Science

'My purpose here is to encourage and to contribute to a revival of political philosophy.' These words stand at the beginning of one of Claude Lefort's most prominent articles (Lefort 1988: 9) – based on a talk he delivered at Nancy and Lacoue-Labarthe's Centre for Philosophical Research on the Political. And indeed, there can be no doubt as to the significance of Lefort's work for contemporary political philosophy and, in particular, for democracy theory. What Lefort has elaborated is one of the most powerful theorizations of the political, of democracy and totalitarianism, which can help us better to grasp the primacy of *political* thought in relation both to science and to the 'pure' thought of philosophism. His theory is invaluable for a thorough analysis of the political difference because, apart from an 'ontologic' theory of the political, Lefort offers a historical genealogy of the Machiavellian moment – the moment of society's ungrounding and political regrounding.

Unfortunately Lefort's theory has fallen victim to what seems to be the fate of all successful theories: *sloganization*. There are two Lefortian phrases or topoi which can be encountered in numerable articles and books. The first portrays our current condition as being governed by the 'the dissolution of the markers of certainty'. The second announces that in democracy 'the place of power is empty'. Most accounts of Lefort stop here – no further details are given, no theoretical context or background is established. These 'slogans' – and isn't this what defines a slogan? – are supposed to speak for themselves. However, they don't.

As it is possible to give an utterly banal reading to these two claims, I suspect that it is not clear to many of those who quote them that these claims fulfil a more profound role in Lefort's theory: their role is to point towards a dimension of the social which throughout the present study we call, for lack of a better term, its *ontological* dimension. If this is overlooked, it is not surprising that they are taken as statements about *ontic* facts of life – that is, facts *within* society. Thus, the claim to the 'dissolution of the markers of certainty' would be reduced to the trivial insight that many a thing is uncertain in our modern times (a banality which has been elevated to the level of 'science' by risk theory). In a similar fashion, 'the emptiness of the place of power' in democracy could simply be reduced to the claim that in democracy no arbitrary power is exercised. Put into the context of Lefort's theory, however, something is said about society's ontological condition: in the case of the empty place of power, it is obvious that power does not disappear – it remains there as something which is emptied: as a dimension whose factual (or ontic) content may disappear while the dimension as such stays operative. And 'the dissolution of the markers of certainty' is not only a particular phenomenon, but defines the universal, that is, ontological, *horizon* of our condition.

Understood in the strong sense – as claims about the ontological condition of society – these claims tell us something important about Lefort's theory. First, he is what we call a contingency theorist. Our very certainty about the dissolution of certainty already indicates that the roots of the latter phenomenon lie at a deeper ontological level than a commonsensical reading would expect. Therefore we should not confuse a weak notion of *uncertainty* with the ontologically strong notion of *contingency* appertaining to every social identity. And, in a second and not unrelated sense, Lefort is a post-foundationalist. Both contingency and the emptiness of the place of power indicate that society is not built on a stable ground: they designate the absence of social or historical necessity, the absence of a positive foundation of society. What they also designate, though, is that the dimension of ground does not simply disappear, since it remains present *as absent*. In this chapter I will try to show why and how Lefort's theory is located within the post-foundational paradigm, to what extent it is centred around a strong notion of antagonism (as originary division), and how the difference he makes between *la politique* and *le politique* – politics and the political – ties in with

Lefort's post-foundationalism.[1] This means that, in order to sub-stantiate our main thesis, we will have to demonstrate the way in which this difference *as difference* is an indication or 'symptom' of the groundless nature of society.

The way Lefort defines the political – as distinguished from politics – is closely related to his idea of philosophy as distinguished from science. To reinterpret the political, we must break with the scientific point of view in general and with the viewpoint of political sciences and political sociology (1988: 11). While Marxism understands politics as part of the superstructure and, for this reason, as being determined by the economic base (the relations of production), political science and sociology live in a different illusion: they con-struct their object matter through the delineation of particular facts. This means, political facts are differentially determined vis-à-vis their relation to other particular facts such as, for instance, economic, juridical or aesthetic facts. Thought is subjugated to the imperatives of exactitude and definition; and the way in which particular facts are established attests to a 'desire to objectify'(1988: 12) on the part of the scientist. In this way a hard and fast separation between subject and object is established: the ideal of a neutral subject is posited – the scientist – who is *exterior* to his/her object of knowledge and whose intellectual operations are entirely detached from social life. Only under this condition can the scientist keep a neutral distance towards the supposedly objective world of facts and retain its supposed objectivity at the same time. Neutrality and objectivity can only be retained, though, if the risk of making judgments is avoided. The scientist must abstain from judging and from 'mere opinion', since s/he has to ignore distinctions whose criteria cannot be supplied – otherwise the fiction of neutrality would collapse. What this ideology of science fails to recognize, though, is that the object is always already invested with meaning, that judgements are risky (because they cannot be arithmetically calculated), but nonetheless necessary, and that, as a consequence, neutrality is impossible. So, by pretending to neutrality and objectivity, the ideology of science systematically ignores 'the difference between legitimacy and illegitimacy, between truth and lies, between authenticity and imposture, between the pursuit of power or of private interests and the pursuit of the common good' (ibid.).

Nobody can escape these basic distinctions, since it is through them that the world is made meaningful for us. To succumb to the illusion of occupying a place not affected by these distinctions means denying one's own situatedness in the world. This is precisely the mistaken belief of bourgeois or positivist science. Positivist scientists aspire to a high-altitude point of observation beyond the horizon of the social, thus denying – and therein Lefort follows Merleau-Ponty's critique of science – that they themselves are part of the world which they observe. Philosophy, on the other hand, accepts that one cannot escape the world and has to take the risk of judging. Yet Lefort's critique of science is supplemented by a critique of philosophy as a discipline haunted by the 'phantom of pure thought' (Lefort 2000: XL). By this he understands thought organized into conceptual systems whose internal consistency remains intact under any circumstances, since they are supposedly constructed independently of any relation with the world – untouched by historical events, that is. Against philosophy as pure thought Lefort calls for a non-metaphysical form of *thinking* as 'an unlocalizable and indeterminable question that accompanies all experience of the world' (249).

It is because thinking – as an infinite form of interrogation – is not concerned with a positive object of thought, but rather 'built' on the constitutive absence of an ultimate foundation, that Lefort can conceive of it as an 'adventure'. One cannot hope for any definite answer, one cannot rely on a solid ground, and still one has to indulge in making judgements. As interrogation, it is impossible for thinking to define and construct its concepts and criteria upon a positive foundation. On the contrary, as Lefort (1978: 20) claims, it is the absence of such positive foundation that can and must serve as the only foundation or law available to philosophical thought. If this is the case, then Lefort's own central concepts – in particular, the concept of the political as differentiated from the concept of politics – must not be understood in the way we usually think of concepts. Rather, in opening up an indeterminate field for interrogation, they indicate the very absence of a positive foundation for thinking and acting.

4.2 Politics and the Political

By aspiring to a point of high altitude, science pretends to look at society from a position external to, or beyond, the social whole. Assuming such a detached stance, it is clear that science is not in a position to think or respond to the *event*, i.e. it is not, as philosophy is, prepared 'to think what is itself seeking to be thought' (2000: xl).

What the subject of science looks out for are value-neutral and positive facts or laws, which correspond to social domains. Thus the very domain of science is established through the delimitation of social domains and the delimitation of disciplines. That is to say, what corresponds to the division of the social into particular domains and sub-domains is, on the side of science, an inner splitting of disciplines and sub-disciplines. From this vantage point, politics – as a particular social sub-system – becomes the subject matter of a positive science, be it political science or political sociology. On the other hand, it is the very tradition of philosophy to pursue an interrogation of what transgresses the limits of every particular social domain. And here is where Lefort starts to develop a concept of the political as the proper 'field of interrogation' of philosophical thought.

In his contribution to one of the readers of Lacoue-Labarthe and Nancy on the retreat of the political,[2] Lefort lays out his version of the political difference as a conscious reaction both to the Marxist view of politics as a mere superstructure and to the sociological view, which, by delineating political facts as distinct from other facts, then forcing them into specific systems of relation and, finally, combining them into the overall system of society, reduces politics to a particular social sub-system among many. This scientific 'fiction', for Lefort, has the effect that modern democratic societies are now characterized by the 'delimitation of a sphere of institutions, relations and activities, which appears to be political, as distinct from other spheres which appear to be economic, juridical, and so on' (1988: 11). Thus, the introduction of a differentiation between *la* and *le politique* in Lefort has to be seen in the light of his critique of science and his defence of philosophical thinking as 'thinking of the political' ('*la pensée du politique*').

Such thinking of the political distances itself from a mere science of politics by inquiring into the origin of the principle of differentiation between social spheres (or social systems) in modernity, i.e. their ontological foundation, rather than describing their differences in merely ontic terms. Its starting point, thus, is the event that constituted that differentiation, not the description of the supposed 'objectivity' of those systems. Lefort insists that this event of differentiation between particular social systems – and, hence, the modern view of politics as a particular sub-system – does itself have a political meaning, which raises the question as to the very form and institution of society. Let us quote this key paragraph in extenso:

The fact that something like *politics* should have been circumscribed within social life at a given time has in itself a political meaning, and a meaning which is not particular, but general. This even raises the question of the constitution of the social space, of the *form* of society, of the essence of what was once termed the 'city'. The political is thus revealed, not in what we call political activity, but in the double movement whereby the mode of institution of society appears and is obscured. It appears in the sense that the process whereby society is ordered and unified across its divisions becomes visible. It is obscured in the sense that the locus of politics (the locus in which parties compete and in which a general agency of power takes shape and is reproduced) becomes defined as particular, while the principle which generates the overall configuration is concealed. (Lefort 1988: 11)

In this central passage Lefort insists that the political – as the very form and mode of institution of society – *both* appears *and* is occulted. This double movement is the specific meaning Lefort gives to the notion of the 'retreat of the political', which now amounts to a forgetfulness or oblivion of the difference between politics – as a sub-system or mode of action – and the political as society's *grounding dimension*, which, for Lefort, also is the *form-giving* dimension of society. 'Interpreting the political' means inquiring into the question that once inspired political philosophy and was announced already in Greek theory of *politeia* – 'what is the nature of the difference between forms of society'? To ask this question means 'breaking with the viewpoint of political science, because political science emerges from the suppression of this question'. The form of oblivion typical for political science consists in the latter's desire to objectify, whereby it forgets 'that no elements, no elementary structures, no entities (classes or segments of classes), no economic or technical determinations, and no dimensions of social space exist until they have been given form' (11).

So we can refer to the political as the moment of institution of the social, which is defined by Lefort as 'the generative principles of its "form"' (2000: 226). The 'form' itself is also called by Lefort the 'symbolic dispositive' of a given society – and we will soon see in greater detail how the symbolic dispositive is structured in modern society and how mutations occur within it.[3] At this stage it must suffice to point out only a few elements of the symbolic institutionalization of modern society's form. In so doing, it should be underscored that Lefort does not completely deny the historical emergence of a particular field of politics – even as this modern differentiation of social sub-spheres does not touch at the 'enigma' of society's institution (229). The field specific to politics is defined by Lefort as 'the field of competition between protagonists whose mode of action and programmes explicitly designate them as laying claim to the exercise of public authority' (1988: 226–7). The emergence of politics as a specific field rests on a series of institutional preconditions which – in their most fundamental sense – turn around the questions of power and conflict. Lefort notes that 'the delineation of a specifically political activity has the effect of erecting a *stage* on which conflict is acted out for all to see (once citizenship is no longer for a small number) and is represented as being necessary, irreducible and legitimate'. The form of modern democratic societies is thus characterized by the institutionalization of conflict. And the origin of power, in modern democratic societies, is no longer linked to the field of religion, nor is it linked, as we will see, to law and knowledge. This in turn is the condition for politics to emerge. What remains occulted, though, is *the very form and condition of the possibility of distinguishing between social spheres*: 'it is therefore true that something can be circumscribed as being *politics* [*la politique*]. The one thing that remains hidden from the gaze of the scientific observer is the symbolic form which, as a result of the mutation in power, makes this new distinction possible: the essence of the political [*du politique*]' (227–8).

In this quotation Lefort makes a (quasi-)transcendental move: at stake is that which makes it possible for politics to emerge as a specific form of action or a particular social sphere: the political (respectively, the very difference between politics and the political). Hence the conditions of politics are not only historical conditions of emergence, but also structural conditions of possibility. Politics and the political are not two separated ontic realms, but rather they are intrinsically intertwined, whereby it is only on the basis of its very absence as an ontic being that the political can serve as the condition of possibility of politics. As Dick Howard observed: 'The political is a *symbolic* presence whose existence as a real absence makes possible political change' (1989: 8). By way of refining the argument, it would therefore be more precise to say that politics and the political serve as *mutual* conditions of (im)possibility due to their play of presencing/absencing. And it is only in modernity that this play is revealed, in the moment in which politics emancipates itself from other sources of legitimation and emerges as an autonomous activity: in the event of what we called 'the moment of the political'. Political theory, as a theory of the political (chiasmatically differentiated from politics), hence assumes the status of what in the previous chapter we have called a first philosophy (a term whose further elaboration we will have to postpone umtil our discussion in the concluding chapter). Political thought can assume such status because its object is not politics in the narrow sense but the *instituting and form-giving dimension* of society eo ipso. Beyond this grounding dimension of the political, there is no form, no stage, no meaning.

4.3 Conflict as Foundation: Society's Double Division

Let us return now to the question of power and conflict, which will turn out to be at the very core of the problem of the political in Lefort. We will see that, at the very root of the formation of society, we encounter an even more basic division as condition of (im)possibility of any formation or form-giving process. The division is primary because it cannot be related to any foundation prior to itself. As Lefort's former collaborator Marcel Gauchet put it: 'Division is neither derivable nor reducible' (1976: 17). So if one wants to abandon the search for an origin of the political *beyond* or *prior to* the political itself, this 'radical interpretative leap' is necessary. Society is 'founded' by way of the originary division which is the division between society and itself *as its other*.

By claiming that the very possibility of society is conditioned by its division, Lefort and Gauchet once more put in place a transcendental argument: division is the condition of possibility of society. But what makes this transcendental argument *post*-foundational and thus *quasi*-transcendental? It is, of course, the fact that it is not a positive principle which founds society and lies at the origin of everything social, but an irresolvable negativity with respect to society's self-identity. This negativity – *division* – cannot be deduced from empirical, 'positive' facts. Thus, social identity cannot be grounded in anything other than the separation of that identity from itself: its self-externalization. Only through division and by turning itself into its Other can society establish *some* identity. This argument is an abstract and general one, with implications for any form of identity. While in Lefort and Gauchet it is formulated from within the radius of Merleau-Ponty's thinking – with its emphasis on the irresolvable chiasm or intertwining between inside and outside – it also bears a clear resemblance to the deconstructive argument. All these cases (and we could add the third one of Lacanianism) rely heavily on the Heideggerian figure of chiasm, and in all of them it is assumed that there can be no identity without it being differentiated from its very outside: and yet, the outside does not have an independent life of its own but – as condition of possibility of the inside – is present on the inside ('contaminating' the inside, as Derrida would have it), thereby again hybridizing the border between inside and outside. Hence every identity is precarious to some degree, for it relies on something which necessarily escapes it.

Now we see that the originary division – which, as it will soon become clear, operates at the 'outer border' of society as much as it runs through what Merleau-Ponty would call the inner 'flesh' of society – is a necessary condition for society to acquire some shape and self-understanding. Philosophical interrogation must start with 'a primal division which is constitutive' of social space, with what Lefort (1988: 225) calls the 'enigma' of the relation between inside and outside. The 'enigma' of the chiasm between inside and outside is shown in the symbolic gestures that *power* makes towards the outside. The role of power is precisely to institute society by *signifying* social identity – and only by relating to this representation/significa- tion of identity can people relate to the space in which they live as a coherent ensemble (which implies that, in turn, a social space entirely devoid of power would not allow for any orientation, and that the signification of social identity *is* power). Power works within the symbolic order. And if the institution/foundation of society occurs at the symbolic level alone, then it necessarily has to be *staged*: this is what Lefort calls *mise-en-scène*. It might be staged in different ways: the 'fabrication of Louis XIV' (Burke 1992), for instance, differs from the ways in which power is staged in democracy as that place which cannot be institutionally occupied once and for all. In the latter case, one might venture to say, an open-ended play is enacted on an empty stage – and yet the theatre of power is not abandoned. Just as there cannot be a society without power, there cannot be power without representation – ergo: no society without the staging of a 'quasi- representation of itself' (Lefort 1988: 12).

So the irreversible event which Lefort calls the 'democratic inven- tion' did not lead to the disappearance of power as such. What occurred historically was a mutation at the symbolic level which affected the way society's unity is staged: its *mise-en-scène*. At the same time, it affected the way society is formed – which Lefort calls its *mise-en-forme* – and the way in which society is given meaning – its *mise-en-sens*. These three aspects cannot be separated: the way in which society is staged by the instance of power simultaneously gives form to it (without power, society would be an amorphous, formless mass); and it also gives meaning to it, because the basic distinctions between true and false, just and unjust, legitimate and illegitimate are what makes social space intelligible for us. It is this dimension of 'the political' – in the sense of the instituting principles of a given symbolic dispositive – which both *forms* and *gives meaning* to the social by *representing it to itself*.

This is what Lefort refers to when famously claiming that in democracy the symbolic place of power is empty: in the moment of the democratic revolution – when the monarchic dispositive mutated into the democratic dispositive – a mutation of the stage of power took place. In the monarchic dispositive, the power of the king 'pointed towards an unconditional other-worldly pole, while at the same time he was, in his own person, the guarantor and representative of the unity of the kingdom' (17). The king could fulfil this role because he was equipped, as it were, with *two bodies*. Lefort relies here on Kantorowicz' account (1957) of medieval theories about the two bodies of the monarch. According to Lefort, the image of the self-representation of the *Ancien Régime* was the image of the body. And, by analogy to the *corpus Christi*, the body of the monarch was thought of as being divided into his earthly, mortal body and a celestial, immortal, collective body incarnating the unity of the kingdom. His two bodies enabled the monarch to mediate between the immanent ('earth', society) and the transcendent (the divine legitimacy of the social order). On the one hand, the body of the monarch belonged to a sphere *outside* society, on the other hand this was precisely the reason why society projected its imaginary 'organic' unity onto his body. The latter stands – as synecdoche – for the body of the mystic community of the entire kingdom.

The king's two bodies allowed for an effective mediation between inside and outside, 'between mortals and gods or, as political activity became secularized and laicized, between mortals and the transcendental agencies represented by a sovereign Justice and a sovereign Reason' (Lefort 1988: 17). The monarchic dispositive, however, is less stable than it might appear. The conditions of its very failure are already present within the dispositive itself. This form of incarnation of community had to cope with an internal contradiction, since the fact that a mediation between society and its outside is necessary in the first place reveals a primordial division. So his two bodies do not only enable the king to incarnate the social whole, they also openly attest to the fact that the king *is not identical with himself* – and hence, society is not identical with itself either.

The linkage between the earthly realm and the transcendent legitimatory ground of society, formerly incorporated in the king's body, is finally broken in the moment of the disincorporation of the king. Within the democratic revolution, this moment – a *moment of the political*, if there ever was one – is symbolically condensed in the decapitation of Louis XVI. What is staged by that spectacle is not only the decapitation of his earthly body, but also the disincorporation of the mystical, transcendent body of the king, which leaves the place of power empty and cuts the link between society and its transcendent legitimatory foundation. But, while power is freed of any positive or substantial content, it does not disappear as a dimension:

> it remains the agency by virtue of which society apprehends itself in its unity and relates to itself in time and space. But this agency is no longer referred to an unconditional pole; and in that sense, it marks a division between the *inside* and the *ouside* of the social, instituted relations between those dimensions, and is tacitly recognized as purely symbolic. (1988: 17)

The point not to be missed here is the circular or chiasmatic relation between the ontological condition of primordial division and the always historical forms of its staging. Yet even the ground of the social in its absence, if, *pace* Lefort, this absent ground is conceived as the place of power emptied of the king's body, must itself be understood as the contingent outcome of an historical event: the democratic revolution. The 'ontological' conditions of possibility are themselves premised upon the historical possibility of conditions. Modernity, from a Lefortian perspective, becomes by and large equivalent with the terrain opened up by the democratic revolution. And yet, paradoxically perhaps, these contingent historical conditions have turned into an unsurpassable horizon that necessarily assumes the status of a 'super-hard' transcendentality. Once the democratic revolution has occurred, every regime – democratic or not – will have to come to terms with the absence of an ultimate ground and with the unbridgeable chasm of division that opens up in place of such a ground.[4]

Before returning to the aspect of the staging and institutionalization of the democratic dispositive, we have to discuss a second dimension of division. Lefort argues that the main feature of the democratic dispositive consists in the acceptance of social division. But it is not only the division between society and its outside that has to be accepted, more than that it is the *inner* divisions of society, the inner conflicts between different interests and classes, between ruler and ruled, oppressors and oppressed, exploiters and exploited – and eventually between political competitors. Thus, Lefort and Gauchet discern a further axis on which social negativity and conflict operate, so that the social is finally constituted on *two* axes of the political. The first axis has just been described as society's self-alienation: in establishing its self-identity, society divides itself and erects an outside vis-à-vis itself which will be incarnated by the instance of power. An antagonism emerges between society and its outside. Now we find out that a second separation or division takes place on the inside of society: here it is the irresolvable tension and opposition between its members which constitutes the antagonism. Together these two axes of division, these two primordial dimensions, make up the very kernel of the political being of society.

4.4 The *Machiavellian Moment* according to Lefort

After having examined the first axis of the originary institution – society's self-externalization – we can now turn to the second axis: the internal division of society. This aspect illustrates the extent to which Lefort and Gauchet's theory is, indeed, a conflict theory. Class antagonism is nothing which could be resolved at a distant point in the future, after the means of production have been socialized and the state has withered away. Yet this conflict is not only irresolvable, it is also necessary for society to institute itself. It is one of the main sources of social cohesion. This might sound counter-intuitive and paradoxical. How can conflict – the irresolvable struggle between men – be one of the main sources of social cohesion? The answer can be found in the fact that it is through conflict that individuals and groups posit themselves within a common world. Through their antagonism – in which the organization, the *raison d'être* and the goals of society are under debate – the antagonists affirm themselves as members of the *same* community.

Far from destroying society as a whole, division in fact implicates a dimension of totality. And totality is implicated precisely by the 'figure of absence' (Gauchet 1976: 25) that is revealed at the heart of social division. This absence emerges from the incapacity of any social actor to master the meaning of society as a whole, since the indefinite play of social division will always prevent single actors from monopolizing it once and for all. So through antagonism a dimension of totality *does* emerge, even though it is not, as some might think, the outcome of the positive presence of a social ground but of the absence of any such ground. For, if the dimension of radical antagonism guarantees that nobody can incarnate the meaning of the whole, that any such pretension can and will be debated, this leads to the conclusion that the truth of the social totality cannot but lie in the debate as such. The dimension of totality is in no way discarded; rather, it is invoked as an effect of a never-ending debate, which makes it impossible for any group to master the meaning of the social whole.

If we want to understand where Lefort's positive evaluation of conflict derives from, it is imperative to turn to his earlier studies on Machiavelli, for it was Machiavelli's thought which allowed Lefort to break with the Marxist postulate of the secondary nature of conflict. With this break Lefort inscribes himself, as a social post-foundation-alist, into the 'Machiavellian moment'. For how could anybody other than Machiavelli, Lefort asks, 'grant a greater role to the event, to the incessant mobility of things in the world, to the every renewed test of complexity?' (2000: 126)

Between 1956 and 1972, Lefort worked on his *thèse d'état*, his 'interrogation' of the Machiavellian *œuvre*, which was to become an 800–page book (1986b). For Lefort, and this is not yet an original claim, Machiavelli in fact is the inventor of political thought proper. But Lefort builds his interpretation around a more radical claim. Machiavelli's discovery – which allowed him to found modern political thought – is the discovery that an irreducible conflict exists at the centre of every polity. Machiavelli thus becomes a philosophical forerunner of the moment of the political, which would only become pertinent historically with the democratic revolution. In the ninth chapter of the *Prince*, Machiavelli declares that the nobles on one side and the people on the other are engaged in an irresolvable struggle due to their opposing *umori*. While the 'humour' or desire of the nobles is to command and to oppress, the desire of the people, on the other hand, is not to be commanded and not to be oppressed (1986b: 382). This constitutive and irreducible opposition between the people and the nobles *precedes* the particular social circumstances or traditions in which they are situated. Conflict, as negative ground of society, precedes any *factual* reasons for conflicts in the plural. And if conflict is to fulfil its role as negative foundation of society, then it follows that the difference between conflict as ground and factual conflicts in the plural must be radical by nature: conflict as ground cannot be just one more of many factual conflicts, but must be located at a radically different level. If we allow ourselves to take up philosophical terminology, the matter can again be stated in terms of the ontological difference: the 'ontological' condition of antagonism is prior to the 'ontic' circumstances under which it is expressed. Wherever there is society – no matter how it is ontically structured – there is internal antagonism at the ontological level. Here we take recourse to Heidegger's quasi-concept of ontological difference not only for heuristic reasons. Heidegger's influence can indeed be traced within Lefort's own texts – even though he only occasionally mentions Heidegger's name. Parallels between Lefort and Heidegger on this account have also been perceived by Hugues Poltier (1998: 147) and Bernard Flynn (1992: 182). The fact that Lefort does not cite Heidegger is explained by Flynn as sign of a certain suspicion on Lefort's part concerning Heidegger's 'systematic denegation of the emergence of the political as such' (1996: 183).

On the other hand, such pure ('ontological') originary conflict – which is the ultimate core of the 'being' of the social – has to find a symbolic outlet if it is not to destroy society. At the most extreme point, a society of *pure* antagonism, a society without the symbolically regulating dimension of power in the Lefortian sense, would amount to a Hobbesian state of nature and hence could not be called society at all. So what results is a chiasm or intertwining between politics and the political rather than their 'distinction' or even opposition. Politics and the political stand in a relation of *reversibility*: 'The analysis of the forms of political society therefore leads to the examination of the forms of action, and vice versa. There are two poles of experience and two poles of knowledge, and the gap is irreducible. Or to say it in a modern language: Reflection on the political and reflection on politics are at once distinct and intertwined' (Lefort 2000: 138).

It is obvious that the Lefortian theory of democracy is located within the 'Machiavellian moment'. For Machiavelli it is the symbolic dispositive of the republic – as the regime of freedom built on the sovereign rule of law – which allows for recognition of conflict as well as for regulation of the opposition between people and nobles, which makes it impossible for any party entirely to dominate/oppress the other. In a sense, this makes Machiavelli not only the first 'antagonism theorist', by placing emphasis on an irresolvable conflict at the core of every possible society, but also the first one to develop a theory of 'agonism' as the symbolically regulated form of antagonism (regulated, for instance, through the arrangement of a mixed constitution). It is important, however, to stress once more that 'regulation' in no way entails the 'sublation' of the opposition between nobles and the people into a harmonious or even homogenous community. Radical antagonism never disappears; it has to be accepted as the condition of possibility of society. Yet, deconstructively speaking, this condition of possibility simultaneously acts for society as its condition of impossibility. From the viewpoint of conceptual history, this has been clearly perceived by Gisela Bock in her essay on 'civil discord' in Machiavelli: '[I]t is only in the republican order that the discords among the various human *umori* can and must be expressed; on the other hand, it is these very discords that continually threaten it. They are both the life and the death of the republic' (1990: 201).

4.5 The Real as Disturbance and the Imaginary as Concealment

When analyzing the prominent role the *umori* play in Machiavelli, it is important for Lefort to underscore the fact that Machiavelli did *not* rely on anthropological assumptions concerning human nature. Even if this were the case, the positive 'content' of these assumptions would not affect the argument as to the originary division, since the latter is construed in merely 'negative' fashion: Lefort observes that the nature of the two humours, and, as a consequence, of the two classes is entirely *relational*. Their very existence is based on their confrontation. Resolve this originary confrontation and, together with society, the identity of the two classes will disappear, since they exist only by virtue of their mutual confrontation. If we look at the matter from this angle, the relation between the two classes does not appear to necessitate any positive substance behind their identity but rather emerges from a primordial lack of a positive substance. The purely negative relation between the two classes of the *umori* points to a lack that *precedes their positive content*. In this sense Lefort can claim that a class only exists through the lack by which it is constituted in relation to another class (1986b: 382).

Any social bond must pass through the conflictual experience of this void, through the experience of a constitutive absence at the very heart of society. From a Lacanian viewpoint, it is of course tempting to see in this void the place of the subject. The introduction of such a Lacanian theory of the divided subject has the great advantage of allowing us to redefine 'human nature' in a non-essentialist way and to retrace the void behind all positive anthropological assumptions. The subject is marked by a void as much as society – and, for that matter, as much as every identity. Yet to what extent do other analytic concepts play a role in Lefort? The most obvious candidate is, of course, the concept of the 'symbolic'. It is clear, for Lefort, that there can be no society without the symbolic dimension. As Bernard Flynn observes, Lacan's notion of the symbolic order is given by Lefort a 'Merleau-Pontyan' turn: 'For Lefort, the Symbolic Order is that which deploys the "within and without"; it is what operates this distinction – the symbolic structure of society is neither within nor without' (1992: 185). One could say that for Lefort the symbolic defines the very way in which the chiasmatic, instituting dimension of society – its self-externalization – is operationalized and institutionalized. In its most basic form, as 'symbolic system' of society, this dimension is specifiable as 'a configuration of the signifiers of law, power and knowledge' (Lefort 1986a: 186). While in the 'monarchic' dispositive these signifiers are unified or incorporated in the single signifier of the body of the king, in the symbolic dispositive of democracy they are disjointed. The relation we establish with, or towards, the dimension of the originary division can only be symbolic.

In like manner, this could suggest thinking about the originary division in terms of 'antagonism as real' (Žižek 1990). Notwithstanding the fact that, from a Lacanian viewpoint, Lefort's usage of terms like 'the real' and 'reality' is not always consistent, in some passages he comes quite close to a Lacanian understanding of the real as that which disturbs the process of every symbolization and functions as a name for radical contingency for the absent foundation of antagonism. Simultaneously, a further category is required to name the complementary process of denial and concealment of the original division. For if society can only be established through a process of self-division – which both enables and disables a certain degree of social coherence – then society can never reach a state of full reconciliation with itself. There will always be attempts at 'covering up' the fact that, at the place of society's ground, the only thing we discover is an abyss. These 'cover-ups' (a 'folding over of social discourse on to itself', 1986a: 202) Lefort calls processes of concealment which operate through the dimension of the 'imaginary'. Such concealment, which indicates a profound inability to accept the instituting distance of society to itself, must always fail in the final instance – due to the ontologically *necessary* character of the disturbing cause of the real. These 'failures' of, and 'discordances' within, the process of occultation allow 'what we can now justly call the *real* to appear'. Lefort, in a manner not entirely dissimilar to Lacan and theorists influenced by Lacan, thus defines the real in purely empty or negative fashion as 'that which marks the impossibility of achieving concealment' (197).

Concentrating for a moment on the imaginary dimension will allow us to re-approach the grounding question regarding the originary and instituting division of society once again – this time, however, from its 'reverse side', the side of its concealment or occultation. For this side Lefort retains the traditional term ideology, which could justifiably be defined as the *discursive actualization* of the imaginary dimension. This actualization might take place in different ways, yet the main problem of every ideology is to come to grips not only with the 'logical' impossibility of closure, but also with the irreversible *historical* event of the democratic revolution. Neither can the event of the democratic revolution be reversed nor can the paradoxes that were instantiated by it be resolved – even as ideology aims at precisely such a de-paradoxization.

Totalitarianism, the most radical form of ideological concealment, is marked by the democratic revolution in particular, since totalitarianism is nothing other than the mutation and prolongation of its features: totalitarianism both inverts and at the same time radicalizes the features of the democratic revolution, and therefore must not be confused with pre-democratic forms of government like tyranny or despotism, as Lefort, like Arendt, repeatedly insists. Rather, it is one of the two major directions in which the democratic revolution can evolve: democracy and totalitarianism; and, since it is rooted in the democratic revolution, totalitarianism cannot be clearly and definitely separated from democracy. The reason is the following. Since society is thrown back on itself at the moment of its institution (or 'invention'), it necessarily resorts to the fantasies of total domination of the social space, of omnipotent knowledge and all-knowing power.

As with all forms of imaginary concealment, the defining characteristic of totalitarianism must be seen in its occultation of the original division and the empty place of power. By merging society and power, it closes and homogenizes social space. Power will be reincarnated and its place occupied first by a party claiming to be different from traditional parties and to represent the people as a whole. The latter will be identified with the proletariat, which will be identified with the party, then with the politburo and ultimately with what Lefort, taking up an expression of Solzhenitsyn's, calls the 'Egocrat'. In contradistinction to the monarch, who was not identical with himself, the Egocrat, who seeks fully to incarnate the place of power *within* society, is in possession of a single body only: *corpus mysticum* and *corpus naturale* are indistinguishable. The Egocrat coincides with himself as much as totalitarian society coincides with itself.

So the main feature of totalitarianism – with respect to the founding conflict – is that any form of antagonism will be concealed, and a homogenized and self-transparent society will be postulated: 'social division, in all its modes, is denied, and at the same time all signs of differences of opinion, belief or mores are condemned' (1988: 13). This means that the originary division is erased, in the sense that the Egocrat incarnates the 'People-as-One', that is to say, society without internal division and antagonism. But, since that division can never be completely erased as an ontological dimension and will continue to surface in the form of disturbances of the imaginary concealment, it has to be *displaced*. In order for the 'People-as-One' to be presented as a totality, as full identity, a relation to some sort of outside is inevitable. What acts as the new outside is a series of internal substitutes representing the 'enemy within': the kulaks, the bourgeoisie, the Jews, spies, and saboteurs. And yet totalitarianism is entangled in a paradox. Its goal is to get rid of internal division, but in order to achieve that goal an enemy has to be produced: 'division is denied . . . and, at the same time as this denial, a division is being affirmed, on the level of phantasy, between the People-as-One and the Other' (298). Totalitarianism needs the enemy as a reference point and thus relies on division at the very moment when the latter is decried.

To summarize: every modern form of ideology consists in the denial of both the instituting role of division and the emptiness of the place of power. Yet with the democratic revolution it has become impossible permanently to occupy that place of power, which has effectively been disincorporated. While in the past this external place was occupied by the gods or, in a supplementary way, by the transcendent body of the monarch, such a transcendent or foundational outside – an actually existing outside with a positive content independent of society's identity – is unthinkable within the democratic dispositive: nothing and nobody can any longer legitimately claim being a natural inhabitant of the outside and incarnating an external point of reference. The outside has long been abandoned by the gods, and power – the representational form of that outside – has been 'emptied'. Philosophically speaking, after the decline of foundationalism nobody can justifiably claim having unhindered epistemic access to a transcendent sphere of knowledge: such epistemic foundationalism is simply the scientific form of *ideology*: the 'enterprise of phantasy which tends to produce and to fix the ultimate foundations of knowledge in every sphere' (1986a: 299).

4.6 Democracy as 'Ontic Institutionalization' of the Originary Division

After having discussed the phenomenon of original division from its reverse side – imaginary concealment – let us recapitulate where precisely the difference between the democratic dispositive and forms of ideology is situated. In both the democratic and the non-democratic dispositive, it is a fact that only with recourse to the instance of power, which represents its outside, can society imagine itself as *one*. In both cases, power offers society a 'point of reference', which has to be external to the social (i.e. has to be represented as being external) in order to function as reference for the social whole, for we can only establish the totality of something by referring to a point or place which is not itself part of that totality, which is external to it. *Every* society – democratic or not – achieves its identity through such a division. But if this logic applies to *every* society, where does the difference lie between a democratic and a non-democratic dispositive?

Here it is important once more to emphasize that the post-foundational answer to this question must not be confused with the *anti*-foundationalist answer. The 'dissolution of the markers of certainty' does not lead to a dissolution of *all markers*, to the dissolution of the symbolic dimension as such. The latter assumption would, of course, characterize the standard foundationalist critique of anti-foundationalism: according to its foundationalist critics, anti-foundationalism assumes that, if we did not have any stable ground, any guiding principle (of ultimate values, rational truth, and so on), any certainty regarding our social affairs – then everything would be allowed. We would be in total confusion, without any orientation and deprived of any symbolic framework within which we could position ourselves. For Lefort, and this is what makes his theory *post*-foundational rather than anti-foundationalist, this does not constitute a stringent conclusion. It is true that what functions as the Other of society is not a positive, transcendent principle or ground, yet on the other hand, the dimension of the outside – the instituting 'ground' – cannot completely disappear either, if society is still to have an identity; and who would deny that it is in need of some sort of identity? Lefort makes it very clear that a point of reference is still required, though within a democratic regime it has to be established in a different, a purely non-substantive way. What characterizes the democratic dispositive, then, is that it keeps the place of power empty and refrains from positing any ground other than its self-division. Yet the different forms of ideology have taught us that the groundlessness of the social and the emptiness of power can be denied and occulted. Hence, something more is required for the democratic dispositive to be realized: the emptiness of the place of power has to be *institutionally* recognized (as much as the groundlessness of society has to be theoretically accepted by post-foundational political thought). The democratic dispositive hence provides an institutional framework that guarantees the *acceptance* of the groundlessness of the social.

How is this paradoxical goal of the institutionalization of groundlessness achieved within the democratic dispositive? The following set of 'arrangements' – which should not be understood as mere mechanical applications, even if they have to be operationalized on the 'ontic' level – is worth being mentioned. We have touched on the first one already: the disincorporation of the place of power is accompanied by 'the disentangling of the sphere of power, the sphere of law and the sphere of knowledge'. Power is in constant search of its own base of legitimation because the principles of justice and of knowledge are no longer incorporated in the person of the ruler (1988: 17–18). Within the democratic dispositive, therefore, the boundaries between these spheres of activity have to be recognized. What we witness is the respective *autonomization* of the spheres of law, knowledge and power – they all develop and define their own norms and principles of legitimacy, and it is totalitarianism which seeks to tear down the walls between these spheres and re-centre society around a single legitimatory ground.

The fact that such a single ground disappears, though, does not imply the disappearance of the *questions* of social institution. Since they cannot rely on any external source of 'founding', they turn into questions of autonomous *self*-institution of society. And it is *within* society where all questions of autonomous self-institution are negotiated. This is made possible by the separation of civil society from the state. Furthermore, a public space is carved out of civil society, in which no monarch, no majority and no supreme judge can decide which particular debate is legitimate and which one is not. Democracy is 'founded upon *the legitimacy of a debate as to what is legitimate and what is illegitimate* – a debate which is necessarily without any guarantor and without any end' (1988: 39).

This never-ending debate – which forms public space – was secured by the declaration of human rights (Gauchet 1989). The notion of human rights points to a territory which, as a consequence of the disentangling of power, law and knowledge, is located beyond the reach of power. Human rights are declared within, and by, civil society itself and are part of its auto-institution. They do not constitute a new positive ground, they do not consist of a certain set of pre-established eternal principles: they are characteristically open with respect to their content. Although human rights, in principle, expose all particular established rights to questioning (Lefort 1986a: 258), they guarantee however that one right cannot be questioned: *the right to have rights*, as Lefort formulates it with reference to Hannah Arendt. Once acknowledged, human rights enable more and more social groups to claim their right to have rights. Lefort's point is that the extension of human rights to more and more groups is absolutely necessary for democracy to exist. The constant call for inclusion of more and more groups (today, for instance, for the rights of homosexuals, jobless people, or immigrants) into the category of those entitled to have rights is what generates democracy again and again.

This generative principle of fighting for further inclusions into the ever-enlarging space, once opened up by the declaration of human rights, is, obviously, conflictual in nature and thus accompanied by the *institutionalization of conflict* in democracy (Lefort/Gauchet 1971). Universal suffrage therefore belongs to the most important elements of the democratic dispositive. This might sound trivial, but the ultimate meaning of universal suffrage, according to Lefort, is not to elect representatives of the people – which, in a sense, is only a 'side effect' of elections. Its real meaning is, first, to give rules to political competition which guarantee the periodic evacuation of the place of power, thereby recalling its ontologically 'empty' status; and, second, to move social conflict (conflicts of interests and class conflict) onto the symbolic stage of politics. This mechanism rests on a process of *disincorporation* at the moment of elections, when citizens who are entangled in different social contexts experience what Lefort calls the 'disincorporation of the individual' (1986a: 303). They are abstracted and converted into numbers. The unity of society is broken apart into numbers at the moment of election: 'Number replaces substance' (1988: 19).

What is actually symbolically represented in the moment of election, then, is not the will of the people in its unmediated emanation: quite on the contrary, it is the fragmentation, division and conflictuality of society which is staged. It follows that the will of the people is nothing unitary, because the fact that it has to be counted out attests to its fragmentation. This is why 'the people' does not exist. And, in addition to that, it also disproves the critique of democracy as 'merely formal'. Such a critique usually insists that democratic elections mask and mystify the 'real' economic power relations, since elections are not about distributing 'real' or factual power. What is overlooked is that elections are not, in the first place, about the distribution of 'real' power anyway, since their function is to stage and symbolize conflict and power *as real*: their paradoxical role is to serve as institutional *markers of uncertainty*.

All these aspects of the democratic dispositive contribute to the institutionalization of society's originary dimension: division. What makes division originary is the impossibility of a positive ground. It is because society's identity cannot be forged in relation to a positive ground that society has to find its ground in itself, by way of self-division. Such a quasi-transcendental claim about the general condition of identity-formation makes sense only if it holds for *every* modern society. The difference between democracy and totalitarianism is not that the latter has access to a positive ground while the former hasn't. What distinguishes democracy from totalitarianism and other forms of ideology is that in democracy the general condition of the absence of a positive ground is not occulted but institutionally recognized and discursively actualized.

This, however, can only be a paradoxical enterprise, because it is impossible fully to institutionalize something purely negative and absent into a presence. If this institutionalization completely succeeded, we would be left with full presence, and the dimension of absence would be entirely lost. Absence as such cannot be institutionalized. Therefore, institutionalization or discursive actualization has to aim at something slightly different: the *recognition* of absence as absence, that is, the recognition of the impossibility of founding society once and for all. Symbolic frameworks are provided, which allow for the acceptance of interrogation, debate, questioning, and conflict as that which *generates* democracy. Groundlessness is openly *staged* in democracy and the constitutive role of division is culturally accepted (it enters the 'flesh of the social'). So we can summarize the main points of this chapter by saying that what characterizes democracy is not so much the logic of groundlessness and self-division, but the recognition of that logic as constitutive. Accepting it as constitutive obviously does not make the dimension of ground disappear. Rather, the ground is emptied of any positive content and retained as something which is absent. This is what makes democracy – and Lefort's theory of democracy – post-foundational. For, unlike any other form of society, democracy is founded upon the recognition of the very absence of any definite foundation.

All this is theorized by Lefort on the premise of his general aim at renewing political thought. Even as the process of such renewal has to be understood, *pace* Merleau-Ponty, as a general philosophical process of interrogation, the latter turns, with Lefort, into a form of doing precisely political philosophy. Philosophical interrogation is, at its most fundamental level, *political* interrogation. Although Lefort does not explicitly state this consequence, it must be drawn from the premises of his theory. Since if philosophy, as well as the process of thinking as interrogation, always takes place *within* society – and does not fly above it – and if, in addition, the symbolic framework of society is always instituted *politically*, then it follows that interrogating whatever phenomenon appears within society's horizon will necessarily involve interrogating society's political institution. To the extent that philosophical interrogation takes place within society, it will, at the most fundamental level, be *political* philosophy – as it will have to interrogate the symbolic and imaginary ways in which all social being is put on stage, is given meaning, and is given form *politically*.

Notes

1. One should mention here Lefort's early collaborator Cornelius Castoriadis, who also employs a specific version of the political difference. To put it in a nutshell, for Castoriadis the dimension of *explicit power*, by which he understands '*instances capable of formulating explicitly sanctionable injunctions*' (1991: 156), should be called *the political*, while true *politics*, on the other hand, 'amounts to the explicit putting into question of the established institution of society' (159).

2. Lefort's phrase 'thinking of the political (*du politique*)' – and therein the implicit but systematic differentiation between *le politique* and *la politique* – is traced by Hugues Poltier (1998: 126) back to the end of the 1970s.

3. We resort to the term 'symbolic dispositive' as a translation for Lefort's '*dispositif symbolique*', despite the fact that 'dispositive' does not exist as an English word, because it seems advisable to remain as closely as possible to the original term which serves Lefort as a terminus technicus. Other translations could also be 'symbolic formation', 'arrangement', or 'conjuncture'.

4. This does not preclude the possibility that the break with ancient sources of legitimacy is less than total and that modernity remains partially haunted by the spectre of the king's transcendent body. Lefort's idea of the permanence of the theological–political (1988: 213–55) seems to point precisely in this direction.

Chapter 5
The State and the Politics of Truth: Alain Badiou

5.1 Against Political Philosophy as a Philosophy of *the Political*

Badiou's work constitutes one of the rare examples in current theorizing of a post-foundational philosophical *system* – and there is hardly a contradiction here between a post-foundational stance and systematic philosophy. For Badiou, true philosophy is always systematic, yet it is not systematic in the sense of being centered around a keystone: 'if by "system" you mean, first, that philosophy is conceived as an argumentative discipline with a requirement of coherence, and second, that philosophy never takes the form of a singular body of knowledge but, to use my own vocabulary, exists conditionally with respect to a complex set of truths, then it is the very essence of philosophy to be systematic' (1994: 85). The aim of this chapter is not, of course, to give an exhaustive account of Badiou's system. What I will try to do is to trace Badiou's attitude to and his role within current political philosophy. This is not an easy task, since Badiou – contrary to Lefort – aims at nothing less than the *destruction* of political philosophy. If Claude Lefort's aim is to re-invigorate political philosophy, then in the eyes of Badiou it is a fundamental imperative for contemporary thought to 'finish with political philosophy'. However, what I will claim is that Badiou can legitimately be located within the group of post-foundational theorists whose work, for lack of a better name, we have labelled the 'Heideggerian Left' in current political philosophy. Yet we will also see that the post-foundational effects of his theory are limited because of some foundationalist injunctions on Badiou's part, which find expression in a certain philosophism and a particular form of ethicism – a side-effect of his deliberate denigration of political philosophy.

It might perhaps come as a surprise that Badiou should be located within the Heideggerian camp, as most often he is presented and presents himself as a sort of anti-Heideggerian, yet in French post-war thought the traces of Heidegger's influence remain visible even where they are openly disavowed. Jacques Derrida once remarked that 'for a quarter century, Heidegger was never named in any book by those who, in France, were forced to recognize in private or in public much later that he had played a major role in their thought (Althusser, Foucault, Deleuze, for example)' (1993: 190). Since I hope some of the Heideggerian themes in Badiou will become apparent throughout this chapter, may it suffice for the moment to point out the most obvious line of filiation: Badiou's decision to entitle his magnum opus *Being and Event* (*L'Etre et l'événement*) can clearly be understood as a reference to his early mentor, Jean-Paul Sartre, and his major work *Being and Nothingness*. Yet Sartre himself, who belonged to the first generation of French Heideggerians, was of course alluding to Heidegger's *Being and Time*, and it goes without saying that neither in the case of Sartre nor in the case of Badiou is the choice of title an arbitrary one. What remains in place in this series of titles is *Being*, while the second term in each one indicates the differential perspective through which being (or *beyng*) is approached. In Badiou's case, it is the notion of event, which in itself bears a deeply Heideggerian mark – even as the idea of a 'fundemantal ontology' (or 'first philosophy') is displaced by Badiou to the field of mathematical set theory. So Badiou *can* be allocated to the group of left Heideggerian theorists, who all share a series of common theoretical tropes or figures (also to be encountered in Badiou's work) and, most importantly, who all employ the conceptual difference between 'politics' and 'the political', or between '*la politique*' and '*le politique*'. And, already in the title of Badiou's magnum opus, we can get a first glimpse at the way in which this difference will be philosophically constructed by him.

In the following I will try, through a systematic presentation of Badiou's 'political thought' (or, rather, of the corners of his thought concerned with political thruth-procedures), to illustrate the extent to which the latter actually displays the group of post-foundational family resemblances outlined in Chapter 2 (contingency, event, conflictuality, groundlessness) – notwithstanding Badiou's rather misleading self-representation as an anti-Heideggerian, *anti*-post-foundational Platonist. Admittedly, as such a self-proclaimed new Platonist, Badiou stands at the most extreme point of the spectrum of post-foundational theory. Some would even say he holds an antagonistic position with respect to most other social post-foundationalists. Peter Hallward (1998: 88), for instance, goes as far as claiming that 'Badiou's mature work provides the most powerful alternative yet conceived in France to the various forms of postmodernism that arose after the collapse of the Marxist project . . .'. In the same fashion, Jean-Jacques-Lecercle (1999: 7) claims that Badiou's position of a *Platonism of the manifold* 'is a lonely place, as he opposes everything continental philosophy of the post-structuralist kind has been about'. However, this may only seem so if we take Badiou's declarations at face value. A closer look will reveal that Badiou's Platonism – supposedly standing in radical opposition towards anything post-foundational – is a Platonism of the most peculiar kind. There is a strong element of provocation involved. Badiou's self-styled Platonism should thus be taken as *strategic coquetry* following from a serious intent, or simply as '*serious* coquetry': 'Our century is fundamentally anti-Platonist. So there's an element of coquetry in calling yourself a Platonist, which I am, profoundly' (1994: 87). How can one be profound and coquettish at the same time? I hope that the following will show that there are many more similarities between Badiou and his alleged adversaries, the modern 'sophists' (including theorists like Lyotard, Derrida, Lacoue-Labarthe and Nancy), than there are incompatibilities – some of which will be discussed at the end of this chapter.

Let us start by considering the premises upon which Badiou's attack against political philosophy is based. From the point of view of the political difference, it is of importance that Badiou relates the category of *the political* (*le politique*) precisely to 'traditional' political philosophy, while retaining the category of *politics* (*la politique*) for his own intellectual enterprise. For Badiou (1998a: 19), political philosophy describes a programme by which politics is 'reified' into an invariable and objective given of universal experience, i.e. the political, and eventually consigned to the realm of ethical norms. In the classical tradition of political philosophy, politics was subordinated to a normative evaluation and quest for the 'good State' – it was thus subordinated to questions of the legitimation of sovereignty. The political philosopher will turn out to be the beneficiary of that process in three ways: first, s/he will be the analyst of the brutal and confused empiricity of real politics; second, s/he will be the one to determine the principles of a 'good' politics or polity, which are in line with the exigencies of ethics; and third, s/he can avoid the risk of becoming the militant of a truth-related political process (engendered, for Badiou, by the intervention of thinking/acting) by withdrawing into the non-activity of *judgement*. Thus, politics no longer describes, as it does for Badiou, the subjectivizing truth-processes of militants, but is reduced to 'free judgement' and the exchange of opinions within a public sphere.

It is Hannah Arendt who serves as Badiou's main target and stand-in for political philosophy at large, since for Arendt truth is not a category of the political sphere. Accordingly, from Badiou's point of view, this implies: ' "Politics" is neither the name of a thinking (if one agrees that every thinking, where its philosophical identification is concerned, is linked in one or the other way to the theme of truth) nor the name of an action' (1998a: 20). A political philosophy which advocates the plurality of opinions by excluding the notion of truth is devoted, in the last instance, to the promotion of the particular politics of parliamentarism. Behind the abstract notion of *the political* we thus find *a particular politics*, the politics of parliamentarism ('Talking about "the political" here means masking the philosophical defense of a politics', 25), legitimated by the notion of pluralism – the plurality of opinions within the public sphere. Against the 'ontological' characterization of the political as plurality (of opinions), Badiou makes a stand for the *singularity* of politics. By this he does not mean that there is only one politics, rather he seeks to underline that the effective plurality of politics in his sense ('[t]here is no simple plurality, there is only a plurality of pluralities', 31) is always induced by subjects which are different. Each of them is defined by his or her singular relation to a truth-event and *not* by their mutual exchange of opinions under the common norm of pluralism.

Today's parliamentary states are, according to Badiou, regulated by three norms: economy, which is why Badiou also speaks about 'capitalo-parliamentarism'; the national norm; and democracy as such – constructed as a norm vis-à-vis despotism and dictatorship (including the freedom of opinion, association and movement). 'Capitalo-parliamentarism', regulated by these norms, does not simply describe a political regime or form of government, but the parliamentary mode of *the state* – which is defined as the particular way in which elements (or sub-sets) are *ordered* within a situation.[1] Obviously, Badiou is highly critical of, if not inimical to, representative democracy in the parliamentary mode. 'Democracy' (and, in particular, Western liberal democracies), for Badiou – and herein he retains a Marxist point of view – is an intrinsic part and element of capitalism ('it is always entangled in the domination of the proprietors', 1991: 31), in that democracy politically supports and secures the private ownership of the means of production. While history knows different other ways of using the term democracy (the Athenian way, the republican way of the French revolution, the socialist–revolutionary way of general assemblies, of workers councils, and so on), in today's propaganda democracy signifies a form of government limited to the party–state.

After the collapse of the former party–states of the East, 'capitalo-parliamentarism' seems to be the only version of democracy left. Yet the disappearance of the socialist states only covers up the effectual triumph of 'vulgar' Marxism, the capitalist version of *economism*, by which the absolute and unrivalled primacy of the market is assumed. The pluralism on which Western democracy prides itself only covers up a regime of the One: 'We are, politically, under the regime of the One, and not under that of the multiple. Capitalo-parliamentarism is the tendentially unique mode of politics, the only one which combines economic efficiency (hence the profit of the proprietors) with popular consensus' (1991: 37). It has become the only way to imagine democracy *and* it is a regime of the One, since 'capitalo-parliamentarism' implies the subordination of politics under a single sphere: the state, thus annulling politics proper, that is, annulling 'la politique *comme pensée*', as Badiou (36) would have it. Real politics is thus subsumed under and, in the last instance, confounded with the state. And it is only on the premise of the state's ruin (in the ruins, as it were, of the criminal state of 'actually existing' socialism, for instance) that the history of politics – far from ending with the collapse of the eastern–European regimes – can commence.

The three 'capitalo-parliamentary' normative functions of the economy, the nation and democracy characterize the parliamentary state as *a* politics (*une* politique) that is oriented towards the State. A politics – which is always *particular* and 'statist' by nature – must therefore be distinguished from what Badiou calls *the* politics (*la* politique) in general. But what is *the* politics? Before a more detailed outline of '*la* politique' is presented, it should be stressed that Badiou does not proceed through definitions, if by definitions we understand an assertion which would link politics to a particular object. Badiou is entirely against any objectifying approach to politics, since philosophy in Badiou's sense, as thinking, does not have an object: 'The "political" object in particular does not exist for it' (1998a: 72). This is one of reasons why philosophy should not be confused with political theory – which objectifies *la politique* into *le politique* – since 'politics [*la politique*], just like philosophy, has no object and is not subordinated to the norm of objectivity' (73). Since there is no object of politics (there is only the militant subject), there can be no definition of politics. Of course, Badiou himself is never tired of providing definitions, but not definitions in the sense of an objective predication, but axiomatic definitions that do not refer to any empirically given 'object' outside the processes of thinking. And he consequently denounces political science, which also 'objectifies' politics and reduces an objectless field in which truth can appear to the 'extrinsic' object of the party–state. In this anti-positivism and anti-objectivism, traits of the Heideggerian criticism of the metaphysics of technology and science are clearly discernible. The corresponding claim is made by Badiou about politics: politics proper must not be confused with today's 'technologized' politics, with the bureaucratic management of the affairs of the state – which is only part of a larger process of technologization and does not enter what Badiou calls truth-procedures or the conditions of philosophy.

It is at this point that Badiou is closest to Heidegger – at least to a certain Heidegger. For Badiou, the great power of Heidegger's thought results from his effort at 'suturing' philosophy to the poem, a move that allowed him to position poetry against positivistic objectification: 'the great force of Heidegger consists in having crossed a properly philosophical critique of positivistic objectivity, of the deployment of technology and the forgetfullness regarding the thinking of being, with a profound understanding of what is at stake, through these very questions, in the poem' (Badiou 1990: 4). While Badiou tends to disassociate himself from this strategy (for Badiou, our own epoch needs to 'de-suture' philosophy from the poem), he retains the Heideggerian distinction between truth and knowledge ('One thus has to distinguish the regime of knowledge from that of truths, herein I agree, and this is a Heideggerian theme', 10), which then is transformed by Badiou into the Lacanian notion of an *unsymbolizable real* as that which is subtracted from language and knowledge. So what is typical for Badiou's Heideggerianism is his translation of Heideggerian themes into post-Lacanian terminology, which sometimes makes it hard to trace back those themes to their Heideggerian and Sartrean roots.[2]

5.2 Politics of the Real

From the viewpoint of politics (*la* politique), both democracy and so-called totalitarianism are figures of the state. What unites liberal, Marxist and fascist conceptions is their common suppression of real politics and its replacement by the complex of state and economy, as something which occupies the totality of the visible. Yet the state in itself, while certainly being a term of the political field, is *a*-political by nature (Badiou 1985: 108–9). So it is democracy and totalitarianism together (and in their seeming opposition) which constitute the terrain for the apogee of the political. The Soviet paradigm is built on nothing other than the political, in the form of the universal pretension of the state, on which the parliamentary democracies are built as well – even though they were long in a position to hide behind the more obvious statist façade of totalitarianism. For this reason, the problem starts when democracy and totalitarianism are presented in terms of an opposition. Instead, '[d]emocracy and totalitarianism are two epochal versions of the accomplishment of the political [*du politique*] in its twofold category of tie and representation. Our task concerns politics [*la politique*] to the extent that it positions occurrences of un-tying in the order of the irrepresentable' (17).

So one has to disconnect politics (*la* politique) from the fiction of the communitarian or social bond as well as from the fiction of representation, that is, from the two main fictions of the political (*le* politique). Where representation is concerned, Badiou makes it more than clear that he is entirely against the representation of anything social (be it the proletariat, the class, or the nation) within or with the help of politics. For him, politics does not represent anything, it is a procedure of *irrepresentation*. And it is only to the extent that it escapes the logic of representation that politics touches on the real, whose logic is entirely different: the real works in the mode of the '*futur antérieur*'. Consequently, 'the time of real politics is the *futur antérieur*' (107). That is to say, a political subject (say, the proletariat) cannot be represented, because it does not exist in the social prior to its political construction: it is established as a subject only retroactively, through the very process of faithfully linking up with a truth-event (say, the revolution). Consequently, for Badiou, *real* politics always means politics of *the real*, and political organization means '*organisation du futur antérieur*' (109).

In Lacan, of course, the register of the real has to be strictly differentiated from that of reality, and hence, for the Lacanian Badiou, the politics of the real cannot be related to the level of empirical facts and social data either. Their realm is not the register of politics, but the realm of *the police*, if by police we understand the 'amplifier' of the pre-given, that is, the management of already established facts. Police is always the 'police of facts' (96). A thinking/acting of politics, on the other hand, always must *substract*[3] itself from the order of being, the state or the police – i.e. from the order of the necessary – and, quite literally, seek to achieve the impossible. In order to do this, that is to say, in order to allow for the event to occur, one has to leave aside all the facts and be faithful to something which is not a given fact of reality but an evanescent interruption of the real: 'The possibility of the impossible is the ground of politics [*de la politique*]. It is massively opposed to everything we are taught today, including politics being the management of the necessary. Politics [*la politique*] starts with the same gesture by which Rousseau clears the ground of inequality: leaving aside all the facts. It is important for an event to arrive to leave aside all the facts' (78).

Again, what is of course incompatible with a true politics that belongs to the register of the real is the notion of the social bond. Politics, like the real, belongs to the order of the event, not to the order of the bond (1985: 20). Political philosophy, for Badiou, is nothing but the fiction of the political as social bond. It is a fiction because political philosophy, in its search for the *legitimate* bond, inscribes politics into the narrative and linear figure of the novel: the fiction of a measurement, according to a philosophical norm, of the *good* state, or the good revolution. The disturbing event of politics is thereby sublimated into the fiction of the political as, on the one hand, bond (or social relation) and, on the other, representation under an authority (or political sovereignty).

The name for the place of all relations is *the social* – which is where all relations of oppression and exploitation are located. This implies for Badiou that the social is also the order of differences. As such, it belongs, in our words, to the 'ontic' level, which is of no importance for Badiou's theorization of the event as that which disturbs and interrupts the ontic. The level of the social is characterized by rites, mores, traditions and beliefs, by imaginary formations such as religions, sexual representations, etc. This level is cherished today by the ideology of multiculturalism. Badiou is not interested in differences as such, because every truth disposes of differences or renders them insignificant. With admirable sobriety he writes: 'Every modern collective configuration involves people from everywhere, who have their different ways of eating and speaking, who wear different sorts of headgear, follow different religions, have complex and varied relations to sexuality, prefer authority or disorder, and such is the way of the world' (2002a: 27). Badiou remains totally unimpressed where the proponents of multiculturalism would be most fascinated. The reasons for his disinterest should have become clear by now: the infinite multiplicity belongs to the level of beings ('*ce qui est*'), while truth belongs to the entirely different register of the event ('*ce qui advient*'): 'Only a truth is, as such, *indifferent to differences*' (27). One may suspect that once more we encounter in Badiou something like a radicalized notion of the ontological *difference as difference*, his '*distinction directrice*' between 'being' and 'event', and Badiou's highly original point, if he were to submit to this Heideggerian vocabulary, would then be that this 'radical difference' whose play grounds all ontic differences, is precisely what *escapes* the ontic order of differences (thus being indifferent to differences).

Event, perhaps the key concept in Badiou, signifies nothing other than the disruption of the order of the ontic, or, in Badiou's words, the disruption of the state of the situation. An event cannot be predicted as it constitutes a break with all available knowledge, procedures or calculations that could allow for a prediction. Events, as Lecercle (1999: 8) has it, 'flash like bolts of lightning, and truths emerge'. Therefore, an event does not itself belong to the situation – which is why it serves as a supplement to it. The reason for this is clear: were the event part of the situation, it would be subsumable under the rules of that very situation and nothing new could originate from it. So it must come, as it were, from outside and yet somehow have a place in the situation in order to be 'effective'. Hence the event must be, at one and the same time, supplementary with respect to the situation *and* placed or situated within the situation.

Yet one has to be careful not to substantialize the event. The supplement of the event is, at the very same time, its eclipse: to be precise, the event can only be experienced as something that has vanished, it only exists, as it were, in its own eclipse. Badiou proposes to think of the event as 'the evanescent', as 'something whose very being is to disappear', as, in our words, a figure of contingency: 'I think of the event as a totally chance, incalculable, disconnected supplement to the situation. It will be recorded in its very disappearance only in the form of a linguistic trace, which I call the "name" of the event, and will supplement the situation with next to nothing' (1994: 87). So, strictly speaking, what supplements a situation is not the event itself (which has always already disappeared), but the *name* of the event: there must be an *intervention of naming that which, in itself, has vanished.*

We can thus conclude the following: An event itself is incalculable and whether or not it occurs is a matter of chance. In our terminology: the event is a figure of contingency. As soon as it occurs – or 'happens' – it has already disappeared. It nonetheless has a *site* within the situation, which lies at the borders of the situation's constitutive void. It is therefore possible to trace the evanescent event with the help of a *name*, which is supernumerary in relation to the situation (the name cannot be part of the situation prior to the event and its naming).

If we ask what exactly it is that is disturbed and disrupted by the event, then we will find as a complementary term the *state* (in its broadest sense). According to the Badiouian nomenclature, an event constitutes a rupture or disturbance with respect to the state of a situation. A situation, for Badiou, is always an infinite multiple: it consists of an infinite series of elements belonging to it – no matter whether it is a mathematical, a historical, a political, or an artistic situation. So if every situation is, by definition, open, what makes it possible to determine whether a given element belongs to it or not? The state is nothing but the operation by which the elements or sub-sets of a situation are codified as belonging to it and the situation itself can thus be counted as One (Badiou 1998a: 158). The state of the situation owns the power to define relations, qualities and properties of the situation's elements. It is the order of the sub-sets of a given situation, and, as such, constitutes the situation's *language*, which 'aims at showing how an element belongs to such and such a subset' (Badiou 1994: 87). And, to the extent that the state imposes order and objectivity on a situation, it is not by chance that there is a certain vicinity between the state of a situation and the political notion of the state.

If we now re-apply this theory of the event to Badiou's usage of the notion of politics and the political respectively, one can provisionally encapsulate the result in the following formula. Politics is what interrupts the fiction of the political. It cuts off all representation and *de*-relates all social relations. Politics therefore lies beyond the realm of the social. It is exceptionary in relation to the social.[4]

Such theorization of the political difference is certainly inspired by the debates at the Centre for Philosophical Research on the Political. In his *Peut-on penser la politique?*, a text which originated at the two conferences in 1983 and 1984 at the Centre, Badiou agrees with Nancy and Lacoue-Labarthe that there is a *retrait* or a *crisis* of the political at the moment of the political's apogee. For Badiou, this crisis is shown most clearly by the crisis of Marxism, yet what is at stake is a much larger phenomenon ('the crisis of the political in its entirety', 1985: 21, 'the planetary crisis of the political', 34), consisting precisely in the dissolution of representation and of the fiction of the social bond: 'What the crisis of the political unveils is that all ensembles are inconsistent, that there is no such thing as France or proletariat, and that, for the same reason, the figure of representation, much like its obverse: the figure of spontaneity, is itself inconsistent . . .' (13).

The 'retreat of the political' in Badiou's sense corresponds to a crisis of closed ensembles or sovereignty of the One in general. The text on the back-cover of the small book makes it utterly clear: 'Thinking politics [la *politique*], first and foremost means refuting the political [le *politique*]: renouncing it as an (imaginary) illusion of "making One" in form of identifications (the party, the union, classless society), of a confinable fact, of a reliable prediction' (1985). What differentiates Badiou from Nancy and Lacoue-Labarthe is his usage of the political difference with reversed premises: politics does not designate, as it does for Nancy and Lacoue-Labarthe, the order of power and of the police but, on the contrary, the order of truth and of the event. However, what is of much greater importance is that, even where he changes the premises, Badiou retains the political difference as difference between *la* and *le politique*. It seems that, wherever we turn in political 'left Heideggerianism', be it to the Lacanian or the deconstructive trajectory, we encounter the need to retain this difference.

In fact, such 'reversal' of terms within the political difference is far from uncommon, particularly when it is an expression of a point of view critical of traditional political philosophy. Etienne Balibar, for

instance, warns against the transformation of *politics* – whose emancipatory pathways are always singular – into a 'representation of *the
political*' (2002: 35). And for Jacques Rancière (1999), whose work is
comparable with Badiou's on this account, politics in the radical sense
(what Rancière calls *la politique* and others would call *the political*)
has to be differentiated from politics in the sense of *police* or *policing*.
While the latter is defined as the set of procedures whereby powers are
organized, consent is established and places and roles are attributed
within society, the former is precisely what is antagonistic to policing:
true politics – as a process of equality – effectuates a break with the
order of policing, thus demonstrating the contingency of the latter.
Politics emerges at the conflictual meeting point between the (non-
political) condition of equality and the logic of policing. In this sense,
politics is the practical proof of society's post-foundational condition:
'The foundation of politics is not in fact more a matter of convention
than of nature: it is the lack of foundation, the sheer contingency of
any social order. Politics exists simply because no social order is based
on nature, no divine law regulates human society' (1999: 16).

5.3 A 'Politics' of Truth: Equality and Justice

Before further engaging with the post-foundational aspects of Badiou's
notion of politics, let us locate the latter in relation to the conceptual
framework of his philosophical system (see 1985: 76–7): A pre-political
situation is defined by Badiou as a complex of facts and statements
wherein a setback for the regime of the One is discernible and where
there is, consequently, an irreducible Two (also described by Badiou as a
point of irrepresentability and as an empty set). Since Badiou calls the
state or structure of the situation the mechanism through which the
situation is *counted as one* (as *this* situation) and thus located within the
sphere of representation, an event must be theorized as the *dysfunction*
of the regime of the One. It is the remainder which cannot be absorbed by
this regime and which is always the product of an act of interpretation.
What he then calls an intervention is constituted by the supernumerary
facts and statements by which the event is interpreted as *an event* (and
the political subject is, far from being the 'agent' of all this, the retroactive outcome of an interpretatory intervention). As we said before, an
event has to be named as an event and its name must not belong to the
situation. Politics is that which, through an intervention, gives consistency to the event.

The last nameable political event, in Badiou's eyes, was the revolution of October 1917. The political events between 1968 and 1980 – the events to which Badiou himself, as a Maoist, adheres – have not yet received their definite name. They remain 'obscure' because they call into question the previous protocols of political nomination – but this does not exclude the possibility that they be named (and thus fixed as an event) many years later. Nevertheless, on a more general level one can specify a series of conditions that have to be met for an event to be designated as political. I would like to mention three. First, the 'material' of the event must consist in a collective: 'An event is political if the material of this event is collective, or if the event cannot be attributed to anything other than to the multiplicity of a collective' (1998a: 155). By collective Badiou does not refer to a certain number of people – collective is not a numerical concept, but it is that which is established in the relation of the militants to universality. The truth-event of politics addresses itself to everybody who proceeds from the event. Second, as an effect of the collective character of the political event, politics presents the infinite character of every situation. A situation is by definition open, it is never finite (in this, Badiou dismisses the Heideggerian theme of finitude and 'being-towards-death', but without grounding the situation in anything other than the void of infinity – which means that the result is still *post*-foundational). Emancipatory and egalitarian politics – and, for Badiou, every politics worth that name is egalitarian and universalistic – immediately convokes this infinity of the situation. Third, if we define the state of a situation as the power to count the sub-sets of the situation as one, thereby making representable the situation as *this* situation, then it follows that such politics of infinity must be directed against the power which, by way of making it countable, would otherwise 'close' the situation and render it finite. Thus, true politics always triggers operations of repression by the state and brings to light the state's excessive power. In this sense, one can say that politics has a *provocative* function.

This kind of thesis implies that the essence of politics is emancipatory. In other words, if true politics is directed against the state by definition, then there is no politics worth the name which is not emancipatory (1991: 54). Now, as it was indicated earlier, the 'moment of politics' – the moment where the state is confronted with the disruption of a political event – is also the moment of *truth*: political truth only begins on the occasion of rupture and disorder, that is, when 'business as usual breaks down for one reason or another' (Hallward 2002). Without truth-event there is no politics in the strict sense, there is only the rule of the state and of the apolitical differences of the social. Yet such truth-event, for Badiou, has certain implications for the normative or perhaps philosophico-'ethical' level of emancipatory politics, since it is closely connected to the interrelated concepts of *justice* and *equality*.

Badiou calls justice 'the name by which a philosophy designates the possible truth of a political orientation' (1999b: 29). It is important to note that justice is one of philosophy's names for a truth-event: it is a philosophical designation, rather than concrete political programme. Justice can also serve as a good example of the extent to which the Badiouian concepts intermesh. If the truth-event is defined by its disruptive quality and justice is one of the philosophical attributes of truth, then justice too occurs in the anti-statist and anti-social form of disruption: 'justice, far from being a possible category of state and social order, is the name which designates the principles at work in rupture and dis-order' (31). Such an approach entails an entirely anti-essentialist understanding of justice. Justice is not defined by any predicate or positive content ('the just'), but only occurs in the 'negative' or undefined moment in which the social bond disintegrates: 'We have too often wished that justice find the consistency of the social tie, while it can only name the most extreme moments of inconsistency' (32).

What was said about justice must therefore also be said about what Badiou calls the 'equalitarian political maxim': equality is a completely 'negative' concept in the sense of not being grounded in the positive substance of a common good; nor should equality be instituted with respect to any positive reference: the only possible reference is the *non*-reference to the state of the situation, to the principle of classification and order (1990: 24). For the same reason, equality cannot be defined: one must not turn equality into a positive programme or an egalitarian policy (at least, such a policy would be exactly that, a policy, and not politics in Badiou's sense). So, in sum, equality does not refer to anything objectively given or to any concrete goal we have to achieve: the effect of the equalitarian axiom related to a truth-event will rather be, as in the case of justice, 'to undo the ties, to desocialize thought, to affirm the rights of the infinite and immortal against finitude, against Being-for-death' (32). Justice and equality are thus interrelated concepts where justice 'is the philosophical name for

the equalitarian political maxim' (30), and the politics of emancipation which imposes an equalitarian maxim, for Badiou, 'is a thought
in act' (31).

If equality is nothing that exists in the social world, but rather an
axiom of thought that works as a prescription, that is to say, if it is
defined by Badiou as *an ethical maxim*, it eventually appears that it is
impossible to talk about real politics (as a politics in which truth,
justice and equality are inextricably linked) without having to enter
the register of the ethical at the same time. Indeed, Badiou's whole
system, despite its apparently 'pure' mathematical inclinations towards set theory as a general ontology, seems to be evolving towards
a generalized ethics.[5] What we encounter in Badiou is an ethics of
truths (and, in the political sphere, of equality), which derives from a
Lacanian ethics of the real based on the *possibility of the impossible*.
Such ethics of truths escapes the order of the symbolic by definition.
Since the truth-event belongs to the order of the real, it cannot be
mediated or communicated. Therefore the ethics of a truth cannot be
an ethics of communication: 'It is an ethics of the Real, if it is true that –
as Lacan suggests – all access to the Real is of the order of an ecounter'
(2002a: 52). In other words, while the event cannot be communicated,
it can be encountered. Hence one of Badiou's reformulations of his
ethical imperative: 'Never forget what you have encountered!' or, in
the shortest version: ' "Keep going!" [*Continuer!*]' (52).

'*Continuer!*' is the formula of fidelity. Continue in being faithful to
the event! Badiou's ethics is centered around the general principle of
faithfully continuing a truth-process. To give consistency to the event
implies giving consistency to, and persevering within, the rupture. In
other words: Never break with the rupture! (Such a break would give
way to the unhindered continuation of the previous situation and the
regime of opinions.) A political organization of militants (i.e. the
subject in the field of politics) is nothing but the collective product of a
process of fidelity towards an event. The reason why an ethical (if not
religious) term like fidelity is so important within the framework of
Badiou's system lies in the fact that it functions as the main operator
of subjectivation: there is a subject only if there is a process of fidelity
– if a subject, through their fidelity, gives consistency to an event. We
remember: an event for Badiou is defined as a supplement to a given
(ontic) situation of multiple beings, and while the former is connected
to the notion of truth and to the real, the latter is always restricted to
the realm of opinions. Subjectivation occurs only if a *decision* is taken

to be faithful to the event against the world of pre-established rules and opinions. Such fidelity creates a rupture within a given situation: a rupture that belongs to the Lacanian order of the real (as something that disturbs the symbolic 'order of things'). At the same time, *a truth* is produced in the situation. One more definition of truth would thus be the following: 'I shall call "truth" (*a* truth) the real process of a fidelity to an event: that which this fidelity produces in the situation' (2002a: 42). A truth is produced by the decision of a subject to remain faithful to an event. What is important to understand, however, is the retroactive logic of subject-formation: the subject only exists to the extent that it actively declares his/her fidelity to the event – it *does not precede* the event. At no point in this circular relation between subject, decision and event do we encounter something of the sort of a ground or Archimedean point. And, of course, fidelity is always optional, never necessary. It consists in an ungrounded decision (a decision for the truth-event), which is grounded only in undecidability and uncertainty. As a result, there always remains the possibility of treason – of non-continuing.

5.4 The Grace of Contingency and the Evil of Foundationalism

Badiou's key concepts – fidelity, truth, infinity, universality – seem to give his philosophy a somewhat Christian ring. Is there a secret, or not so secret, Christian model upon which Badiou's atheistic philosophy relies to some extent? His little book on Saint Paul and the foundation of universalism seems to point in this direction. Badiou, as a matter of fact, places the birth of Western universalism (to which he himself still subscribes) in early Christianity. While it is not an original idea to associate universalism with Christianity, Badiou gives it an interesting twist by retracing the foundational moment of universalism to the Paulinian intervention – and it should not surprise us that, from Badiou's point of view, Paul in many ways had a similar role for Christianity to the one that Lenin had for Bolshevism. This intervention consists in Paul's 'emancipation' of Christianity from all particular or 'communitarian' traditions of both Jews and Gentiles. (For instance, he spoke out against circumcision, as a rite by which a particularist link would be retained between Christianity and the Jewish religion: such a link, in turn, would exclude the non-circumcised Gentiles from Christian universality). Paulinian universality is empty in the sense of being beyond the level of cultural or religious particularisms and social differences. Every particularity constitutes a potential stumbling-block, as true universality must be *for all* – which is the maxim of universalism: 'The One is only insofar as it is for all: such is the maxim of universality when it has its root in the event' (2003: 76).

As Badiou sustains, the source of such empty universality – since it is not some particularity, as in the model of politics proposed by Ernesto Laclau (1996a), where every universality is hegemonized by some particularity – can only be evental. In other words, in Badiou there is a necessary co-belonging of the One, of universality and singularity, since the correlate of an event can never be some particularity, it must always be the universal (in Paul, all of humanity, including former Jews and Gentiles) and the singular of the event. In Paul's case, the event consists in nothing other than Christ's death and resurrection. Once more Badiou detects a certain similarity between the exemplary modern model of an event – the revolution – and the Paulinian model. The resurrection of Christ in its evental aspects ('Christ is, in himself and for himself, *what happens to us*', 48) has the same structure as modern revolutions: it is a political truth-procedure which disrupts the previous discursive regime. It is an event in the strict Badiouian sense of the term and, as such, does not belong to the realm of the particular, but to the realm of the singular–universal. For this reason, the universal–singular event of Christ is of a completely different order than the *historical person* by the name of Jesus, who belongs entirely to the realm of the particular.

While this will sound familiar, given the general exposition of Badiou's theory, the most spectacular modernization of a Paulinian category is to be found in the post-foundational re-framing of 'grace' as a figure of contingency. The event (of Christ's death and resurrection) *is grace* – it is neither foreseeable nor calculable, and it cannot be subject to proof. The phenomenon of grace therefore derives directly from the *incalculability* of the event:

> For Paul, the event has not come to prove something; it is pure beginning. Christ's resurrection is neither an argument nor an accomplishment. There is no proof of the event; nor is the event a proof. (2003: 49)

The event does not prove anything nor can it be proven in turn (it can only be axiomatically declared), since it is of the order of the incalculable: 'Christ is precisely incalculable' (50). So, if it cannot be calculated, it must have the nature of a gift. It is then a matter of grace whether or not we are touched by an event. Subjects are constituted by the evental grace:

> The pure event is reducible to this: Jesus dies on the cross and resurrected. This event is 'grace' (*kharis*). Thus, it is neither a bequest, nor a tradition, nor a teaching. It is supernumerary relative to all this and presents itself as pure givenness. As subject to the ordeal of the real, we are henceforth constituted by evental grace. (2003: 63)

Badiou calls for a *materialism of grace* based on the event. And if we understand 'grace' as a figure of contingency, he calls for nothing other than *a materialism of contingency*. So, what Badiou says about one of Paul's main teachings could equally be said about the post-foundational exigency of contingency: 'We are no longer under the rule of law, but of grace' (74). We no longer live under the law, we are subjected to contingency. Law, according to Badiou, is always predicative, particular and partial, and it always belongs to the order of the state (by which, as we saw, Badiou understands that which denominates and controls the parts of a given situation), while the evental truth is beyond number, predicate and control. Grace, on the other hand, 'is the opposite of law' (77). It is a *post*-foundational category that subverts the foundations of the law and the state. Yet it is far from being entirely *anti*-foundational. He is not at all interested in erasing all figures of foundation. On the other hand, however, it would be misleading to call his theory, as it is sometimes done (even by himself), foundational: a ground is maintained but it is the ground of contingency. For Badiou, a subject has to be founded indeed, but it is founded upon grace, that is to say, upon contingency: 'this foundation binds itself to that which is declared in a radical contingency' (77).

If it is true that Badiou's philosophy secretly relies on the Christian paradigm as its model (or one of its models), one can suspect to find a conceptual role for what is in Christianity the function of *evil*. And I submit that, while grace is constructed as a figure of contingency, evil in Badiou is in fact presented as a figure of essentialism and foundationalism. Evil is, in our own terms, the attempt at *grounding the ungroundable*. This claim can easily be substantiated, if we remember the way in which Badiou's post-foundationalism is systematically constructed. The place from where the event occurs is the place of the void of a given situation. What serves, in Badiou's system, as the absent ground of a situation is hence conceptualized by him according to the figure of the *void* (2002a: 68). Together with the event, this grounding void is *named*. The event that, for instance, Karl Marx signifies for political theory consists in his naming of the proletariat as the foundational yet disavowed void of bourgeois society. So every situation is founded upon something which it excludes: the void.

This is where evil may enter the scene: *terror* (and what Badiou calls the 'simulacrum' of a truth-procedure) occurs where it is not the void of a situation that is convoked by an event, but the *plenitude* of that situation. The Nazis for instance, by misnaming their absolute community as a national-socialist 'revolution', presented the void of the previous situation as plenitude. In such case, the void is filled with a substance (the simulacrum of an 'event-substance'), let's say the substance of the totality of a people. The result is a closed particularity of, for instance, 'the Germans' or 'the Arians'. To remain faithful to such simulacrum will eventually lead to war or massacre. So one can speak about a simulacrum of the truth-event, if what is convoked is 'not the void but the plenum'. If, in such fashion, *substance* is put on the political agenda, a given community will become closed and 'always approaches this kind of racial, biological, or territorial conception' (1994: 124) of the plenum. In the words of his commentator, Jean-Jacques Lecercle (1999: 9): 'If the celebrated "event" is not a hole in the situation but an already existing (and discernible, and nameable) aspect of it, we have not a process of truth but a *simulacrum* of truth'.

Here, Badiou introduces into his system a term that is complementary to the void, calling it the 'unnameable point' of a situation. While the disavowed void must be named, if an event is to occur, the 'unnamable point', as one might suspect, is precisely that which must *not* be named in a situation. Every truth-procedure implies such a 'limit case', a point that must remain without name. Where the truth-procedure of politics is concerned, Badiou argues that the unnamable point is 'community' in a substantialized sense: 'More and more, I am tempted to think that in emancipatory politics the community in a racial or biological sense is strictly an unnamable point. In order for politics to remain emancipatory, the community must not be named as such' (1994: 123). The unnameable of a truth-procedure relates to the real in being the *symbol* of that which must escape symbolization.

Yet, such unnameable should not be confused with the Kantian thing-in-itself, as it is, in principle, communicable (it does not constitute a limit to communication as such); rather, it is the symbol of the pure real of the situation. And, as Badiou makes it clear, in the case of politics, the substantial community or the collective is the unnameable, since every attempt at politically naming the community leads into disastrous evil. This has implications for the notion of truth, which must never assume total control over a given situation. Truth is *non-total* in that it must respect the unnameable point, and it is precisely the function of evil to present truth as total: 'When a truth is forced beyond its unnamable point, the consequences are necessarily ruinous, even criminal' (124).

5.5 The Danger of Ethicism

By *both insisting* on a notion of ground or truth *and simultaneously detotalizing* it, Badiou definitely locates himself within the ambit of post- rather than anti-foundational theories (not to mention foundationalist theories). His 'philosophy of politics', however, leaves open a couple of troubling questions. Above all, one might wonder whether the Badiouian politics of the immediate and unconditional can still reasonably be called a politics – or whether one should not rather speak about an ethics in the first place: a rigorous and uncompromising ethics of the unconditional, by which Badiou steps out of the Machiavellian moment of the conditioned, i.e. of power and strategy. It is in this sense, not in the sense of his self-styled Platonism, that Badiou may eventually give in to the foundationalist temptation. From Laclau and Mouffe's post-Gramscian (and in this sense Machiavellian) starting point, to which we will turn in the next chapter, one would arrive at the very different result of a politics of the conditioned – and of the conditional. One should certainly not underestimate the great benefits of Badiou's stance: by radicalizing most post-foundational concepts (event, contingency, and so on) which constitute the family resemblances of left Heideggerianism, he sharpens our view and presents us with a clear and distinct version which, in this respect, is without comparison. His work could thus be understood as a thought experiment in which post-foundationalism is stressed to the extreme – with all the dangers involved in such exercise.

However, Badiou's claim that the political act of 'vertically' linking up a subject with a truth-event is a matter of 'thinking' ('*la politique comme pensée*'), and not at all a matter of 'horizontally' organizing a new political will out of dispersed elements, as Gramsci would have it, leaves him open to the charge of philosophism. Like Nancy, who exhibits a tendency towards philosophism as well, Badiou is highly critical of political thought and seeks and proposes a general ontology as first philosophy – in his case: mathematical set theory. In addition, Badiou exhibits a strong tendency towards what could be called 'ethicism' – a danger not hidden in ethics as such, but in the subsumption of politics and of the political under the ethical. By constructing the political side of his theory around the notion of fidelity, as he does in his *Ethics* and his *Saint Paul*, Badiou privileges an ethical perspective on politics. As a result, political action becomes an ethical, even quasi-religious effort at remaining faithful to a specific event through one's thinking and acting. In that way, politics – and not only politics, but also science, love and art – is subordinated to the overarching imperative *Continue!*, whereby ethics (and not, as one would expect, mathematics or set theory) silently takes over the role of a *prima philosophia* from set theory. As an unexpected consequence, Badiou's small book on ethics turns into the cornerstone of his whole 'system'.

This surprising move – overlooked by most commentators – certainly has consequences for our view of politics, since a rigorous and uncompromising ethics of the unconditional is entirely at odds with our political reality. By grounding his theory of politics on the unconditional (the 'real'), Badiou steps out of the Machiavellian moment of the *conditioned*, that is, of power and strategy. But how shall we imagine a purely 'ontological' politics of the real, completely emptied of any 'ontic' content or context of political reality? To be sure, Badiou will always maintain that every politics occurs in a specific situation, but this implies that politics will always take place on an uneven 'ontic' terrain and not only in relation (of 'fidelity') to a truth-event. In other words, politics does not take place on the vertical axis between the militant subject and the event only, but also on a horizontal axis, that is, between a multiplicity of struggling actors (or subjects), all placed at different positions on an uneven, intransparent and power-ridden terrain. With such denial of the necessity of 'horizontal' political articulation Badiou unwillingly joins ranks with Hardt and Negri and their notion of the multitude. For Hardt and Negri, starting from entirely different premises from those of Badiou, the multitude 'directly opposes Empire, with no mediation between them' (2001: 393). Horizontal articulation between different actors of the multitude is as superfluous for Hardt and Negri as it is for Badiou, as one can always jump vertically from, in our terms, the ontic into the ontological.

But what if we cannot have immediate access to the ontological sphere, what if politics will always be tainted by compromise, strategy and a political realism in the Machiavellian rather than the Lacanian sense? In politics, to put it in the language of political science – which surely remains foreign to Badiou, but here at least draws on an expression of his early master Sartre – we will always be confronted with a 'dirty hands' problem. In Badiou, however, we will search in vain for a theorization of actual 'ontic' politics. He does not tell us how we are supposed to enact a 'politics of truth' on an always uneven and compromising terrain. Since in the so-called real world politics cannot simply be about fidelity, as this would imply the exclusion of any dimension of strategy, one could argue that there is a significant danger that such expulsion of the strategic might very well lead to an expulsion of politics per se in favor of the most radical form of *Gesinnungsethik*.[6] Isn't there a danger that such ethical 'politics' will eventually lead to a moralizing and self-righteous attitude, since it does not acknowledge the 'dirty hands' problem (the fact that one's own politics will always be less than pure, less than perfect, less than ethical)? Wouldn't such ethicization of politics prove to be politically disabling, if only for the reason that one will always be sure to find oneself on the right side, the side of an ethical, emancipatory politics?

While in Badiou the specificity and autonomy of the political is reduced (or, as Badiou himself would have it, 'sutured') to the ethical, from a more realistic point of view regarding politics – for instance, from Laclau and Mouffe's Gramscian point of view, to which we will turn next, but also from Lefort's Machiavellian perspective – one would arrive at the very different conclusion that there can be no such thing as a pure 'politics of the real' (at the most, there could be an ethics of the real while politics always takes place on the level of 'reality').[7] But Badiou is not the only one on the Heideggerian Left who conceives of politics in ethical terms. In fact, this is one of the most striking family resemblances among many post-foundational political theorists (with Laclau/Mouffe and Lefort as noticeable exceptions), and it constitutes a point of convergence between Badiou and his rivals, denounced as the deconstructive 'modern sophists', including Derrida or Nancy and Lacoue-Labarthe. Deconstructivists and Lacanians alike tend to frame our relation towards the event in exclusively ethical terms, that is, in terms either of an infinite *responsibility* towards the other-as-other, respectively a promise of an event-to-come, or of an infinite *fidelity*. The tendency to ethicize politics, which Badiou shares with the latter thinkers, can make both paradigms appear rather remote sometimes from our actually existing political world of compromise and alliance-building. Of course, there is no point in playing the arbitrator, precisely because, in order to arrive at a political theory proper, one would have to leave the very terrain of ethics, thus in a certain respect stepping outside the plane of both theoretical paradigms.

The difference between both paradigms – the Lacanian and the deconstructive – has to be located on a different plane. A striking divergence can be detected with respect to the rarity or ubiquity of the political event or the moment of the political. In the case of Badiou's theory, but also in Rancière's case, we witness a theoretical *rarification* of the political event. In Badiou, a truth-event occurs only on exceptional occasions – it may happen, as in the case of Saint Paul, only once a lifetime. As Badiou's commentator Hallward puts it: 'True politics is exceptional, an exception to the contemporary cliché that "everything is political".' And: 'The instances or "modes" of so exalted an understanding of politics are rare by definition' (Hallward 2002). Similarly, for Rancière, 'politics doesn't always happen – it actually happens very little or rarely' (1999: 17). A deconstructive approach, on the other hand, would rather opt for the ubiquitous and 'shattered' (Nancy 1991: 82–109) nature of politics. Accordingly, Badiou's idea of the rarity of the political event and his tendency to turn politics into a heroic act have been criticized from a deconstructive position by Simon Critchley: 'I see politics as everywhere, as being a really quite banal, or rather mundane, call to forms of mobilization that begin from the place where you are, where you are working (or where you are not working), the place where you are active and where you are thinking' (2005: 296). And, in this respect, Laclau as well must be located in the deconstructive camp: social relations constitute, as we will see, a sedimented form of an initial yet forgotten political institution that can be reactivated at any time. Hegemony is a struggle that never stops.

For the same reason, politics cannot be the privilege of an emancipatory and egalitarian Left – as it is always enacted as a strategic game on an uneven terrain, ridden with conflict and power struggles. Badiou is lead to his ethical injunction because he cannot accept a single terrain of intermingling forces (in which the ontological is only present as a dislocating and disturbing absence), but rather upholds the strict separation between a politics of truth and the state. Because of his radical rejection of any form of mediation or representation in politics (which for Badiou is always immediate), no room, is left for strategy and mediation. The strict opposition – rather than *difference* – between a politics of truth and the state hence involves the danger of ruling out any possible cross-contamination between the event as the (absent) ground on the one hand and the state on the other. That is to say, by radicalizing the ontological difference and hypostatizing the ontological side, Badiou runs the risk of putting the *play* of the ontological difference to a halt. What results is a dualistic narrative according to which the great and rare emancipatory event is opposed to the always repressive machinations of the State.

Notes

1. One can clearly see how political questions are linked to Badiou's general ontology, according to which sub-sets are categorized by the state of the situation as elements belonging to this situation. The multiplicity of a set, as we will see in a moment, is thus *counted as One* by the state.

2. A case in point is the Badiouian-Lacanian notion of the subject (the subject of lack), which in the original Lacanian formulation relies heavily on the Sartrean idea of an irresolvable *lack-of-being*, which in turn relies on a Kojèvian–Hegelian reading of Heidegger's notion of finitude (see Marchart 2006).

3. 'Subtraction' is Badiou's *terminus technicus*: 'The point where thinking substracts itself from the State, thus inscribing that substraction into being, constitutes the very real of a politics [*d'une politique*]'. (Badiou 1991: 57)

4. To the extent that politics only emerges in the moment of exception (Badiou 1985: 19), one can suspect a certain structural parallel to Schmitt's argument as to the *Ausnahmezustand* – a parallel Badiou himself would perhaps not concede, even as it would position him close to another, more openly left-Heideggerian thinker: Giorgio Agamben (1998).

5. It is most likely that Badiou himself would not subscribe to this account, as for him there is no such thing as a general *ethics*, there can always only be an *ethics-of*: 'Ethics does not exist. There is only the *ethics-of* (of politics, of love, of science, of art)' (2002a: 28). However, seen from a point of view outside of Badiou's system, one can detect a generalized ethics not only as motivating force, but also as the main operational principle behind most of Badiou's concepts or the linking of these concepts – so that I would submit, as will be elaborated at the end of this chapter, that Badiou's politics is actually *an ethics*.

6. One might argue that the ethical moment of the unconditional and the political moment of the conditioned are not mutually exclusive. Even as one might concede this, it still remains clear that Badiou does not – and perhaps cannot, given his model – provide us with any theory regarding the very workings of politics on the ontic level. The result is that 'real politics' is confined to very 'rare moments' – an aspect which might prove politically disabling under more ordinary conditions. Not everybody happens to walk a road to Damascus.

7. It therefore does not come as a surprise that Badiou is strictly opposed to theorists such as Laclau and Mouffe, André Gorz, or Alain Touraine, who turned towards social movements and gave up the idea of a radical separation between emancipatory politics and the 'state of the situation' in which it takes place. From Badiou's point of view, 'they have been won over, politically, to the established order' (Badiou 1998b: 121).

Chapter 6
The Political and the Impossibility of Society: Ernesto Laclau

6.1 The Impossibility of Society

> Any advance in the understanding of present-day social struggles depends on inverting the relations of priority which the last century and a half's social thought had established between the social and the political. This tendency had been characterized, in general terms, by what we may term the systematic absorption of the political by the social. The political became either a superstructure, or a regional sector of the social, dominated and explained according to the objective laws of the latter. Nowadays, we have started to move in the opposite direction: towards a growing understanding of the eminently political character of any social identity. (Laclau 1990: 160)

In the above quotation, Ernesto Laclau indicates a large part of the aim of his theoretical enterprise, and, to some extent, of Chantal Mouffe's theoretical enterprise. Their aim is to reverse the order of priority between the social and the political. The assumption that the political has been systematically 'absorbed' by the social places the Laclauian enterprise in the framework of theories that share Schmitt's neutralization thesis and Arendt's colonization thesis, as they were discussed in Chapter 2 respectively. However, contrary to Max Weber, who can be considered the actual source of the absorption thesis, no pessimistic or even fatalistic conclusions as to the irreversibility of this absorption or enclosure of the political in the 'iron cage' of an increasingly bureaucratized and managed society are drawn, since the political essence of the social can be *reactivitated*: and this is the very task of, among other post-foundationalist theories, deconstruction and hegemony theory. How does Laclau proceed about showing the primacy of the political? And how does he define the political and the social in the first place?

To recapitulate our own starting point: one hypothesis underlying our argument throughout this investigation is that the difference between politics and the political, so prevalent in current political theory, in a way 'mirrors' the one between the political and the social, since, as far as society is not identical with itself (as social post-foundationalists claim), politics too becomes internally split into a dimension which internally belongs to the social ('politics' as a social sub-system) on the one hand, and, on the other, a more fundamental or radical dimension ('the political'), which grounds and regrounds the social from without, or, rather, from an ultimately *impossible* outside. Thus what is named by the term 'the political' is the moment of the institution/destitution of the social or society respectively. In one of his interviews where he aims at clarification concerning these concepts, Laclau maintains having developed the two notions of the social and the political in terms of two counterpositions: 'One is the relationship between the social and the political, the other the distinction between the social and society'. Let us quote the paragraphs in which Laclau defines these pairs, starting with the second distinction, the one between the social and society:

> I understand 'society' to mean simply the possibility of closure of all social meaning around a matrix which can explain all its partial processes. That would be, for instance, the position of classical structuralism. On the other hand, if one takes a more poststructuralist position – the impossibility of closing any context and among them the social context as a unified whole – what you have are marginal processes which constantly disrupt meaning and do not lead to the closure of society around a single matrix. When we have the social defined in this sense as something which creates meaning but which makes closure impossible, I tended to speak of 'the social' instead of 'society.' That was an early distinction. For example, that is precisely the argument which is being presented in the article on the impossibility of society. (Laclau 1999: 146)

If we go back to that very article on the impossibility of society, originally published in 1983, we find Laclau stating that 'the social only exists as the vain attempt to institute that impossible object: society' (1990: 92). In *Hegemony and Socialist Strategy*, jointly written with Chantal Mouffe and published two years later, that argument was to be elaborated upon. One may even hold that it is in this very short and condensed article, 'The Impossibility of Society', that one can find the Laclauian enterprise formulated *in nuce*. So what exactly does Laclau intend with his assumption of the impossibility of society?

Laclau recognizes from a historical point of view that the concept of social totality has entered a state of crisis. This crisis is particularly obvious in the case of the Marxist base-superstructure model of society, where economic base and politico-ideological superstructure together form the totality of the social. In the Marxist imaginary it was possible to describe and define that social totality, since it had taken the form of an intelligible positive object. The totality asserted by the Marxist model operated, Laclau maintains, as an underlying principle of intelligibility of the social order, that is to say, an immutable essence behind the superficial empirical variations of social life. Laclau calls this kind of totality that presents itself as a recognizable object of knowledge a *'founding totality'* (because knowledge can be founded upon it), against which he proposes accepting the *'infinitude of the social*, that is, the fact that any structural system is limited, that it is always surrounded by an "excess of meaning" which it is unable to master and that, consequently, "society" as a unitary and intelligible object which grounds its own partial processes is an impossibility' (1990: 90). In other words, 'society' does not serve as the *ground* of social processes and, in this sense, does not constitute a *founding totality*. However, Laclau does not stop at this point (if he did, he would simply be an *anti-*foundationalist), since the impossibility of society is a *productive* one.

The reason for this lies in the fact that the social is structured by, and through, a double movement of fixation/defixation. On the one hand, the 'infinitude of the social' – something which is simply a metaphor for the fact that the social cannot, by principle, manage to suture itself into a closed totality – guarantees that the social is always overflown by the 'excess of meaning' surrounding it and, consequently, its very meaning becomes defixated into an infinite play of differences which Laclau calls *the discursive*. Since the complete defixation of meaning, however, is as much an impossibility as its complete fixation is (for a universe without any fixed meaning would be a psychotic universe), we must assume a counter-movement as well, so that, on the other hand, it is possible to launch partial attempts to effect this 'ultimately impossible fixation': there has to be an attempt to limit the play of difference. The precondition for this to work is that totality is not merely absent but – to phrase it once more in post-foundational terms – remains present in its very absence: ' "totality" does not disappear: if the suture it attempts is ultimately impossible, it is nevertheless possible to proceed to a relative fixation of the social through the institution of nodal points' (91). Society-as-totality is an impossible object, but it is precisely because of its impossibility that it functions as condition of possibility for the social, whereby the latter is understood as the discursive terrain on which meaning is being partially fixed into nodal points. Thus, we have to conclude that society is *both* impossible *and* necessary.

In *Hegemony and Socialist Strategy*, after having deconstructed the history of Marxism in a remarkable tour-de-force, Laclau and Mouffe start again building their theory of politics as hegemony by 'renouncing the conception of "society" as founding totality of its partial processes' (1985: 95).[1] Here again, it becomes clear that they do not propose an *anti*-foundationalist theory but a *post*-foundationalist one, since the dimension of ground does not disappear without a trace, but rather serves, through its very absence, as 'negative' foundation which must remain present: 'We must, therefore, consider the openness of the social as the constitutive ground or "negative essence" of the existing, and the diverse "social orders" as precarious and ultimately failed attempts to domesticate the field of differences' (95–6). To paraphrase Laclau and Mouffe, we can say that the only ground upon which to build our attempts to fix the field of difference, to create meaning, is an *abyss*: we build upon the very openness of the social. And yet without that openness – an openness indicating the impossibility for the social to turn itself into society-as-totality – we would not be in a position to start building nodal points of meaning in the first place. The social and society, then, stand in a mutual relation of constant play (in the Heideggerian sense), where the social seeks to overcome its own openness by turning itself into society, which is only gradually possible in so far as the latter remains *impossible*: 'If the social does not manage to fix itself in the intelligible and instituted forms of a *society*, the social only exists, however, as an effort to construct that impossible object. Any discourse is constituted as an attempt to dominate the field of discursivity, to arrest the flow of differences, to construct a centre' (112). But how does this attempt at domination occur? Here it becomes clear that the establishment of these nodal points of the partial fixation of social meaning is the role of politics. This necessarily leads us to a more primary distinction that Laclau establishes, namely the one between the social and the political.

6.2 Social Sedimentation and the Event of Reactivation

Laclau holds the distinction between the social and the political to be of higher relevance (compared to the distinction between the social and society), because it is at this stage that the encounter with the workings of politics becomes obvious. In the case of this difference, Laclau is concerned again with the question of *grounding* – however, the perspective changes. The social is scrutinized now not from the point of view of society as its unachievable horizon (the horizon of an impossible yet necessary totality), but from the political point of view of its institution. In a sense, what comes into focus is the 'source' and not so much the 'goal' of social practices (whereby, as it goes without saying, the notions of 'source' and 'goal' have to be used very cautiously and only for heuristic reasons). By changing focus, Laclau relates the difference between the social and the political to Husserl's distinction between sedimentation and reactivation:

> The way I am presenting the argument is that we live in a world of sedimented social practices. The moment of reactivation consists not in going to an original founding moment, as in Husserl, but to an original contingent decision through which the social was instituted. This moment of the institution of the social through contingent decisions is what I call 'the political'. (Laclau 1999: 146)

Thus, Laclau proposes to think of the social as the terrain of sedimented discursive practices. By contrast, the political is defined as the moment of the institution of the social as well as the moment of the reactivation of the contingent nature of every institution. By pointing to the contingent nature of the social, the political intervenes, making it clear that the social cannot rely on a stable ground. Hence the political points to the *absent ground* of the social and, at the same time, substitutes for that absence by (re)grounding the latter. But before giving a more detailed account of Laclau's notion of the political, I would like to approach the problem from the angle of the *workings* of the political/the social in the way it is indicated in the above quotation. What is indicated there is the double movement of hegemonic articulation. On the one hand, hegemonic articulation, if it succeeds, can lead to what Laclau – referring to Husserl – calls 'sedimentation' or the 'sedimented forms of "objectivity"'. This is the field of the ostensibly objective or, as Barthes would have termed it, the 'naturalized' *social sphere*, as it must be distinguished from the political moment of rearticulation. Following Husserl, sedimentation is a name for the routinization and forgetting of origins – a process that tends to occur as soon as a certain articulatory advance has led to a hegemonic success. In Laclau's terminology, this movement describes the successful fixation of meaning into solid topographies that need to be conceptualized as sedimentations of power. Laclau conceptualizes these sediments as *space*, they spatialize the temporal moment of pure dislocation into a choreography. Traditions are nothing but such routinized practices. 'Insofar as an act of institution has been successful,' Laclau holds, 'a "forgetting of the origins" tends to occur; the system of possible alternatives tends to vanish and the traces of the original contingency to fade. In this way, the instituted tends to assume the form of a mere objective presence. This is the moment of sedimentation' (1990: 34).

Yet inasmuch as these spatial, 'ossified' sediments can, on the other hand, be reactivated, there also exists a temporalization of space or an 'extension of the field of the possible'. In the words of Laclau/Husserl, we are confronted with a moment of 'reactivation', with a process of defixation of meaning. In this case, more and more elements, levels and places are perceived as being contingent in their relational nature. This is the moment of the *dislocation* of a given spatial system through time – time being precisely the category that *prevents* social sediments, once and for all, from becoming firmly established. This is a non-reciprocal process. As Laclau attempts to explain, space can hegemonize (i.e. 'spatialize') time, but time does not hegemonize anything at all, since it is a pure effect of dislocation (1990: 42).

The complete constitution of society – as a fully self-sufficient entity – is impossible, because the identity of every 'system' (which is always 'spatial' in Laclau's sense) has to refer to a constitutive outside, which is at once the condition enabling it *and* making its complete closure and self-identity impossible. And one of the ways in which this outside shows itself phenomenologically is *time*. However, one has to go one step further, since it follows from this that time is not itself identical with politics. The constitutive outside of space is what is radically different with respect to the system – something which cannot be explained from the inner logic of the system itself, or which has never had any prescribed place in the topography. Yet it occurs *within* such topography as its dislocation, disturbance, or interruption: as *event*. Laclau calls this moment of the reactivation of spatial sediments 'the moment of the political' – which is strictly correlative to what must be called Laclau and Mouffe's main contribution to contemporary political thought: the concept of antagonism.

Let us recall what 'antagonism' originally names in Laclauian theory: the equivalential division of a discursive field – which, in the tradition of Saussurian linguistics, is initially conceived of as a system of differences – into two camps. Each pole – resulting out of the condensation of differences into a chain of equivalence – annuls its respective positive, differential content, since the only 'identical something' that holds the chain together is a common orientation towards 'what it is not': its negative, threatening outside. In the extreme case of complete antagonization, the identity has become purely negative (in a relation of complete equivalence, the differential positivity of all elements is dissolved) and thus can no longer be represented or symbolized – except through the very failure of symbolization as such: 'This is precisely the formula of antagonism', Laclau and Mouffe hold, 'which thus establishes itself as the limit of the social' (1985: 128). This limit is further characterized as being *internal* to the social, for if it were simply separating two territories (= external limit) it would constitute a new difference: 'Society never manages fully to be society because everything in it is penetrated by its limits, which prevent it from constituting itself as an objective reality' (127). Speaking in discourse-analytic terms, the boundary of a given signifying system cannot be signified, but can only manifest itself in the form of an interruption or breakdown of the process of signification. The function of the excluding boundary, being both condition of possibility and condition of impossibility of meaning, thus consists in introducing an essential ambivalence into every system of difference constituted by the very same boundary. In *New Reflections*, this ambivalence (called 'subversion' in *Hegemony*) is called 'dislocation' and is described phenomenologically as 'event' or 'temporality'.

This moment of antagonistic negativity and dislocation is exactly where contingency has to be located as an event which *reveals* that things could be otherwise: 'if antagonism *threatens* my existence, it shows, in the strictest sense of the term, my radical contingency'

(Laclau 1990: 20).[2] Contingency, therefore, is not identical with accidentality in the sense of pure chance. The status of the conditions of existence of a given significatory system is not accidental (derived from pure chance, as in a game of dice), but these conditions are contingent because they cannot be derived from the internal logic or rationality of the system as such. Laclau maintains that, 'if negativity is radical and the outcome of the struggle not predetermined, the contingency of the identity of the two antagonistic forces is also radical and the conditions of existence of both must be themselves contingent' (20). Contingency thus stands to necessity in a relation of subversion: Necessity can only partially limit the field of contingency, which in turn subverts necessity from inside. As a result, the line between the contingent and the necessary is blurred. But the crucial point lies in the fact that the existence of that line, that is to say, of the general (and thus quasi-transcendental) difference between the necessary and the contingent, is *not* contingent but necessary: 'as identity depends entirely on conditions of existence which are contingent, its relationship with them is absolutely necessary' (21). Or, to put it differently: while the conditions of existence of any identity/ objectivity/system are *contingent* with respect to the system in question, they are *necessarily* so.

Now, what is conceptualized by Laclau as the moment of antagonism defines, in turn, his notion of the political: 'The sedimented forms of "objectivity" make up the field of what we call the "social". The moment of antagonism, where the undecidable nature of the alternatives and their resolution through power relations become fully visible, constitutes the field of the "political"' (35). The important point here, and the point which links the difference between the social and the political to what we call, *pace* Heidegger, the grounding question, is that, according to Laclau, 'social relations are constituted by the very distinction between the social and the political' (ibid.). And, in what must be described as a typical quasi-transcendental deconstructive move, Laclau substantiates his claim:

If, on the one hand, a society from which the political has been completely eliminated is inconceivable – it would mean a closed universe merely reproducing itself through repetitive practices – on the other, an act of unmediated political institution is also impossible: any political construction takes place against the background of a range of sedimented practices. The ultimate instance in which all social reality might be political is one that is not only not feasible but also one which, if reached, would blur any distinction between the social and the political. This is because a *total* political institution of the social can only be the result of an absolute omnipotent will, in which case the contingency of what has been instituted – and hence its political nature – would disappear. The distinction between the social and the political is thus ontologically constitutive of social relations. (Laclau 1990: 35)

How does this relate to the difference between politics and the political? Although at some points in *New Reflections* Laclau seems to distinguish between the political and politics only implicitly, it can be inferred that politics, in fact, is a category in its own right, which has to be explicitly distinguished not only from the social, but also from the political as such. As we will see, many readers of Laclau felt inclined to make this distinction – although there is some confusion as to the precise nature of the distinction. In his paper on deconstruction and pragmatism, however, Laclau himself is more precise as to this distinction: there he defines the political as the '*instituting moment* of society' (1996b: 47), and politics as 'the *acts* of political institution' (60; my emphasis). Therefore, the difference seems to lie between the ontological *moment* of the political and the latter's ontic *enactment* (which is termed 'politics').

6.3 Politics and the Political – a 'Laclauian' Difference

While the difference between politics and the political has assumed some prominence with theorists close to Laclau (Žižek, Mouffe) or relying on the Laclauian framework (Dyrberg, Arditi, Cholewa-Madsen, Stäheli), it is only implicitly present in Laclau, for instance when he deplores that 'the dominant vision of the political in the nineteenth century, prolonged into the twentieth by various sociologist tendencies, had made of it a "subsystem" or "superstructure", submitted to the necessary laws of society' (1996b: 47). Even as it is not spelled out in Laclau's work in terms of a 'definition', it is still safe to say that the political difference is present in Laclau's own work, and, in addition to that, that it is without doubt a 'Laclauian' difference, given its prominence in theorists connected to Laclau's work.

Most closely connected, of course, is Laclau's collaborator Chantal

Mouffe, who, in order to clarify 'agonistic pluralism', introduces the 'distinction between "politics" and "the political"', defined as follows:

> By the 'political', I refer to the dimension of antagonism that is inherent in human relations, antagonism that can take many forms and emerge in different types of social relations. 'Politics', on the other side, indicates the ensemble of practices, discourses and institutions which seek to establish a certain order and organize human coexistence in conditions that are always potentially conflictual because they are affected by the dimension of 'the political'. I consider that it is only when we acknowledge the dimension of 'the political' and understand that 'politics' consists in domesticating hostility and in trying to defuse the potential antagonism that exists in human relations, that we can pose what I take to be the central question for democratic politics. (Mouffe 2000: 101)

As Mouffe underlines in her most recent book *On the Political*, to make a distinction between politics and the political, as she understands it, implies a further distinction, between a political-science approach that restricts itself to the empirical domain of politics and a political-theory approach, 'which is the domain of philosophers who enquire not about facts of "politics" but about the essence of "the political"' (2005: 8). While the latter – the instituting moment of society – can be understood in a variety of ways (not at least in the Arendtian way of what we called in Chapter 2 the associative paradigm), Mouffe's proposal is to think of it in terms of an ineradicable antagonistic dimension, constitutive of human society – while the former refers to 'the set of practices and institutions through which an order is created, organizing human coexistence in the context of conflictuality provided by the political' (9).[3]

In a similar fashion, Benjamin Arditi makes explicit the latent differentiation in Laclau's *New Reflections* between politics and the political, also focusing on the antagonistic nature of the political, as opposed to the 'sublimating' nature of politics. The political, in Arditi's words, is the 'living movement, the magma of conflicting wills', whereby conflict serves as its very ontological condition (1994: 21). Like Mouffe, his main point of reference here is Carl Schmitt, whom he follows in conceiving of the political as a '*form* of confrontation (as friend–enemy) that can originate in religious, economic, moral or other fields', and 'does not necessarily require an intervention of that which society formally recognizes as part of the field of politics' (18). Other Laclauians like Torben Bech Dyrberg (1997; 2004; see also Cholewa-Madsen 1994) basically follow that route by attacking the liberal attempt to reduce the political to a social sub-system. Such reduction of the political to a sub-system of society is 'besides being itself a political act, a normative imposition whose purpose is to prevent the politicization of social relations and the conflicts that may go with it' (Dyrberg 1997: 188).

Interestingly, however, the difference between politics and the political is maintained, even where the respective slots occupied by politics and the political are reversed, that is to say, where the political is described in a way corresponding to how we would usually describe politics and vice versa. Consider the respective definitions in Jacob Torfing's book on *Laclau, Mouffe and Žižek* (1999). In his glossary, Torfing defines the political as 'the institutional order of the state, which provides the primary terrain for the struggle between hege-monic agents who seek to place themselves in a position from where they can "speak in the name of society"', while he defines politics as the taking of a decision in an undecidable terrain: 'As such, politics is simultaneously a constitutive and a subversive dimension of the social' (304). It should be obvious by now that Torfing ascribes to 'the political' the role of the political sub-system as it is institutiona-lized in the state apparatus, and to 'politics' the more fundamental or radical role of institution/destitution of the social. He keeps the slots – the signifiers politics/the political – but reverses the semantic content. He justifies this choice, which runs counter to most readings of Laclau and Mouffe – by referring to their ambiguity on this matter: 'As Laclau and Mouffe are ambiguous on this score I have felt free to call the constitutive dimension of the social "politics", and to denote the institutional level of the state "the political"' (294).

This example of an inverse reading of the notions of the political and politics is not without significance for our discussion. And, as a matter of fact, it is far from constituting a 'misreading': Torfing very clearly and correctly detects and accepts the constitutive, reactivatory function of time as well as the sedimentary function of spatialization. He simply names them in reverse manner. This terminological 'devia-tion' is of some interest for the genetico-historical part of our project, but of almost no interest at all for the theoretico-conceptual part: while in Torfing's usage the terminology comes closer to the common Anglo-American usage, the 'logic' stays the same. There is still an unbridgeable gap between the two levels. So the significance of the example of Torfing's usage of the political difference lies in the fact that it further clarifies the predominance of the *difference as difference* vis-à-vis the signifiers indicating its respective 'content' – for the radical difference between the political and politics can be *maintained* even as their respective meaning is reversed.

Similarly, it is important to realize that, within the camp of left Heideggerians, the political difference can easily be theorized from the perspectives of – seemingly – diverging theoretical positions such as deconstruction or Lacanianism. From Slavoj Žižek's Lacanian position, the political difference, which in our investigation was framed along the lines of the deconstructive and Heideggerian notion of difference-as-difference, is described as a *gap* of impossibility. Since I would hold, against Žižek himself, that there is no basic incompatibility between a Lacanian ontology of lack and a Derridian ontology of difference (on their relation see Marchart 2006, where it is argued that these approaches, including the Deleuzian ontology of abundance, have in common that all three elaborate what might be called an *unstable ontology*), it is indeed possible to employ Lacanian vocabulary to describe the phenomenon of society's absent ground as it is mirrored conceptually in the politico-political difference: For Žižek, this difference, which he detects in Rancière (as difference between '*la politique/police*' and '*le politique*'), in Badiou (as difference between 'being' and 'truth-event'), in Balibar (as difference between the imaginary universal order and '*égaliberté*'), and in Laclau (as difference between a particular political demand and an impossible universal dimension), constitutes what Žižek calls 'the basic opposition between two logics', where in all cases 'the second point is properly political, introduces the gap in the positive order of Being'. In all cases, various forms of opposition are erected 'between Substance and Subject, between a positive ontological order (police, Being, structure) and a gap of impossibility which prevents a final closure of this order and/or disturbs its balance'. As Žižek knows, however, the two sides of the opposition cannot be conceived as simply external as 'the space for the political Truth-Event is opened up by the symptomatic void in the order of Being, by the necessary inconsistency in its structural order' (1999a: 233). Translated into the vocabulary of our own investigation: the political difference points at the absent ground of the social, the fact that society is an impossibly (yet necessary) object. It is from this perspective that we have to understand the political difference.[4]

6.4 Discourse Theory as Political Ontology

Given the radical ontological dimension of Laclau's theory of the political, and given our previous investigation into the question of a political 'first philosophy', we have to draw these consequences that Laclau himself seems hesitant to draw, since it follows neatly from the premises of his theory that (a) Laclauian hegemony or discourse theory is, essentially, a *political ontology*; and (b) such political ontology must assume the status of a *prima philosophia* or 'first philosophy' (in a qualified sense, of course).

In fact, everything in discourse theory as formulated by Laclau seems to point in this direction of a political ontology. The question upon which the argument hinges is whether discourse theory, as developed by Laclau, counts as a *regional* or as a *general* theory of the production of meaning? Is it a theory of *political* signification only, or does it provide us with a theory of signification as such? Now, if the logic Laclau develops covers, as he explicitly states, 'language (and by extension all signifying systems)' (1996a: 37), then it seems to be difficult to maintain that this can be done by a regional theory of political signification. It would certainly require a general theory of signification. To be more precise, what is developed by Laclau is a quasi-transcendental argument as to the possibility of signification *as such*. But, insofar as this argument is in itself politicized by Laclau, what we encounter is not only a theory of 'political signification' but a 'political theory' of signification.

I have already presented the contours of this theory. Let us recapitulate. According to Laclau, a certain degree of systematicity is necessary in order for a certain degree of meaning to arise, and the systematicity of the system can only be guaranteed by a limit which is not by nature differential but antagonistic. If the systematicity of the system – which Laclau also calls the 'being' of the system – is a direct result of the exclusionary limit, then antagonism serves as the system's ground – while simultaneously subverting the identity of the system. It lies in the deconstructive nature of the argument that pure systematicity of the system, i.e. 'full being', is unreachable – even as 'effects of systematisation' can and must be realized if there is to be meaning at all. Hence we will not have any systematicity, nor will we have any meaning at all, without at least some form of antagonism. So a certain degree of antagonization is a necessary precondition for meaning to arise. Without antagonism – no meaning.

So it is apparent that, when a post-Saussurian argument is presented as to the construction of meaning, it is presented as a general argument, which applies to all forms of meaning and signification, not only to political ones. On the other hand, however, the category of antagonism – which is crucial to the argument – is the category of the political. And from here we have to conclude that, if antagonism is necessary for the construction or temporary stabilization of all meaning, then *all* meaning is, at its roots, political. It appears to me that these radical implications of the discourse-analytical argument have been systematically overlooked. But if the consequences of the argument are fully accepted, we will find in discourse theory, at least implicitly, something of the order of a political ontology. To wrap the argument together, three points are crucial. (1) The political logic of signification, as developed by Laclau, applies to the construction of all meaning, not only to political meaning – which implies that seemingly non-political meaning systems are, in fact, constructed 'politically' via exclusion and antagonization. (2) Since there is no social reality outside signification or beyond meaning, a theory of signification amounts to a theory of *all possible being*, that it is to say, it amounts to an ontology. For this reason it is not by accident that Laclau constantly employs ontological vocabulary, for instance in discussing, in his and Chantal Mouffe's response to Norman Geras (in Laclau 1990), the difference between the 'being' and the mere 'physical existence' of things (whereby the realm of 'being' entirely coincides with the realm of the discursive, and the mere physical existence of an object will always have to be mediated through discourse). So, to the extent that all 'being' is discursively constructed and, conversely, the discursive constitutes the horizon of all 'being', discourse theory, implicitly or explicitly, constitutes an ontology. And (3), if we put the political and the ontological aspect of discourse theory together – the claim that discourse theory constitutes a general theory of signification which is a political theory, and the claim that the latter constitutes what a philosophically trained observer would call an ontology – it follows that we are confronted with nothing other than a *political ontology*.

This argument deserves a couple of specifications. First of all, if all meaning is political by nature, how can we account for all those seemingly apolitical meaning structures? This question was addressed by Laclau in *New Reflections*, when he brought into the picture the differentiation between the social as the realm of sedimented practices and the political as the moment of their institution/reactivation. We can now specify that these two concepts do not designate two entirely different worlds: one political, one apolitical or social, but one has to think of them as two sides of the same coin. They represent two different *modes* of the political: the social mode of the political is not non-political or apolitical, but rather is characterized by the oblivion or forgetfulness of its instituting moment, which is the moment of the political. For this reason Laclau speaks about 'the primacy of the political over the social' (1990: 33).

Where the question of political ontology as a *first philosophy* is concerned, it is interesting that, for the sedimented social practices, Laclau gives a series of examples of *seemingly* unpolitical situations – situations which supposedly do not entail any denial, negativity or antagonism: the relationship with a postman delivering a letter, buying a ticket at the cinema, or going to a concert. Again, somebody might ask: is it not obvious that these situations lie outside the jurisdiction of political ontology? I suppose the correct answer would be *no*, because rather than being 'unpolitical', these are social practices the political origins of which have been forgotten. Yet their origins remain political in potentiality because they can be reactivated at any time, that is, whenever the event of (re-)antagonization occurs, for instance with a strike of the postal service. So the social has to be conceived of as a kind of 'sleeping mode' of the political, and we can imagine instances of antagonization in which 'going to a concert' can turn into a political manifestation. Wherever we look, we will find the political at the root of social relations.

There is a further reason, although connected to the previous one, why all social identity remains within the ambit of the political: social relations are always *power* relations. Again, power and identity have to be located at the *ontological* level. They are ontological categories in the sense that they apply to the whole realm of being and not only to certain regions of the social: 'the construction of a social identity is an act of power and . . . identity as such *is* power' (31). Seen from this angle, identity, 'being' and power are the same, since, as Laclau continues, '[w]ithout power there would be no objectivity [that is, no 'being', OM] at all' (32). The political ontology amounts to an 'ontology of power', which in turn determines the nature of social inquiry, which is '[t]o study the conditions of existence of a given social identity, then, is to study the power mechanisms making it possible' (32).[5]

This brings us finally back to the question of political ontology as 'first philosophy': Why call it 'first'? As I have said repeatedly, the qualifier 'first' must not be used in the sense of 'foundational'. On the other hand, however, what we call ground – and this is where we part company with all forms of scientism, positivism or even *anti*-foundationalism – remains present in its very absence. In Heideggerian post-foundational thought the question of *ground* does not simply disappear but is displaced by the constitutive play between institution and dislocation. Consequently, the meaning of the qualifier 'first' will have to be displaced too. A first philosophy would not be a philosophy which provides all other philosophies with a stable ground. Rather, it must be understood as a form of thinking or philosophizing that seeks to establish the quasi-transcendental conditions of the process of grounding and ungrounding. And, given that the process of grounding/ungrounding must be conceived of as an intrinsically *political* one, and that *ontology* must necessarily be conceived of as *political ontology*, the difference between the ontological and the ontic will necessarily be reframed in terms of the difference between 'the political' and 'politics'.

To bring this discussion to a preliminary end before resuming in the concluding chapter, the overall argument we tried to present was as follows.

A case has been made for discourse theory having the status of an *ontology*. As a matter of course, the nature of 'being' changes from the perspective of discourse theory – the field of objectivity is now understood in terms of the *discursive*. The theory of 'being' turns into a theory of the production of *meaning*. Still to call it an ontology, then, is a philosophical way of indicating the radical implications of such a theory, as it does not only apply to language in the usual regional sense of the term, but to the very horizon of all 'being'. And if, as our second claim was, *being-as-being* – objectivity as such – is intrinsically political (because it rests on an act of political inception which became sedimented within the social), then such ontology must be conceived of as a *political* ontology. So, in opposition to other current philosophies such as Badiou's, where politics is only one out of four regional 'ontologies' (love, art, science, politics), from the perspective of discourse theory *every* ontology would be, in its essence, political. And, since such a political ontology is not concerned with a regional aspect of beings but with the ground and horizon of all possible being, we may justifiably speak about a *prima philosophia*.

6.5 The Seventh Day of Rest

From what has been said so far, it should be clear that Laclau's theory has to be located at the antagonistic end of the scale of social post-foundationalism. While being largely in agreement with other non-foundationalists, Laclau abstains from any peaceful deliberational or conversational argument and definitely positions himself at the opposite, non-consensual or dissociational, end of the scale. Directed at Rorty's anti-foundationalist conversationalism, he argues that the points of divergence are at least as important as the points of convergence: 'The latter exist because, in both cases, we are dealing with non-foundationalist constructions of meaning, but the idea of a "conversational" grounding seems to add the further assumption of a necessarily peaceful process, as if the non-foundational nature of the grounding involved the "civilized" character of the exchange' (1996b: 60). This, according to Laclau, does not follow at all. And the reason lies, of course, in the very insurmountable facticity of antagonism, which is lacking in the associational accounts. In a similar way, Chantal Mouffe reacts to Hannah Arendt's and others' non-foundational *agonism without antagonism*: 'This antagonistic dimension, which can never be completely eliminated but only "tamed" or "sublimated" by being, so to speak, "played out" in an agonistic way, is what, in my view, distinguishes my understanding of agonism from the one put forward by other "agonistic theorists", those who are influenced by Nietzsche or Hannah Arendt, like William Connolly or Bonnie Honig' (2000: 107). The distance Mouffe wants to keep with respect to the theorists mentioned has to do with the fact that, behind the ontic play of agonism cherished both by Nietzscheans and by Arendtians, she detects the more fundamental, ontological category of antagonism – even as Mouffe herself, in a second step, argues for its institutional 'taming' into democratic agonisms.

The Habermasian variant of consensual deliberation does not lead much further. Not only because it disavows the radical notion of antagonism, but also because, according to Laclau, it is nothing but a weaker version of foundationalism, since it establishes an external tribunal (of undistorted communication) from which to judge and thus to fix the play of politics: 'If meaning is fixed beforehand either, in a strong sense, by a radical ground (a position that fewer and fewer people would sustain today) or, in a weaker version, through the regulative principle of an undistorted communication, the very possibility of the ground as an empty place which is politically and contingently filled by a variety of social forces disappears' (1996a: 58–9). It is clear, of course, that Laclau, on the other hand, does not fall into the trap of an extreme anti-foundationalism and equally attacks those Baudrillardian versions of postmodernism which assume, on the basis of a critique of foundationalism, the implosion of *all* meaning. This does not constitute a valid conclusion, because 'the impossibility of universal ground does not eliminate its need: it just transforms the ground into an empty place which can be partially filled in a variety of ways (the strategies of this filling is what politics is about)' (59). There is no way of getting around the strategic moment that is based on the ineradicability of power, contingency, and antagonism.

All this attests to the fact that Laclau's theory constitutes one of the foremost formulations of political and social post-foundationalism. While denying any possibility of an ultimate ground, he does not give in to the temptation of doing away with the dimension of grounds in the plural and with the process of constant and always necessarily partial *grounding*. This involves an ontology of power and the priority of the political over the social. In his own words:

> [S]ince there is no original *fiat* of power, no moment of radical foundation at which something beyond any objectivity is constituted as the absolute ground on which the being of objects is based, the relationship between power and objectivity cannot be that of the creator and the *ens creatum*. The creator has already been partially created through his or her forms of identification with a structure into which s/he has been thrown. But as this structure is dislocated, the identification never reaches the point of a full identity: any act is an act of reconstruction, which is to say that the creator will search in vain for the seventh day of rest. (1990: 60)

Notes

1. This is most clearly expressed in the following quotation from *Hegemony and Socialist Strategy*: 'The incomplete character of every totality necessarily leads us to abandon, as a terrain of analysis, the premise of "*society*" as a sutured and self-defined totality' (Laclau/Mouffe 1985: 111).
2. This *revelatory* function of dislocation and antagonism is achieved when gaps, breakdowns, and interruptions occur at the ontic level of beings. The dislocatory event brings with it an

effect of unconcealment, which is the second consequence: the ontological level shows itself as lack in the ontic level. 'It is this effect of unconcealment that splits the opposing forces between their "ontic" contents and the character of mere possibility – that is, inception, pure Being – of those contents' (Laclau/Zac 1994: 30). Without this antagonistic 'split', 'no ontological difference would be possible: the ontic and the ontological would exactly overlap and we would simply have pure presence. In that case, Being would only be accessible as that which is the most universal of all predicates, as that which is beyond all *differentia specifica*. And that would mean it would not be accessible at all . . . But if nothingness were there as an actual possibility, any being which presents itself would also be, to its very roots, mere possibility, and would show, beyond its ontic specificity, Being as such. *Possibility*, as opposite to pure *presence*, temporalizes Being and splits, from its very ground, all identity' (ibid.). For a detailed discussion of the ontological difference in Laclau's work see Marchart (2004).

3. It should be noted that Mouffe explicitly compares the political difference to Heidegger's ontico-ontological difference, whereby 'politics refers to the "ontic" level while "the political" has to do with the "ontological" one. This means that the ontic has to do with the manifold practices of conventional politics, while the ontological concerns the very way in which society is instituted' (Mouffe 2005: 8–9).

4. It is from this perspective of the structural impossibility of the social – the void at the heart of Being - that Žižek draws two Lacano-Hegelian conclusions that, once more, illustrate the split at the centre of the modern concept of politics: '(1) the very notion of politics involves conflict between the political and apolitical/police – that is, politics is the antagonism between politics proper and the apolitical attitude ("disorder" and Order); (2) for this reason, "politics" is a genus which is its own species: which, ultimately, has two species, itself and its "corporatist"/police negation' (1999a: 233).

5. Against this interpretation of discourse theory as political ontology, it could be objected that the category of *dislocation* in Laclau is more primary than the one of antagonism, and that dislocation is not intrinsically political (and that, consequently, the ontology in question is not political either, nor does it have

the status of a first philosophy). However, dislocation as such functions in the first place as a negative limit concept, to indicate that there will never be such a thing as an entirely closed system or an eternally stable meaning structure. The whole point is that, at the very moment we do *encounter* dislocation in our social experience, we have already constructed it in a certain way. Dislocation will therefore always occur within the horizon of being (the social), and it is clear that all examples given by Laclau for a seemingly *non*-antagonistic form of signification are far from being non-political. It might be possible that, in a given situation, the social sedimentations will be dislocated (for instance, by an earthquake or a volcanic eruption), without their *antagonistic* roots becoming apparent. In this case, the meaning of the event might be negotiated outside political discourse in the ontic sense (as the 'wrath of God', for instance), but this does not mean that the forgotten politically instituting moment of these sedimentations disappeared without trace, it just remains forgotten until returning in the form of antagonism. A volcanic eruption might be constructed as a natural phenomenon or as the 'wrath of God', but in either case a whole network of power relations (of the discourse of modern science, or of the belief-system of the Catholic Church) will have to be in place already, instituted politically, if such construction is to be successful.

Chapter 7
Founding Post-Foundationalism:
A Political Ontology

> [P]olitical philosophy is not, or rather not immediately, concerned with 'politics,' but with the 'political'. It is the task of political philosophy to elaborate theoretically the authentic characteristics of the political modality, to form a concept of the political. If this is so, perhaps she should change her name and be called? the philosophy of the political.
>
> Ernst Vollrath (1987: 27)

7.1 Towards a Philosophy of the Political

One of our initial assumptions was that, if our aim is to delineate the contours of current post-foundational political thought, it is not sufficient to develop the conceptual history of the emerging concept of the political. In the present investigation I wanted to go one step further by concentrating on those theories that employ the term within the post-foundational framework of what was described as left Heideggerianism. So let us once more recapitulate the thesis: in most such theories, 'the political' in its difference vis-à-vis 'the social' and 'politics' serves as an indicator of precisely the impossibility or absence of an ultimate foundation of society. As an indicator (but only by way of being differentiated from politics), 'the political' can assume the phenomenal or conceptual form of 'event', 'contingency', 'antagonism', 'freedom', or 'undecidability'. In some theories the political also indicates the moment of partial closure and founding: the moment of institution of society. But, while in all these cases the role of 'the political' might be modified according to the specific theoretical constellation in which it appears, what is still seen as a necessity is the very *differentiation* between the two concepts, of politics and the political. In the last instance, the play of this political difference will have to be understood as nothing but the symptom of society's absent ground.

Yet what is important to realize, and what the last chapter on Laclau has vividly shown, is that ground and abyss, from a *post*-foundational vantage point, must not be understood as two mutually or antithetically exclusive terms. As Laclau himself underlines, *de-grounding* is never absolute, but 'part of an operation of grounding except that this grounding is no longer to refer something back to a foundation which would act as a principle of derivation but, instead, to reinscribe that something within the terrain of the undecidables (iteration, re-mark, difference, etcetera) that makes its emergence possible' (1996a: 79). The very difference between politics and the political, seen from the perspective of our own 'grounding question', that is to say, interrogated *as difference*, would then indeed be part of this terrain of undecidables. So what is at stake in political post-foundationalism is not the impossibility of *any* ground, but the impossibility of a *final* ground. And it is precisely the absence of such an Archimedean point that serves as a condition of possibility of always only gradual, multiple and relatively autonomous acts of grounding. I hope to have shown – by presenting a constellation of left-Heideggerian theorists (and only mentioning, for reasons of space, a couple of others, like Jacques Rancière, Julien Freund, Cornelius Castoriadis, Zygmunt Bauman *et al.*) – how the political difference occurs at the point where the very possibility of a stable or final ground dissolves: the *moment of the political*. It is this disloca-tion of the foundationalist horizon which leads, in political theory, to the development of the radical concept of the political as differen-tiated from politics – for, if no natural ground of society is available any more, we will have to come to terms with the contingent forms of society's institution/destitution, which is the very concern of a *phi-losophy of the political*, as opposed to the traditional idea of *political philosophy*.

Today, post-foundationalists stand – to use a romantic image – among the ruins of what was once considered society's unshakable foundations. Must we view this moment – the crumbling of grounds and the disintegration of the foundationalist horizon – with concern, or even anxiety? Some conservative thinkers (although not all, if we count Oakeshott) may be alarmed. Others from the normative camp, 'Haberrawlsians' mainly, may claim that without some sort of foundation within the realm of the normative we will deliver ourselves to ethical and political nihilism. Yet contrary to such a conservative or normativist view, there are no necessarily pessimistic or nihilistic conclusions to be drawn from the dissolution of the foundationalist horizon – for one of the names of the absence of ground is freedom. As Ernesto Laclau underlines, the 'abandonment of the myth of foundations does not lead to nihilism, just as uncertainty as to how an enemy will attack does not lead to passivity', since the 'dissolution of the myth of foundations – and the concomitant dissolution of the category of "subject" – further radicalizes the emancipatory possibilities offered by the Enlightenment and marxism' (Laclau 1989: 79–80). The main theorists assembled in this investigation – Nancy, Lefort, Badiou, and Laclau – would concur on the point that, even as the political outcome of the dissolution of the markers of certainty is undecidable, this dissolution remains the very precondition for politicization and emancipation. Yet, while, apart from their common employment of the political difference, these theorists share a large series of assumptions concerning contingency, conflict and the evental nature of the political, there are also dissimilarities and disagreements between them regarding the conclusions to be drawn from the withdrawal of ground. In the remaining part of this investigation I will draw attention to a couple of dissimilarities within the Heideggerian Left. And, what is perhaps of even greater importance, I will try to underline the political stakes involved in a post-foundational stance in politics. I will then end by outlining some of the philosophical consequences which, in my opinion, have to be drawn from our discussion of the political difference. These consequences, indicated in previous chapters already, mainly concern the very theoretical status of post-foundational political thought with respect to other areas of thought. A case will be made for the – paradoxical – role of post-foundational political ontology as what once was called 'first philosophy' and of the political difference as the *quasi-transcendental 'ground'* of the social and of society.

7.2 Post-Foundationalism and Democracy

As Ernesto Laclau reminds us, some of the political stakes involved in a post-foundational approach to politics 'founded' on the dissolution of the very myth of foundations consist in an enlarging space for politicization, including *emancipatory* politicization. This weakening of ground may lead to the increasing acceptance of the contingency and historicity of being, which potentially has a liberating effect. Even though it has to be conceded that the same process may result in a paralyzed state of anxiety or in a conservative sceptical attitude, Laclau, on the other hand, tends to stress that human beings 'will begin seeing themselves more and more as the exclusive authors of their world'. People will tend to consider their fate as inevitable where they assume that God or nature have made the world as it is. But if the world is considered the result of the 'contingent discourses and vocabularies that constitute it' (1996a: 122), people may tolerate their fate with less patience and might start developing a more political attitude towards the construction of new, yet always only contingent, foundations.

But again, before too easily assimilating emancipatory politicization with politicization *tout court*, we should pause for a moment. What Laclau delineates in the quotation above are the historical conditions of possibility for an emancipatory politics. It is more than obvious, when observing current political developments, that these conditions do not necessarily lead to the spreading of emancipatory claims, or to the building up of an emancipatory hegemony. And if the latter is not necessarily the outcome of politicization, then we should also be careful not to jump too easily to conclusions concerning the emancipatory or democratic nature of a post-foundational stance in political thought. If we take seriously the notion of a politico-ontological difference, then we should recognize that we will never be able to secure an ontological ground that would found or determine a particular ontic politics (emancipatory or not) – such a move would clearly be self-contradictory. And, as I have mentioned in the Introduction, we can easily imagine a conservative post-foundational scepticism which is not necessarily democratic or emancipatory. So, if to derive a particular politics from a post-foundational stance would be a clear *non sequitur*, then it seems that the only political argument which can be made starting from the political difference is a *non sequitur* argument.

Is this really the case? If no particular politics can be logically derived from a post-foundational stance, does this imply that *nothing* follows? I don't think so, because what a post-foundational stance *does* say is that every attempt at grounding will ultimately fail. To realize this does in fact have implications for our idea of democracy, since democracy is to be defined as a regime that seeks, precisely, to *come to terms* with the ultimate failure of grounding rather than simply repressing or foreclosing it. While all conceivable political regimes, all forms of political order and ordering, are necessarily grounded in the abyss of an absent ground, most of them tend to disavow their abyssal nature. Claude Lefort's argument as to the dissolution of the markers of certainty and as to the emptying of the place of power in democracy implies that democracy is the regime which comes closest to *accepting* the absence of an ultimate ground. And, as Laclau (1996a: 79) would add, such a regime is to remain itself ungroundable: 'Democracy does not need to be – and cannot be – radically grounded. We can move to a more democratic society only through a plurality of acts of democratization.' If this is the case then political post-foundationalism may lead to diverse forms of politics, not necessarily democratic ones. Yet every democracy, if it is worth that name, *will have to be deliberately post-foundational* – a criterion which is not precisely met by everything that goes under the name of 'democracy' today (it is even debatable whether, or to what extent, the current liberal-capitalist regimes of the West meet this criterion). We encounter again the paradox of necessary contingency, this time in the field of democracy theory: democracy has to accept contingency, that is, the absence of an ultimate foundation for society, as a *necessary* precondition. Otherwise it cannot legitimately be called democracy in a strong sense. In short: not every post-foundational politics is democratic, but every democratic politics is post-foundational.[1]

This insight, and here we encounter a major dissimilarity among the post-foundationalists discussed, was largely lost on theorists like Alain Badiou or Jacques Rancière (as well as on most thinkers within the Arendtian tradition of the political). While Nancy (1991: xl) leaves open the possibility of a *politics of the political* (a politics that does not stem from the will towards foundation), thus taking rather seriously the nature of the political difference as *gap* between the political and a particular politics, and while Lefort and Laclau are too much of political realists in the Machiavellian tradition to believe in any 'natural' emancipatory inclination of political post-foundation-alism – for Badiou and other thinkers *true politics* is always, and by definition, emancipatory. The essence of true politics, as a politics directed against the state and connected to a truth-event by way of the declaration of an 'equalitarian maxim', 'lies in the emancipation of the collective' (1991: 54) – everything else would fall, not under the rubric of politics but under that of police. For Rancière, similarly, true politics – as a process of equality – effectuates a break with the order of policing, thus demonstrating the contingency of the latter. In the case of both theorists, hence, 'politics' (as opposed to 'the political' in the sense of traditional political philosophy) is always considered egalitarian and emancipatory. Many theorists located within the Arendtian tradition, upholding a radically emancipatory notion not of 'politics' but of 'the political', would ironically join in with Badiou (who is entirely hostile towards Arendt). While for Badiou 'politics' is only politics if it is emancipatory, for Arendtians the political is only 'truly political' if and only if an associative bond is established through free and public deliberation, unstained by traces of violence. What can be witnessed in either case is the same tendency towards an *emancipatory apriorism.*

Again, such an apriorism is a clear *non sequitur* if we take seriously the ontological difference between politics and the political. What the gap between the ontic and the ontological, between politics and the political indicates is precisely that no particular ontic politics can ever be grounded within the ontological realm of the political, but will always have to be articulated within the space opened by the play of the political difference. Such an articulation might lead in the most diverse political directions, and no emancipatory or democratic outcome can be guaranteed for it in advance. If this is the case, though, then how do we explain why the most sophisticated theorists resort to the *non sequitur* argument of emancipatory apriorism? I submit that the reason might be found not so much in wishful thinking as in the secret subsumption of the political under *the ethical*, of which Badiou's work is an extreme example. Contrary to what some declare to be the main danger of political post-foundationalism, its normative deficit, it is this *ethicism* that can frequently be detected in post-foundation thought. The result, exemplified in our chapter on Badiou, is an ethical displacement of politics.

7.3 The Political Displacement of Politics

The ethical short-cut between the political and an emancipatory politics is one way in which the radical implications of the political difference can be displaced. Yet there are other ways. Apart from the normative and ethical short-cut, a 'displacement of politics' – i.e. of struggle and conflict – with the *juridical* or the *administrative* has been detected by Chantal Mouffe (1993) and Bonnie Honig (1993) in the liberal, communitarian, and sometimes republican strands of political thought. There can be no doubt that, traditionally, political theory is rather hostile towards its very object: politics. More often than not, political thought – from Plato to Rawls and Habermas – is concerned with the establishment or legitimization of a 'good order' which eventually would render irrelevant any form of contestation and conflict. Jacques Rancière (1999) has provided a systematization of what one may call the *figures of displacement* of politics within political thought. In particular he mentions three forms of the political abolishment of politics, named by Rancière 'archipolitics', 'parapolitics', and 'metapolitics', and ammended by Žižek (1999a: 1990) with the concepts of 'ultrapolitics and of postpolitics' (the latter being derivative from what Rancière calls 'post-democracy').

Let us take up and translate Rancière's displacement figures into our own 'lexicon' of the political difference. In *archipolitics*, the ontological side of the political assumes the role of ground for the ontic side of politics, thus eliminating the play of the political difference and fusing the social into the substantial totality of community (what Nancy would call 'communion' or the politics of 'immanentism'). Every politics is anchored within the *arkhê* of the political whose 'truth' – the harmonious essence of a good or just community – is to be determined by the philosopher. In *parapolitics*, the ontological side of the political – as the instituting/destituting instance of antagonism – is eliminated by being dispersed into its ontic doublet of politics, whereby the latter assumes the governmental role of police or policing. This time it is the political which disappears within a politics not of conflict but of competition. One could suspect that today's secret model for parapolitical depoliticization is the market, where antagonists are turned into economic competitors. By way of this parapolitical transformation, the play between politics and the political can be domesticated and becomes governable. In *metapolitics*, the symmetrical version of archipolitics, the ontic side of politics is not 'grounded' within the ontological but is understood as a false appearance of deeper-lying social structures. In other words, politics does not express or enact a supra-historical truth of the political or of community; rather, it is seen as an ideological distortion of social objectivity. And, since the truth of the latter is only accessibly by means of science, the play of the political difference is understood as a mere delusion, behind which either the hard ontic facts of social objectivity or the eternal, iron 'ontological' laws of history have to be discovered.

In *ultrapolitics*, to uses Žižek's term, the political (as the ontological instance of antagonism) assumes full domination over politics. The political adversary is seen as an enemy to be destroyed by all means. Once more, the difference between politics and the political collapses, this time towards the side of the political, which politics is supposed to enact in an *immediate* way. The ontological ground/abyss appears directly within the ontical. This may, in the last instance, result in civil war. While the result of this ultrapolitical collapsing of the political difference towards its ontological side can have catastrophic effects,[2] it might very well be the outcome of an attempt to achieve the opposite: the *postpolitical* foreclosure of the ontological instance of antagonism. In the latter case, the very existence of antagonism at the ground of the social is denied; society is imagined not – in Laclau's words – as an impossible object, but as a world without conflict, where consensus is already established (Tony Blair) or is to be established, if only counterfactually, in the long run (Jürgen Habermas).

These diverse figures of displacement all lead with regularity to the same result. They all seek to put the play of the political difference to a halt, thereby either reducing the political to politics or hypostatizing politics into the political. To the extent that they are figures of traditional 'political philosophy' – the latter being understood as the philosophy of precisely the displacement of politics – they are situated right at the core of philosophical discourse. But, certainly, these figures of displacement are not exclusively philosophical modes of thought, they are very much political in that they are part of our political, institutional, governmental discourses (the postpolitical discourse seems even to have achieved hegemonic status in many countries of the West). One has to conclude that the philosophical displacement of politics is in itself deeply political, that the abolishment of the political is 'ideological' in the only precise sense in which the term 'ideology' may still be employed: the displacement of politics is an act that tries to conceal its own political nature, and thus its own contingency, historicity, conflictuality and ungroundable status. If, on the other hand, democracy and emancipation must be conceived of in a post-foundational way, as it was claimed above, then it is of vital importance for an emancipatory project to defend a post-foundational approach, not only, of course, on the terrain of political debate but also on the terrain of political thought. We can thus apply our previous claim as to the necessarily post-foundational nature of the democratic regime to the question of political thought: not all post-foundational thought is democratic, but democratic thought is always post-foundational.

In this qualified sense, the ideological displacement of politics will always imply the displacement of democracy. For this reason it is imperative for an emancipatory project that aims at deepening and radicalizing the democratic horizon to engage critically with all figures of displacement, both on the terrain of every-day politics and on the terrain of political thought. And for the same reason we must not hesitate fully to assert the consequences of post-foundational political thought, and to do this in the offensive, not in the defensive mode. It will not suffice to proceed on the *via negativa* only, criticizing or deconstructing different figures of displacement. The displacement of politics can only be avoided by putting the political center-stage, that is, by fully endorsing the priority of the political vis-à-vis society and all things social, and by giving space to the play between politics and the political without subsuming one side under the other. In order to do so, and to complete this investigation, we will have to reflect on the very theoretical status of post-foundationalism vis-à-vis competing approaches of social and philosophical inquiry. This will also allow us finally to determine the theoretical status of the political difference *as difference*.

7.4 Political Thought as First Philosophy

The first thing to realize when discussing the theoretical status of a post-foundational political thought which does not entirely discard the notion of an ontological ground (as anti-foundationalists would) is that such political thought assumes the position of what, on a more traditional note, would have been called a *political ontology* – with the proviso that 'ontology' here is employed with deconstructive reticence. It has been argued throughout this investigation that the political difference, in a sense, 'mirrors' the post-metaphysical difference between the ontic and the ontological, as it was theorized by Heidegger *as difference*. Now the time has come to determine more clearly this sense in which the political difference mirrors the ontological difference. Let us approach the problem by first reflecting on how a post-foundational political ontology must be understood, and then by determining the very status of such ontology.

Traditionally, the term ontology designates the science of being-qua-being. That is to say, ontology does not cover a regional sphere of the world, a particular realm or ontic species of beings, but the very horizon of being in general (the ontological). As one can see, the ontological difference is already presupposed, explicitly or not, by the very idea of ontology as a philosophical 'discipline' concerned with being-qua-being and not with beings. But, to the extent that the horizon of foundationalism has crumbled, the history of ontology is a history of its disintegration. While ontological inquiry started with Aristotelian metaphysics, it was only with Christian Wolff and German '*Schulphilosophie*' that ontology appeared as a name for a philosophical discipline – only to be increasingly displaced by *epistemology* (a process that culminated in Berkeley, Kant and their modern heirs). It was with Heidegger, but certainly prepared by Schelling, that a more ontological style of reasoning returned, but it did not return in full glory, nor did it always return under the name of ontology. What has occurred was that the idea of Being-as-ground had turned into an entirely dubious notion. At the end of this process, where we stand today, ontology is available in no other form than, to use Derrida's term (1994), 'hauntology' – an ontology haunted by the spectre of its own absent ground. And here one clearly sees how the deconstructive claim that 'the great chain of being' is constitutively *out of joint* has been prepared by Heidegger. The never-ending play of the difference between ontological being and the realm of ontic beings injects a 'ground/abyss' of radical instability into the field of being, and thus into the discipline of ontology. It is only in the sense of *hauntology*, that is to say, as an ontology lacking its very object (being-as-ground), that the term ontology may still be employed.

But why, then, should we adhere to the notion of ontology and not abandon the terrain of metaphysical questioning as such? In fact, one answer, proposed by Heidegger, Derrida and Nancy, would be that simply to desert does not yet render dysfunctional today's many attempts at epistemological, logical, rational, technical or empiricist *regrounding* which inherit and resume under different names the foundational attempts of classical ontology. Moreover, it is more than questionable that any refuge beyond the horizon of Western metaphysics is readily available. So, not a strategy of evasion or even desertion, but only a form of deconstructive engagement with ontological and foundational discourse will be a feasible strategy. Yet I suspect that this answer, correct as it is, is not fully satisfying as long as it leaves untouched the traditional hierarchies of philosophical thought and the subordination, much criticized by Hannah Arendt, of political thought to a marginal sub-discipline of philosophy. Of course, a 'disciplinary' view of philosophy is overcome and would not be defended by Heidegger or Derrida – nor would the entirety of political thought – given the complicity of many of its strands with the displacement of politics – be worth being defended *tout court*. But only on rare occasions is it realized that a post-foundational approach to philosophical problems bears radical consequences since only *the political* can step in as a supplement for the absent ground. And this implies that any (post-foundational) ontology – every *hauntology* – will necessarily be a *political* ontology, which cannot any longer be subordinated to the status of a region of philosophical inquiry.

Everything within the most radical strands of post-foundational political thought points in this direction, while its proponents do not dare to draw the full consequences. Let us remember Laclau's claim that '[a]ny advance in the understanding of present-day social struggles depends on inverting the relations of priority which the last century and a half's social thought had established between the social and the political' (Laclau 1990: 160). After the political has been reduced to a regional sector of society and absorbed by the social, we now have to move, according to Laclau, 'in the opposite direction: towards a growing understanding of the eminently political character of any social identity' (ibid.). What Laclau holds about the political character of any social identity – which is always discursive – of course concerns philosophical discourse as well. Philosophy, a social discourse with no privilege within the realm of the discursive, is eminently political as every single philosophical text and every particular discipline, sub-discipline or region of philosophical thought is founded on the instituting/destituting ground of a political decision. Such instituting decision – ungroundable itself – is the only thing that can supplement the absent ground and 'overcome' the radical un-decidability of the social by effectuating a contingent and always temporary hegemonic closure: 'Once undecidability has reached the ground itself, once the organization of a certain camp is governed by a hegemonic decision – hegemonic because it is not objectively deter-mined, because different decisions were also possible – the realm of philosophy comes to an end and the realm of politics begins' (Laclau 1996a: 123).

Slavoj Žižek, who clearly perceived that, 'for Laclau, the break-down of the traditional closed ontology reveals how features that we (mis)perceive as ontologically positive rely on an ethico-political decision that sustains the prevailing hegemony' (1999a: 174), was not completely mistaken when he compared this Laclauian 'inversion of priority' between the philosophical and the political to the Marxist injunction to pass from philosophical interpretation to practical change. Now to imply, as Žižek does, that 'in both cases the ultimate solution to philosophical problems is practice' (174) may – arguably – hold for Marx, but I suspect that it does not hold for Laclau, since within a post-foundational approach there is no such thing as an *ultimate solution*. I submit that the above quotation should be interpreted in a slightly different manner: far from abandoning the terrain of philosophical and theoretical work in favor of some sort of wild practicism, the end of philosophy and the beginning of politics should not be taken as two successive and mutually exclusive histor-ical stages, but rather as a battle line which, *inter alia*, cuts across the very terrain of philosophical discourse. Under this aspect, the realm of politics must not be conceptualized as entirely exterior to philosophy. Laclau is in certain ways closer here to Nancy and Lacoue-Labarthe's deconstructive approach to the relation between philosophy and politics (see Chapter 3) than he is to Marx's eleventh thesis on Feuerbach.[3]

Let us bring together the Heideggerian/Derridean perspective on the post-foundational *subversion* of the philosophical and the Grams-cian/Laclauian perspective on the political *inversion* of the philoso-phical. If, first, the terrain of philosophical discourse, as a terrain of hegemonic struggle, should not be deserted but rather *subverted*, and if, second, the priority within philosophical thought should be *re-versed* in favor of ontology as a *political* ontology, then we should not hesitate attributing to political ontology a quasi-transcendental and even a (post-)foundational status vis-à-vis other possible ontologies (e.g. Badiou's ontology of mathematics and set theory, or his un-avowed prioritizing of the ethical). It is in this sense that we can propose the following solution regarding the relation between politics (and the political) and philosophy (and the philosophical) – perhaps the only feasible solution within the horizon of post-foundational political thought: their relation should not be construed as one of pure exteriority (which would mean that we could abandon philosophy altogether), but rather as one of mutual im-plication: politics as the 'end of philosophy' occurs as much outside as it occurs within philosophy. Herein the *raison d'être* of a *philosophy* of the political is to be found: in post-foundational political thought, the political, as the 'outside' of the philosophical, is folded back into the philosophical in the form of political ontology as *prima philosophia*.

Why call it *prima philosophia*? Are we not taking a step backward by insisting on the (impossible) necessity of a first philosophy, thus returning to the golden era of metaphysical foundationalism? In the Wolffian system, ontology was designated as '*metaphysica generalis*', inhabiting the function of a *prima philosophia*, a first philosophy with respect to regional metaphysical disciplines such as cosmology, psychology and theology. Obviously, from a post-foundational vantage point a 'first philosophy' cannot be an ontology that provides all other regional philosophies with a stable ground. Rather, it must be understood as a form of thinking or philosophical interrogation that seeks to establish the quasi-transcendental conditions of the process of grounding and ungrounding of all being. In this sense, *first* philosophy means that such a quasi-transcendental inquiry takes into account the play of the ontological difference as the withdrawal of ground. This, again, is the post-foundational or Heideggerian perspective on being-qua-*differencing*. Where the *political* perspective is concerned, everything hinges on whether we understand by 'political ontology' a *regional* or a *general* category, which applies to all regions of being. Now, if political ontology amounts to nothing but an ontology of *the political* (which simultaneously is based on the hauntology of the political difference), then it should clearly not be confused with the traditional regional discipline of political philosophy as a philosophy of *politics* (and yet, it has to be added immediately, the complete disengagement from political theory would most likely be a symptom of philosophism). What is at stake in political ontology is the political nature of being-qua-being, the political nature – in quasi-transcendental terms – of *all possible* being, and not simply the nature of the 'good regime' or a 'well-ordered society'. But what differentiates a political ontology in this sense from a purely deconstructive or Heideggerian account of post-foundationalism is that not only the *withdrawal* of ground is accounted for by insisting on the differential character of the political difference, but also the – contingent and temporary – moment of grounding is theorized as the instituting moment of the political. The perspective on being-qua-differencing is supplemented by a perspective on being-qua-*the political*. The political is constantly retreating due to the ungrounding nature of difference, and yet this retreat is – in a myriad of instances – put to a halt, if always only temporarily, in the moment of grounding.

Since the above claim as to the status of political ontology as a first philosophy may appear as somewhat over-stretched from the perspective of most, if not all, competing approaches, a couple of clarifications might be useful in order to avoid confusion.

First, if we retain the notion of 'ontology', we will not retain it for reasons of philosophical nostalgia but in order to maintain the radical implications of this traditional term. Ontology once referred to the very horizon of being-qua-being, and, given the radical aim of post-foundationalism, what is at stake is not the foundation of a particular being (or region of beings) vis-à-vis others but the ground/abyss of all being. As was mentioned in Chapter 1, the idea of a 'regional' post-foundationalism or a 'non-necessary' contingency does not make sense, as it would leave open the possibility of *some* particular being assuming the status of an ultimate ground (which would simply be a form of foundationalism, not of post-foundationalism). However, it goes without saying that the very term 'ontology' has to be deconstructed from within – which is what Derrida seeks to achieve with the homonym of 'hauntology'. In the Heideggerian context, being-as-ground – as it was posited by traditional ontology – gets constitutively destabilized by the indefinite play of the difference *between* beings and being. But to assume the *withdrawal* of Being (= Ground) via difference does not compel us to become logical positivists or anti-foundationalists and to dismiss ontological questioning altogether. A notion of the political-as-ground remains indispensable for post-foundational political thought, even as the political can never be implemented directly and unmediated by the never-ending play of difference.

Second, transcendental and ontological inquiry are correlative to the extent that they both refer to the conditions of possibility of being-qua-being – and not to an epistemology of being-qua-understanding. That is to say, a quasi-transcendental approach in the post-Heideggerian sense is solely concerned with ontological conditions, not with the conditions or foundations of 'knowing' or 'understanding'. With a political ontology we leave the modern hegemonic terrain of epistemology (which itself had, since Descartes, Kant and the neo-Kantians, displaced the terrain of classical ontology as *prima philosophia*, see Marchart 2006). So, a standard epistemological critique of our approach along the line of questions such as: 'How can you "know" the transcendental conditions you are talking about?', or: 'Isn't your claim as to the ubiquity of the political self-contradictory, as it would necessarily have to be a political and not a "scientific" claim?' – such a critique in the epistemological style loses its meaning once we situate ourselves within the ontological paradigm. Neither does an ontological approach aim at something like 'objective knowledge' of being, nor does it claim 'scientific' status in the restricted sense of the term. In fact, the charge of speaking from a political point of view can wholeheartedly be accepted, given the basic assumption of the political ground of all things social (including, of course, philosophico-theoretical arguments). This assumption is as much a political intervention – proceding from the side of *politics* – as it is a philosophico-conceptual invention of a new term ('the political'). Hence, it is not necessary at all to assume a position 'beyond' or 'above' the horizon of being in order to make ontological claims – a charge that should rather be directed against objectivist approaches of positive science. And, to the extent that every position from which one speaks will always be located within the horizon of the political, every ontological but *also* every epistemological position will be politically overdetermined. One can only take such a position by, precisely, *taking position* – and this is what we do.

Third, the argument as to the priority of the political over the social has so far relied very much on the Laclauian 'dialectics' between political institution/destitution and social sedimentation (see Chapter 6) – whereby social sediments are not *non*-political but political in the, as it were, sleeping mode. That is, their original political roots – the grounding moment of institution called by Laclau 'the political' – have been forgotten within the social but can be reactivated at any time through dislocation and antagonization. This is also the reason why we prefer speaking about *political* ontology rather than *social* ontology. What should be underlined once more is that the realm of social objectivity, the realm of being, is conceptualized by Laclau and Mouffe as the *discursive*: 'the discursive is coterminous with the being of objects – the horizon, therefore, of the constitution of every object' (Laclau 1990: 105). With this claim as to the discursive nature of all social 'being', discourse theory assumes both an ontological and a quasi-transcendental status. Vice versa, ontology and quasi-transcendentalism have to be firmly located within the ambit of the linguistic turn, or rather the 'discursive turn'. Yet to this 'turn' we have to give a further, political twist: the discursive is a *political* concept. This 'twist' finds support in the work not only of Laclau but of other theorists as well. Žižek, for instance, holds, from a Lacanian vantage point, that 'the order of the signifier as such is political and, vice versa, there is no politics outside the order of the signifier' (1999a: 177). A claim reminiscent of Pocock's chiasmatic conception of politics as a language-system and language as a political system (see Chapter 2).

Fourth, one could suspect that the primordial status of political ontology amounts, in Rancière's words, to 'the assertion that everything is political, which comes down to saying that nothing is' (1999: 86) – and hence to just another form of metapolitics. This would only be the case, however, if politics or the political resided within all beings in an immediate way and not by way of 'mediation' through the political difference. A world in which every being is 'political' would equal either a world in which politics (in the ontic sense) has infiltrated all corners of the social, or a world in which the political (in the ontological sense of antagonism) is fully enacted on the entire scale of the social. While the first option would be considered by some a definition of totalitarianism, the second option amounts to a definition of universal civil war. In both cases we would be confronted with a world in which the political difference has collapsed. As should be clear by now, everything within left-Heideggerian political thought agitates against this idea. The claim as to the primordial status of political ontology does not correspond to the commonplace notion of 'everything is political' – even though everything *is* political in the sense of being irresolvably subverted by the instituting/destituting moment of the political, as it is indicated in the play of the political difference. But it is precisely the *irresolvability* of this play that guarantees that both the totalitarian absorption of all social being by politics and the war-like absorption of all social being by the political are doomed to failure in the last instance. Not 'everything is political', but the ground/abyss of everything is *the political*.

7.5 The Political *Difference* as *Political* Difference

Let us exemplify our claim as to primacy of political ontology – understood as a fundamental 'hauntology' of the political – by contrasting it with a current counter-example of an 'ontological ontology'. In a recent voluminous book, Miguel de Beistegui has proposed to revive the idea of a first philosophy in terms of what he calls a *differential ontology*. While there is no space for going into the details of his project, it is clear that a cursory look at it would detect astounding parallels. De Beistegui's aim is to show 'how philosophy can reinvent itself as differential ontology' (2004: 26), proceeding from the Heideggerian notion of the ontico-ontological difference, extended – in de Beistegui's view – by Deleuze. Such a philosophy can only be developed on post-foundational premises. The future of metaphysics has to be thought out of the 'event of un-grounding'. Yet at the same time it has to be thought of as an ontology, since, '[b]y metaphysics, we must now understand neither the science of first principles and highest causes nor the science of beings as onto-theology, but indeed the science of the being of beings' (23), whereby being 'unfolds only in and as dif-ference' (25).

So far, de Beistegui's model can clearly be located within the Heideggerian tradition of post-foundational thought. Like Nancy, however, de Beistegui falls into the trap of philosophism when he assumes that a differential ontology should be an ontology of differential being *as such* and, hence, should be untainted by any particular 'beings' or ontic regions. Although we would agree that any ontology worth its name would have to be concerned with being in general (respectively, with the difference between being and beings), one has to disagree with the implications of de Beistegui's proposal. For, in order to achieve his objective of a differential philosophy that 'is concerned with everything, or with the All' (x), he has to cut off the links between being-as-difference and any regional field of beings, between differential ontology as a 'first philosophy' and all other philosophies: 'At a time when there are literally dozens of branches of philosophy, each specializing in one aspect of what used to be a unified field, each limiting itself to being philosophy *of* science, or art, or ethics, or economics, etc., I wanted to investigate the possibility that philosophy be *of* everything' (335). With this, he explicitly wishes to overcome 'the very shattering and dispersal of philosophy' (12) into regional disciplines. The price to be paid for all this lies in the very emptiness of such differential ontology: in its philosophism. A philosophy that seeks to capture being and 'dif-ference' *as such* will always tend to denigrate the realm of the ontic, of history and of politics. So it is no surprise that politics – or political thought – plays not the slightest role in de Beistegui's book.

Warned by Nancy's and Badiou's philosophism – itself prepared to some extent by Derrida's and Heidegger's philosophism – we propose to take another route. Rather than clinging to a hypostatized notion of 'dif-ference' as such (or *différance*, or *difference-as-difference*), one should take into account that difference will have to work itself out on a particular ontic terrain, and therefore will always be less than 'pure' dif-ference. If it is the case, though, that 'dif-ference' will always be overdetermined by some ontic remainder which resists the pure play of 'dif-ference', then the idea of developing an ontology pure and simple will be doomed to failure. Rather than seeking to cover up such a failure with a discourse of philosophism, one should wholeheartedly accept it and – as in the martial arts – turn weakness into an advantage. If every general ontology will be over-determined by a regional ontology, and if one nonetheless agrees on the necessity of a general ontology, then the latter can only be constructed out of a regional ontology that will have to incarnate this impossible place. Every ontology, which necessarily will be *less* than a pure ontology, has to be grounded in an 'ontic', which necessarily will be *more* than a mere ontic. This also implies that any 'first' philosophy will be a 'second' one, grounded from the side of a 'secondary' discipline, because no first ground is readily available. And, since no such further ground will be available, it cannot be determined by purely philosophical means *which* regional discipline will live up to this task. In actual fact, the ascension of a regional ontology to the always precarious status of a general ontology can only be based, at the end of the day, on a contingent decision. And our decision to grant *political* thought (rather than aesthetics, or ethics, or set theory) the role of a *prima philosophia* is, of course, not so much a 'philosophical' decision based, for instance, on so-called rational grounds, as it is an intrinsically *political decision*: an intervention from the ontic side of politics into the depoliticized field of philosophy.

We are now in a better position, I hope, to determine the exact nature of the political difference in relation to the ontological difference. Throughout this investigation, the political difference has been understood in terms of, and by analogy to, the ontological difference in philosophical thought. It was claimed that the difference between 'politics' (*la politique, die Politik*) and the political (*le politique, das Politische*) mirrors conceptually what in Heidegger is described as difference (*qua difference*) between the ontic and the ontological. As long as the political difference was depicted as just a derivation of the ontological difference, post-foundational political thought remained subordinated to philosophy or to what Heidegger calls thinking. But, if we take seriously the reversal of priority not only of the political over the social – including the philosophical – but also of *political* ontology over the traditional ontology of a *metaphysica generalis* (even in the post-foundational sense of a constitutively *failed* meta-physica generalis), then we have to draw the full consequences: it is the very terrain on which our grounding question as to the political difference-as-difference was posed which gets inverted. Not the political difference is to be understood, as it was claimed in our initial hypothesis, by analogy to the ontological difference, but conversely: the ontological difference – i.e. difference-as-difference – has to be understood in the light of the political difference.

From this it follows that the very difference or differencing – which was alternately named in our investigation 'play', 'event', or 'freedom' – between politics and the political is *in itself* political. Given these considerations, we should not be irritated by the fact that the qualifier 'political' *appeared twice* throughout this investigation: nominalized, it is the name for the ontological 'side' of the political difference (*the* political, le *politique*, das *Politische*), and adjectivized it defines the difference itself as *political* difference, i.e. as the *political in-between* of the political and of politics. So again, on the one hand, the side of the ontological of the ontico-ontological difference is turned, to use William Connolly's term (1995), into something like the '*ontopoli-tical*': we cannot but think about Being other than in the sense of the political; being-qua-being turns into being-qua-*the political*. On the other hand, between this ontopolitical realm of 'being' and the sedimented realm of social beings we encounter an unbridgeable chasm, an abyss, which, by dividing the ontopolitical from the ontic side of politics, at the very same time unites them in a never-ending play (and it is this play which in itself is of a deeply political nature). Heidegger, in order to account for the double inscription of 'being' as both ontological 'Being' and 'difference', resorted for some time to the awkwardly written term *beyng* (*Seyn*) as a name for the event of differencing in-between the ontological and the ontic. This allowed him to retain the semantics of 'beingness' and at the very same time undermine it with an archaic spelling that points at something else. 'Beyng', as a name for difference-as-difference, is nothing completely other than 'being' (or 'beings'), and yet indicates exactly the unsur-passable difference between 'being' and 'beings' – the ground/abyss that opens up in the very event of their differencing. But if we want to abstain from typographical experiments it should suffice simply to point out the double inscription of the political and the fact that the event of differencing between politics and the political – the play that points to the absent ground of society, which nevertheless remains present in its absence – is not a neutral (non-)ground but is of a deeply political nature in itself.

One question remains to be answered, however. Where does this leave us with politics in the ordinary, ontic sense? For if we decide to conceive of the very difference between politics and the political as *political* difference (and not as difference tout court, or difference-as-difference, as in Heidegger's case of the ontological difference or in Derrida's notion of *différance*), then the question could be raised whether we borrow the qualifier 'political' from the side of 'the political' or whether we take it from the side of 'politics'. It is evident that, if one remembers the intertwining or chiasmatic relation between politics and the political, both sides must be involved to some extent. Yet the side of politics (what, in the case of the ontological difference, would be the ontic aspect of the difference) has not yet received sufficient attention.

So, to approach a possible answer to the above question, let us consider an argument by Slavoj Žižek, who has given an interesting Lacanian twist to Lefort's and Laclau's differentiation between ' "politics" as a separate social complex, a positively determined sub-system of social relations in interaction with other sub-systems (economy, forms of culture . . .) and the "Political" [*le Politique*] as the moment of openness, of undecidability, when the very structuring principle of society, the fundamental form of the social pact is called into question' (Žižek 1991: 193). He clearly perceives that such an approach risks the hypothesis that the 'very genesis of society is always "political"' (194). Up to this point Žižek follows Lefort and Laclau in the argument; the twist occurs when Žižek gives a 'symptomatological' reading of politics as a sub-system (or particular form of action). Politics as a sub-system becomes a *metaphor* for 'the political', it becomes 'the element which, within the constituted social space, holds the place of the Political as negativity which suspends it and founds it anew'. As he goes on explaining:

> In other words, 'politics' as 'sub-system', as a separate sphere of society, represents *within* society its own forgotten foundation, its genesis in a violent, abyssal act – it represents, within the social space, what must *fall out* if this space is to constitute itself. Here, we can easily recognize the Lacanian definition of the signifier (that which 'represents the subject for another signifier'): politics as sub-system represents the Political (subject) for all other social sub-systems. (1991: 194)

Žižek's point – reminiscent of Lefort – is that the sphere of politics is not one sub-system among many, rather it is the very sub-system that serves as a symbolic reminder of the ungroundable nature of society, of – in Laclau's words – the *impossibility* of society. Politics, as a metaphor, is the '*One which holds the place of Nothing* (of radical negativity)' (1991: 195). But as, according to Žižek, the metaphoricity of politics in its capacity of stand-in for 'the political', as absent ground of the social, assumes its full potential only in moments of antagonization (in what we have called the *moment of the political*), politics will be reduced 'to being "one among others"' once the social bond, or a new hegemonic order, is re-established. It then becomes again a social sub-system among many.

This observation has the merit of reminding us that there is no political difference without 'politics' on one side of the difference – and that 'politics' is of as much importance as 'the political' on the other side. It also reminds us that 'politics', whether we understand by it the 'political system' or a specific form of action, is not necessarily reducible to other social spheres or forms of action (such as, for instance, work and labor – to use Arendt's distinctions). The observation above only has the disadvantage of missing the Schmittian point that antagonization may occur in *any* social sub-system, not only in the system of politics, and that, as I would add, any form of action may be turned into political action.[4] A more deconstructive approach would put emphasis on the fact that antagonization – like hegemony – occurs all the time, even if to different degrees. *The moment of the political*, when society is confronted with its own absent ground and with the necessity to institute contingent grounds, has always already come and *does not stop coming*. We do not have to wait for the grand historical events of uprisings and revolutions, we always already enact, in the most diverse and 'shattered' ways, the political within the realm of the social.

So the political – and be it in the smallest dose – is indeed everywhere. Yet this 'everywhere' is a peculiar place which nobody has ever seen. The presence of the political as the 'ontological' moment of society's institution, as we have repeatedly stressed, can only be inferred from the absence of a firm ground of society, from our experience of the incompletion of the realm of social beings, as it is indicated by the play of the political difference. Nobody has ever encountered the realm of the 'ontopolitical' *as such*, except in the cracks and fissures of the social which become filled, expanded or closed by – precisely – *politics*. It is in this sense that Žižek's argument as to the metaphoricity of politics is useful: politics may serve as the 'ontic' name for the political in the mode of enactment. An enactment which, conditioned by the political, nevertheless cannot get hold of the political, as it is separated from if by an unbridgeable chasm. Therefore we are not the subjects of this enactment, since, as much as we enact the political, we *are* enacted by the political. As much as the 'event' of the political cannot be brought about voluntaristically, we always bring it about whenever we act. Politics is the name for a paradoxical enterprise that is both impossible and unavoidable – which is why nobody has ever seen 'politics pure and simple' either.

This is why every displacement of politics – where it contains the foreclosure of society's ungroundable nature (and, consequently, the foreclosure of the necessity to provide, politically, for partial and contingent groundings) – is a political move in itself. The denegation of society's groundless nature is merely the *foundationalist* way of instituting society (without ever being able ultimately to *ground* it). It remains a political gesture even in its vain attempt at abolishing politics and/or the political. And, for the same reason, the political fight against the displacement of politics is a fight over the *degree* of ideological displacement or, vice versa, the *degree* of politicization, and not a fight over the ontopolitical which, as such, remains out of reach for every ontic politics. Society, ontopolitically speaking, has always been and will always remain groundless and antagonistic, regardless of the particular politics enacted. Society is groundable only on the insurmountable difference between the social as the realm of sedimented practices and the political as the moment of their antagonistic institution/reactiviation. And politics in itself is torn apart between these two dimensions: the ontic dimension of the social, where politics appears as a particular sub-system or form of action, and the dimension of the political as the instituting ground of all social relations.

Becoming aware of the full philosophical and political implications of the political difference will help us theoretically and practically to cope with the peculiar fact that society is groundless and still the dimension of ground does not disappear without trace. It is true that the metaphysical figures of the past disintegrate, but it is also true that we are compelled to live and engage with their spectres. Post-foundational political thought does not abandon the metaphysical terrain of foundation but seeks to rework and re-define this very terrain politically. Perhaps we have eventually come to the point of reframing the famous Levinasian question as to the fundamental role of ethics, only this time from a political point of view. So, is *the political* fundamental? Given the insights of post-foundational political thought, as I have tried to present them throughout this investigation, the answer can only be the following: yes, the political serves as *ground* as much as it serves as *cause* and *condition* of all social being. Yet, this is a *ground* that can never be reached and still has the status of a foundation, a *cause* that does not determine anything and still produces effects of its absence, and a transcendental *condition* whose emergence is historically conditioned and still assumes supra-historical validity.

Notes

1. This point regarding the 'non-reversible' relation between democracy and post-foundationalism is elaborated upon in more detail in Marchart (2006). Does this not also explain the nature of the relation between Ernesto Laclau and Chantal Mouffe's project of radical and plural democracy vis-à-vis their general theory of hegemony? Many observers have launched a *non sequitur* argument against the fourth and last part of *Hegemony and Socialist Strategy* (1985), where Laclau and Mouffe develop their theory of radical and plural democracy, but it is clear from their argument that a political project of radical democracy does not follow with necessity from a post-foundational historical constellation or from a general theory of hegemony. It simply constitutes one possible political project among others. So we have to conclude, by analogy to what was said before, that while radical and plural democracy will always have to be post-foundational to some extent, the post-foundational horizon of our times is far from being radically democratic in any aprioristic sense.

2. This is most obvious in the case of civil war. But an ultrapolitical approach may also have, it must be added, potentially liberating effects, as in some cases of revolutions. In theses cases, however, revolutionaries will immediately face the less-than-ultrapolitical Arendtian question of how to institutionalize a 'post-foundational' regime of freedom once the moment of liberation has occurred. And this is where the democratic question sets in.

3. Notwithstanding the fact that, of course, the latter can also be interpreted, and has been interpreted, in a myriad of ways; and notwithstanding that in Nancy and Lacoue-Labarthe one can witness, from time to time, a certain philosophism and the tendency to avoid the radical consequences that a truly political inversion of the field of philosophy would entail.

4. Of course, Žižek himself knows this very well, but he does not accept the implication of this fact. To put it in Lacanian terms: if antagonization can occur in any social sub-system, then any sub-system (not only politics) may, under such conditions, assume the metaphorical function of representing the political.

Bibliography

Abel, Olivier (1996), *Paul Ricœur. La promesse et la règle*, Paris: Editions Michalon

Agamben, Giorgio (1993), *The Coming Community*, Minneapolis and London: University of Minnesota Press

Agamben, Giorgio (1998), *Homo Sacer. Sovereign Power and Bare Life*, Stanford: Stanford University Press

Arditi, Benjamin (1994), 'Tracing the Political', *Angelaki* 1/3, pp. 15–28

Arditi, Benjamin (1995), *Politics, Publicness and Difference*, PhD thesis, University of Essex, Department of Government

Arditi, Benjamin and Jeremy Valentine (1999), *Polemicization: The Contingency of the Commonplace*, New York: New York University Press.

Arendt, Hannah (1968), *Between Past and Future*, New York: Viking Press

Arendt, Hannah (1993), *Was ist Politik?*, ed. by Ursula Ludz, Munich and Zürich: Piper

Badiou, Alain (1985), *Peut-on penser la politique?*, Paris: Editions du Seuil

Badiou, Alain (1988), *L'Etre et l'événement*, Paris: Editions du Seuil

Badiou, Alain (1990), 'L'entretien de Bruxelles', *Les Temps Modernes*, 526 (May), pp. 1–26

Badiou, Alain (1991), *D'un désastre obscur. Droit, Etat, Politique*, La Tour d'Aigues: Editions de l'Aube

Badiou, Alain (1992), *Conditions*, Paris: Editions du Seuil

Badiou, Alain (1993), *L'Ethique. Essai sur la conscience du mal*, Paris: Hatier

Badiou, Alain (1994), 'Being by Numbers', *Artforum International* (October), pp. 84–124

Badiou, Alain (1998a), *Abrégé de métapolitique*, Paris: Editions du Seuil

Badiou, Alain (1998b), 'Politics and Philosophy. An Interview with Alain Badiou', *Angelaki* 3/3, pp. 113–33

Badiou, Alain (1999a), *Manifesto For Philosophy*, Albany: SUNY Press

Badiou, Alain (1999b), 'Philosophy and politics', in *Radical Philosophy* 96 (July/August), pp. 29–32

Badiou, Alain (2002a), *Ethics. An Essay on the Understanding of Evil*. London and New York: Verso

Badiou, Alain (2002b), 'One Divides into Two!', *Culture Machine*, 4, electronic document: http://culturemachine.tees.ac.uk/Articles/badiou.htm

Badiou, Alain (2003), *Saint Paul. The Foundation of Universalism*. Stanford: Stanford University Press

Balibar, Etienne (2002), *Politics and the Other Scene*, London and New York: Verso

Ball, Terence (1988), *Transforming Political Discourse. Political Theory and Critical Conceptual Change*, Oxford: Blackwell

Baraldi, Claudio, Giancarlo Corsi, Elena Esposito (1997), *GLU. Glossar zu Niklas Luhmanns Theorie sozialer Systeme*, Frankfurt am Main: Suhrkamp

Barthes, Roland (1994), *Œuvres complètes*, Vol. 3, Paris: Editions du Seuil

Bauman, Zygmunt (1996), 'Morality in the Age of Contingency', in Paul Heelas, Scott Lash and Paul Morris (eds), *Detraditionalization*, Oxford: Blackwell, pp. 49–58

Bauman, Zygmunt (1999), *In Search of Politics*, Cambridge: Polity Press

Beardsworth, Richard (1996), *Derrida & the Political*, London and New York: Routledge

Beck, Ulrich (1993), *Die Erfindung des Politischen*, Frankfurt am Main: Suhrkamp

de Beistegui, Miguel (2004), *Truth & Genesis. Philosophy as Differential Ontology*, Bloomington and Indianapolis: Indiana University Press

Benhabib, Seyla (1996), *The Reluctant Modernism of Hannah Arendt*, London: Sage

Birmingham, Peg (1991), 'The Time of the Political', *Graduate Faculty Philosophy Journal* 14/2 and 15/1, pp. 25–45

Bock, Gisela (1990), 'Civil discord in Machiavelli's *Istorie Fiorentine*', in Gisela Bock, Quentin Skinner and Maurizio Viroli (eds), *Machiavelli and Republicanism*, Cambridge: Cambridge University Press, pp. 181–201

Burke, Peter (1992), *The Fabrication of Louis XIV*, New Haven and London: Yale University Press

Butler, Judith (1992), 'Contingent Foundations: Feminism and the Question of 'Postmodernism', in Judith Butler and J. W. Scott (eds), *Feminists Theorize the Political*, New York and London: Routledge, pp. 3–21

Castoriadis, Cornelius (1991), *Philosophy, Politics, Autonomy*, ed. by David Ames Curtis, New York and Oxford: Oxford University Press

Cholewa-Madsen, Michael (1994), 'Enacting the Political', *Angelaki* 1/3, pp. 29–42

Clarke, Paul Barry (1996), *Deep Citizenship*, London/Chicago: Pluto Press

Condren, Conal (1994), *The Language of Politics in Seventeenth-Century England*, Basingstoke, London: Macmillan

Connolly, William E. (1995), *The Ethos of Pluralization*, Minneapolis and London: University of Minnesota Press

Critchley, Simon (1992), *The Ethics of Deconstruction. Derrida and Levinas*, Oxford and Cambridge, MA: Blackwell

Critchley, Simon (1993), 'Re-Tracing the Political: Politics and Community in the Work of Philippe Lacoue-Labarthe and Jean-Luc Nancy', in David Campbell and Michael Dillon (eds), *The Political Subject of Violence*, Manchester: Manchester University Press, pp. 73–93

Critchley, Simon (2000), 'Demanding Approval. On the Ethics of Alain Badiou', *Radical Philosophy* 100 (March–April), pp. 16–27

Critchley, Simon (2005), ' "Fault Lines": Simon Critchley in Discussion on Alain Badiou', *Polygraph* 17, pp. 295–308

Dallmayr, Fred (1987), 'Politics and Conceptual Analysis. Comments on Vollrath', *Philosophy and Social Criticism* 13/1, pp. 31–7

Dallmayr, Fred (1988), 'Hegemony and Democracy: On Laclau and Mouffe', *Strategies* 30 (Fall), pp. 29–49

Dallmayr, Fred (1993a), *The Other Heidegger*, Ithaca, NY: Cornell University Press

Dallmayr, Fred (1993b), 'Politics and Power: Ricœur's Political Paradox Revisited', in David E. Klemm and William Schweiker (eds), *Meanings in Texts and Actions. Questioning Paul Ricœur*, Charlottesville and London: University Press of Virginia, pp. 176–94

Dallmayr, Fred (1997), 'An "Inoperative" Global Community? Reflections on Nancy', in Darren Sheppard, Simon Sparks and Colin Thomas (eds), *On Jean-Luc Nancy. The Sense of Community*, London and New York: Routledge, pp. 174–96

Dauenhauer, Bernard P. (1998), *Paul Ricœur. The Promise and Risk of Politics*, Lanham and Oxford: Rowman and Littlefield

Derrida, Jacques (1978), *Writing and Difference*, Chicago: The University of Chicago Press

Derrida, Jacques (1990), 'Some Statements and Truisms about Neologisms, Newisms, Postisms, Parasitisms, and Other Small Seismisms', in David Carroll (ed.), *The States of 'Theory'. History, Art and Critical Discourse*, Irvine Studies in the Humanities Volumes, New York: Columbia University Press, pp. 63–94

Derrida, Jacques (1992), *The Other Heading*, Indianapolis: Indiana University Press

Derrida, Jacques (1993), 'Politics and Friendship: An Interview with Jacques Derrida', in Enn Kaplan and Michale Sprinker (eds), *The Althusserian Legacy*, London and New York: Verso.

Derrida, Jacques (1994), *Spectres of Marx*, London and New York: Routledge

Derrida, Jacques (1996), 'Remarks on Deconstruction and Pragmatism', in

Chantal Mouffe (ed.), *Deconstruction and Pragmatism*, London and New York: Routledge, pp. 77–88

Derrida, Jacques (1997), *Politics of Friendship*, London and New York: Verso

Dillon, Michael (1996), *Politics of Security. Towards a Political Philosophy of Continental Thought*, London and New York: Routledge

Doucet, Marc G. (1999), 'Standing Nowhere(?): Navigating the Third Route on the Question of Foundation in International Theory', *Millennium: Journal of International Studies* 28/2, pp. 289–310

Dyrberg, Torben Bech (1997), *The Circular Structure of Power. Politics, Identity, Community*, London and New York: Verso

Dyrberg, Torben Bech (2004), 'The Political and Politics in Discourse Analysis', in Oliver Marchart and Simon Critchley (eds), *Laclau: A Critical Reader*, London and New York: Routledge, pp. 241–55

Fairlamb, Horace L. (1994), *Critical Conditions. Postmodernity and the Question of Foundations*, Cambridge: Cambridge University Press

Farr, James (1989), 'Understanding Conceptual Change Politically', in Terence Ball and James Farr (eds), *Political Innovation and Conceptual Change*, New York and Melbourne: Cambridge University Press, pp. 24–49

Flynn, Bernard (1984), 'The Question of an Ontology of the Political: Arendt, Merleau-Ponty, Lefort', *International Studies in Philosophy* XVI/1, pp. 1–24

Flynn, Bernard (1992), *Political Philosophy at the Closure of Metaphysics*, New Jersey: Humanities Press

Freund, Julien (1965), *L'Essence du politique*, Paris: Sirey

Freund, Julien (1995), 'Schmitt's Political Thought', *Telos. A Quarterly Journal of Critical Thought* 102 (Winter), pp. 11–42

Frye, Charles E. (1966), 'Carl Schmitt's Concept of the Political', *The Journal of Politics*, 28/4, pp. 818–30

Fynsk, Christopher (1991), 'Foreword. Experiences of Finitude', in Jean-Luc Nancy: *The Inoperative Community*, Minneapolis: University of Minnesota Press, pp. vii–xxxv

Gasché, Rudolphe (1986), *The Tain of the Mirror. Derrida and the Philosophy of Reflection*, Cambridge, MA and London: Harvard University Press

Gasché, Rudolphe (1994), *Inventions of Difference. On Jacques Derrida*, Cambridge, MA: Harvard University Press

Gasché, Rudolphe (1999), *On Minimal Things. Studies on the Notion of Relation*, Stanford: Stanford University Press

Gauchet, Marcel (1976), 'L'Expérience totalitaire et la pensée du politique', *Esprit*, 7 (July–August), pp. 3–28

Gauchet, Marcel (1989), *La Révolution des droits de l'homme*, Paris: Gallimard

Gebert, Sigbert (1992), *Negative Politik. Zur Grundlegung der Politischen Philosophie aus der Daseinsanalytik und ihrer Bewährung in den Politischen Schriften Martin Heideggers von 1933/34*, Berlin: Duncker & Humblot, Philosophische Schriften, Vol. 7

Gilbert-Walsh, James (2000), 'Broken Imperatives. The Ethical Dimension of Nancy's Thought', *Philosophy & Social Criticism* 26/2, pp. 29–50

Hallward, Peter (1998), 'Generic Sovereignty. The Philosophy of Alain Badiou', *Angelaki* 3/3, pp. 87–111

Hallward, Peter (2002), 'Badiou's Politics: Equality and Justice', *Culture Machine*, 4, electronic document: http://culturemachine.tees.ac.uk/Articles/hallward.htm

Hallward, Peter (2003), *Badiou. A Subject to Truth*, Minneapolis: University of Minnesota Press

Hardt, Michael and Antonio Negri (2001), *Empire*, Cambridge, MA and London: Harvard University Press

Heidegger, Martin (1957a), *Der Satz vom Grund*, Stuttgart: Neske

Heidegger, Martin (1957b), *Identität und Differenz*, Stuttgart: Neske

Heidegger, Martin (1983), *Die Grundbegriffe der Metaphysik. Welt – Endlichkeit – Einsamkeit*, Frankfurt am Main: Vittorio Klostermann

Heidegger, Martin (1988), *Gelassenheit*, Pfullingen: Neske

Heidegger, Martin (1994), *Beiträge zur Philosophie (Vom Ereignis)*, Gesamtausgabe Vol. 65, Frankfurt am Main: Vittorio Klostermann

Heidegger, Martin (1996), *Wegmarken*, Frankfurt am Main: Vittorio Klostermann

Heidegger, Martin (1998), 'Basic Concepts', transl. by Gary E. Aylesworth, Bloomington and Indianapolis: Indiana University Press

Heidenheimer, Arnold J. (1986), 'Politics, Policy and Policey as Concepts in English and Continental Languages: An Attempt to Explain Divergences', *The Review of Politics* 48/1, pp. 3–30

Heller, Agnes (1991), 'The Concept of the Political Revisited', in David Held (ed.), *Poltical Theory Today*, Cambridge: Polity Press, pp. 330–43

Herzog, Don (1985), *Without Foundations. Justification in Political Theory*, Ithaca/London: Cornell University Press

Honig, Bonnie (1992), 'Toward an Agonistic Feminism: Hannah Arendt and the Politics of Identity', in Judith Butler and J. W. Scott (eds), *Feminists Theorize the Political*, New York and London: Routledge, pp. 215–35

Honig, Bonnie (1993), *Political Theory and the Displacement of Politics*, Ithaca and London: Cornell University Press

Howard, Dick (1988a), *The Marxian Legacy*, second edition, Minneapolis: University of Minnesota Press

Howard, Dick (1988b), *The Politics of Critique*, Minneapolis: University of Minnesota Press

Howard, Dick (1989), *Defining the Political*, London: Macmillan

Howard, Dick (1996), *Political Judgements*, Boston: Rowman and Littlefield

Howarth, David (1993), 'Reflections of the Politics of Space and Time', *Angelaki* 1/1, pp. 43–56

Janicaud, Dominique (2001), *Heidegger en France*, 2 vols, Paris: Bibliothèque Albin Michel

Kantorowicz, Ernst (1957), *The King's Two Bodies*, Princeton, NJ: Princeton University Press

Karatani, Kojin (1995), *Architecture as Metaphor. Language, Number, Money*, Cambridge, MA: MIT Press

Kemper, Peter (ed.) (1993), *Die Zukunft des Politischen: Theoretische Ausblicke auf Hannah Arendt*, Frankfurt am Main: Fischer

Kolb, David (1986), *The Critique of Pure Modernity. Hegel, Heidegger, and After*, Chicago and London: University of Chicago Press

Koselleck, Reinhart (1972), 'Einleitung', in Otto Brunner, Werner Conze and Reinhart Koselleck (eds): *Geschichtliche Grundbegriffe*, Vol. 1, Stuttgart: Klett, pp. xiii–xxvii

Koselleck, Reinhart (1973), *Kritik und Krise: Eine Studie zur Pathogenese der bürgerlichen Welt*, Freiburg/München: Karl Alber

Laclau, Ernesto (1989), 'Politics and the Limits of Modernity', in Andrew Ross (ed.), *Universal Abandon?*, Minneapolis: University of Minneapolis Press, pp. 63–82

Laclau, Ernesto (1990), *New Reflections on the Revolution of Our Time*, London and New York: Verso

Laclau, Ernesto (1994), 'Introduction', in Ernesto Laclau (ed.), *The Making of Political Identities*, New York and London: Verso, pp. 1–8

Laclau, Ernesto (1996a), *Emancipation(s)*, London and New York: Verso

Laclau, Ernesto (1996b), 'Deconstruction, Pragmatism, Hegemony', in Chantal Mouffe (ed.), *Deconstruction and Pragmatism*, London and New York: Routledge, pp. 47–68

Laclau, Ernesto (1999), 'Hegemony and the Future of Democracy: Ernesto Laclau's Political Philosophy', in Lynn Woshma and Gary S. Olson (eds), *Race, Rhetoric, and the Postcolonial*, Albany: SUNY Press, pp. 129–64

Laclau, Ernesto (2005), *On Populist Reason*, London and New York: Verso

Laclau, Ernesto and Chantal Mouffe (1985), *Hegemony and Socialist Strategy. Towards a Radical Democratic Politics*, London and New York: Verso

Laclau, Ernesto and Lilian Zack (1994), 'Minding the Gap: The Subject of Politics', in Ernesto Laclau (ed.), *The Making of Political Identities*, London and New York: Verso, pp. 11–39

Laclau, Ernesto, Slavoj Žižek and Judith Butler (2000), *Contingency, Hegemony, Universality. Contemporary Dialogue on the Left*, London and New York: Verso

Lacoue-Labarthe, Philippe (1989), 'Transcendence Ends in Politics', in *Typography*, Stanford: Stanford University Press, pp. 267–300

Lacoue-Labarthe, Philippe (1990), *Heidegger, Art and Politics*, Oxford and Cambridge, MA: Blackwell

Lacoue-Labarthe, Philippe and Jean-Luc Nancy (eds) (1981a), *Les Fins de l'homme: A partir du travail de Jacques Derrida*, Paris: Galilée

Lacoue-Labarthe, Philippe and Jean-Luc Nancy (eds) (1981b), *Rejouer le politique*, Paris: Galilée

Lacoue-Labarthe, Philippe and Jean-Luc Nancy (eds) (1983), *Le Retrait du politique*, Paris: Galilée

Lacoue-Labarthe, Philippe and Jean-Luc Nancy (1997), *Retreating the Political*, ed. by Simon Sparks, London and New York: Routledge

Lecercle, Jean-Jacques (1999), 'Cantor, Lacan, Mao, Beckett, *même combat*. The Philosophy of Alain Badiou', *Radical Philosophy* 93 (January–February), pp. 6–13

Lefort, Claude (1978), *Sur une colonne absente. Ecrits autour de Merleau-Ponty*, Paris: Gallimard

Lefort, Claude (1979), 'Préface', in *Eléments d'une critique de la bureaucratie*, second edition, Paris: Gallimard

Lefort, Claude (1986a), *The Political Forms of Modern Society. Bureaucracy, Democracy, Totalitarianism*, ed, by John B. Thompson, Cambridge, MA: MIT Press

Lefort, Claude (1986b), *Le Travail de l'uvre, Machiavel*, Paris: Gallimard

Lefort, Claude (1988), *Democracy and Political Theory*, Minneapolis: University of Minnesota Press

Lefort, Claude (1990), Machiavelli: History, Politics, Discourse, in David Carroll (ed.), *The State of Theory*, New York: Columbia University Press, pp. 113–24

Lefort, Claude (1998), *Die demokratische Gesellschaft ist keine Gesellschaft von Individuen. Vortrag anläßlich der Verleihung des Hannah-Arendt-Preises für politisches Denken*, Bremen, unpublished manuscript

Lefort, Claude (1999), *La Complication. Retour sur le communisme*. Paris: Fayard

Lefort, Claude (2000), *Writing. The Political Test*, Durham, NC and London: Duke University Press

Lefort, Claude and Marcel Gauchet (1971), 'Sur la démocratie: Le politique et l'institution du social', *Textures* pp. 2–3

Levinas, Emmanuel (1998), *Ethique comme philosophie première*, Paris: Editions Payot & Rivages

Luhmann, Niklas (1996), 'Complexity, Stuctural Contingencies and Value Conflicts', in Paul Heelas, Scott Lash and Paul Morris (eds.): *Detraditionalization*, Oxford: Blackwell, pp. 59–71

Mansbridge, Jane (1996), 'Using Power/Fighting Power: The Polity', in Seyla Benhabib (ed.), *Democracy and Difference. Contesting the Boundaries of the Political*, Princeton, NJ: Princeton University Press, pp. 46–66

Marchart, Oliver (1998), 'Gibt es eine Politik des Politischen? *Démocratie à venir* betrachtet von Clausewitz aus dem Kopfstand', in Oliver Marchart (ed.), *Das Undarstellbare der Politik. Zur Hegemonietheorie Ernesto Laclaus*, Vienna: Turia+Kant

Marchart, Oliver (1999), 'Zivilgesellschaftlicher Republikanismus: Lefort und Gauchet', in André Brodocz and Gary S. Schaal (eds), *Politische Theorien der Gegenwart. Eine Einführung*, Opladen: Leske & Budrich, pp. 119–142

Marchart, Oliver (2002a), 'On Drawing a Line. Politics and the Significatory Logic of Inclusion/Exclusion', *Soziale Systeme* 8/1, pp. 69–87

Marchart, Oliver (2002b), 'Enacting the Unrealized. Political Theory and the Role of Radical Democratic Activism', in Okwui Enwezor (ed.), *Democracy Unrealized*, Ostfildern: Hatje Cantz, pp. 253–66

Marchart, Oliver (2003), 'The Other Side of Order: Towards a Political Theory of Terror and Dislocation', *Parallax* 9/1, pp. 97–113

Marchart, Oliver (2004), 'Politics and the Ontological Difference. On the "Strictly Philosophical" in Laclau's Work', in Oliver Marchart and Simon Critchley (eds), *Laclau: A Critical Reader*, London and New York: Routledge, pp. 54–72

Marchart, Oliver (2005), *Neu Beginnen. Hannah Arendt, die Revolution und die Globalisierung*, Vienna: Turia+Kant

Marchart, Oliver (2006), 'The Absence at the Heart of Presence. Radical Democracy and the "Ontology of Lack"', in Lars Tonder and Lasse Thomassen (eds), *On Radical Democracy: Politics Between Abundance and Lack*, Manchester: Manchester University Press, pp. 17–31.

Massey, Doreen (1992), 'Politics and Space/Time', *New Left Review*, no.196 (November–December), pp. 65–84

Mattéi, Jean-François (1995), 'The Heideggerian Chiasmus or the *Setting Apart* of Philosophy', in Dominique Janicaud and Jean-François Mattéi, *Heidegger. From Metaphysics to Thought*, transl. by Michael Gendre, Albany: SUNY Press, pp. 39–150

McClure, Kirstie (1992), 'The Issue of Foundations: Scientized Politics, Politicized Science, and Feminist Critical Practice', in Judith Butler and J. W. Scott (eds), *Feminists Theorize the Political*, New York and London: Routledge, pp. 341–68

Merleau-Ponty, Maurice (1973), *The Prose of the World*, Evanston: Northwestern University Press

Meyer, Thomas (1994), *Die Transformation des Politischen*, Frankfurt am Main: Suhrkamp

Meyer, Thomas (2000), *Was ist Politik?*, München: Fink

Mouffe, Chantal (1993), *The Return of the Political*, London and New York: Verso

Mouffe, Chantal (1999), 'Introduction: Schmitt's Challenge', in Chantal

Mouffe (ed.), *The Challenge of Carl Schmitt*, London and New York: Verso, pp. 1–6

Mouffe, Chantal (2000), *The Democratic Paradox*, London and New York: Verso

Mouffe, Chantal (2005), *On the Political*: London and New York: Routledge

Müller, Jan (1997), 'Preparing for the Political: German Intellectuals Confront the "Berlin Republic" ', *New German Critique* 72, pp. 151–76

Nancy, Jean-Luc (1991), *The Inoperative Community*, Minneapolis: University of Minnesota Press

Nancy, Jean-Luc (1992), 'La Comparution/The Compearance. From the Existence of "Communism" to the Community of "Existence" ', *Political Theory*, 20/3 (August), pp. 371–398

Nancy, Jean-Luc (1993), *The Experience of Freedom*, Stanford: Stanford University Press

Nancy, Jean-Luc (1998), 'The Surprise of the Event', in Stuart Barnett (ed.), *Hegel after Derrida*, London and New York: Routledge, pp. 91–104

Nancy, Jean-Luc (2000), *Being Singular Plural*, Stanford: Stanford University Press

Negt, Oskar (1993), 'Zum Verständnis des Politischen bei Hannah Arendt', in Peter Kemper (ed), *Die Zukunft des Politischen. Ausblicke auf Hannah Arendt*, Frankfurt am Main: Fischer, pp. 55–68

Negt, Oskar and Alexander Kluge (1993), *Maßverhältnisse des Politischen: 15 Vorschläge zum Unterscheidungsvermögen*, Frankfurt am Main: Fischer

Neu, Daniela (1997), *Die Notwendigkeit der Gründung im Zeitalter der Dekonstruktion: zur Gründung in Heideggers 'Beiträgen zur Philosophie' unter Hinzuziehung der Derridaschen Dekonstruktion*, Philosophische Schriften, Vol. 20, Berlin: Duncker & Humblot

Norris, Andrew (2000), 'Jean-Luc Nancy and the Myth of the Common', *Constellations* 7/2, pp. 272–95

Oakeshott, Michael (1991), *Rationalism in Politics and Other Essays*, Indianapolis: Liberty Fund

O'Neill, Basil (1993), 'Truth as Fundamental or Truth as Foundational', in Hugh J. Silverman (ed.), *Questioning Foundations. Truth/Subjectivity/Culture*, London and New York: Routledge, pp. 29–43

Palonen, Kari (1985), *Politik als Handlungsbegriff. Horizontwandel des Politikbegriffs in Deutschland 1890–1933*, The Finnish Society of Sciences and Letters: Commentationes Scientiarium Socialium 28

Palonen, Kari (1989), *Die Thematisierung der Politik als Phänomen. Eine Interpretation der Geschichte des Begriffs Politik im Frankreich des 20. Jahrhunderts*, The Finnish Society of Sciences and Letters: Commentationes Scientiarium Socialium 38

Palonen, Kari (1993), 'Introduction: From Policy and Polity to Politicking and Politicization', in Kari Palonen and Tuija Parvikko (eds), *Reading the Political. Exploring the Margins of Politics*, The Finnish Political Science Association, pp. 6–16

Palonen, Kari (1998), *Das 'Webersche Moment'. Zur Kontingenz des Politischen*, Opladen: Westdeutscher Verlag

Palonen, Kari (1999a), *Politics as Activity. Toward a Rhetorical History of the (Re-)Conceptualization of a Concept*, paper given at the Conference of the History of Political and Social Concepts Group, Ecole Normale Supérieure de Fontenay-Saint-Cloud, typescript

Palonen, Kari (1999b), *The Englishman as a Political Animal? Preliminary Observations on the British Mode of Talking about Politics*, typescript

Pateman, Carole (1989), *The Disorder of Women. Democracy, Feminism and Political Theory*, Cambridge: Polity Press

Pitkin, Hannah Fenichel (1972), *Wittgenstein and Justice*, Berkeley and Los Angeles: University of California Press

Pitkin, Hannah Fenichel (1998), *The Attack of the Blob. Hannah Arendt's Concept of the Social*, Chicago and London: University of Chicago Press

Pocock, J. G. A. (1973), 'Verbalizing a Political Act: Toward a Politics of Speech', in *Political Theory*, 1/1, pp. 27–44

Pocock, J. G. A. (1975), *The Machiavellian Moment. Florentine Political Thought and the Atlantic Republican Tradition*, Princeton, NJ: Princeton University Press

Poltier, Hugues (1997), *La Découverte du politique*, Paris: Michalon

Poltier, Hugues (1998), *Passion du politique. La Pensée de Claude Lefort*, Geneva: Labor et Fides

Rancière, Jacques (1995a), 'Politics, Identification, and Subjectivization', in John Rajchman (ed.), *The Identity in Question*, London and New York: Routledge, pp. 63–72

Rancière, Jacques (1995b), *On the Shores of Politics*, London and New York: Verso

Rancière, Jacques (1999), *Disagreement. Politics and Philosophy*, Minneapolis: University of Minnesota Press

Rasch, William (1997), 'Locating the Political: Schmitt, Mouffe, Luhmann, and the Possibility of Pluralism', *International Journal of Sociology – Revue Internationale de Sociologie* 7/1, pp. 103–15

Rasch, William (2002), 'A Completely New Politics, or, Excluding the Political?', *Soziale Systeme* 8/1, pp. 38–53

Reid, Michael (1994), 'The Aims of Radicalism', *Angelaki* 1/3, pp. 183–5

Revault d'Allonnes, Myriam (1998), 'Qui a peur de la politique? Réponse à Alain Badiou', in *Esprit* 12 (December), pp. 236–42

Revault d'Allonnes, Myriam (1999), *Le Dépérissement de la politique. Généalogie d'un lieu commun*, Paris: Flammarion

Richir, Marc (1991), *Du Sublime en politique*, Paris: Editions Payot

Ricœur, Paul (1964), *Histoire et vérité*, Paris: Editions du Seuil

Ricœur, Paul (1965), 'The Political Paradox', in *History and Truth*, Evanston: Northwestern University Press, pp. 247–70

Ricœur, Paul (1998), *Critique and Conviction. Conversations with François Azouvi and Marc de Launay*, London: Polity Press

Rorty, Richard (1979), *Philosophy and the Mirror of Nature*, Princeton: Princeton University Press

Rorty, Richard (1989), *Contingency, Irony, and Solidarity*, New York: Cambridge University Press

Rosanvallon, Pierre (2003), *Pour une histoire conceptuelle du politique*, Paris: Editions du Seuil

Rubinstein, Nicolai (1987), 'The History of the Word *Politicus* in Early-Modern Europe', in Anthony Pagden (ed.), *The Language of Political Theory in Early-Modern Europe*, New York and Melbourne: Cambridge University Press, pp. 41–56

Sallis, John (2001), 'Grounders of the Abyss', in Ch. E. Scott, S. M. Schoenbohm, D. Vallega-Neu and A. Vallega (eds), *Companion to Heidegger's* Contribution to Philosophy, Bloomington and Indeanapolis: Indiana University Press, pp. 181–97

Sartori, Giovanni (1973), 'What is "Politics" ', *Political Theory* 1/1, pp. 5–26

Schmitt, Carl (1963), Der Begriff des Politischen, Berlin: Duncker & Humblodt

Schmitt, Carl (1993), 'The Age of Neutralizations and Depoliticizations', *Telos. A Quarterly Journal of Critical Thought* 96 (Summer), pp. 130–42

Schmitt, Carl (1996), *The Concept of the Political*, London and Chicago: University of Chicago Press

Schürmann, Reiner (1990), *Heidegger. On Being and Acting: From Principles to Anarchy*, Bloomington: Indiana University Press

Schwab, George (1996), 'Introduction', in Carl Schmitt, *The Concept of the Political*, London and Chicago: University of Chicago Press, pp. 3–16

Sellin, Volker (1978), 'Politik', in Otto Brunner (ed.), *Geschichtliche Grundbegriffe*, Vol. 4, Stuttgart: Klett, pp. 789–874

Skinner, Quentin (1988), 'Some Problems in the Analysis of Political Thought and Action', in James Tully (ed.), *Meaning and Context. Quentin Skinner and his Critics*, Cambridge: Polity Press, pp. 197–8

Skinner, Quentin (1989), 'Language and Political Change', in Terence Ball and James Farr (eds), *Political Innovation and Conceptual Change*, New York and Melbourne: Cambridge University Press, pp. 6–23

Sparks, Simon (1997), 'Editor's Introduction: Politica Ficta', in Philippe Lacoue-Labarthe and Jean-Luc Nancy, *Retreating the Political*, ed. by Simon Sparks, London and New York: Routledge, pp. xiv–xxviii

Spivak, Gayatri (1993), 'Foundations and Cultural Studies', in Hugh J. Silverman (ed.), *Questioning Foundations. Truth/Subjectivity/Culture*, New York and London: Routledge, pp. 153–75

Stavrakakis, Yannis (1999), *Lacan & the Political*, London and New York: Routledge

Thompson, John B. (1986), 'Editor's Introduction', in Claude Lefort, *The Political Forms of Modern Society. Bureaucracy, Democracy, Totalitarianism*, ed. by John B. Thompson, Cambridge, MA: MIT Press, pp. 1–27

Torfing, Jacob (1999), *New Theories of Discourse. Laclau, Mouffe and Žižek*, Oxford: Blackwell

Tully, James (1988), 'The pen is a mighty sword: Quentin Skinner's analysis of politics', in James Tully (ed.), *Meaning and context. Quentin Skinner and his critics*, Cambridge: Polity Press, pp. 7–28

Villa, Dana R. (1996), *Arendt and Heidegger. The Fate of the Political*, Princeton, NJ: Princeton University Press

Viroli, Maurizio (1992), 'The Revolution in the Concept of Politics', *Political Theory* 20/3, pp. 473–95

Vollrath, Ernst (1987), 'The "rational" and the "political". An Essay in the Semantics of Politics', *Philosophy and Social Criticism* 13/1, pp. 17–29

Vollrath, Ernst (1989), 'Politisch, das Politische', in J. Ritter, K. Gründer (eds), *Historisches Wörterbuch der Philosophie*, Basel: Schwabe & Co., pp. 1071–5

Vollrath, Ernst (1993), 'Hannah Arendts Kritik der politischen Urteilskraft"', in Peter Kemper (ed.), *Die Zukunft des Politischen. Ausblicke auf Hannah Arendt*, Frankfurt am Main: Fischer, pp. 34–54

Vollrath, Ernst (1995), 'Hannah Arendt: A German-American Jewess Views the United States – and Looks Back to Germany', in Peter Graf Kielmansegg, Horst Mewes and Elisabeth Glaser-Schmidt (eds), *Hannah Arendt and Leo Strauss. German Emigrés and American Political Thought After World War II*, Cambridge: Cambridge University Press, pp. 45–60

White, Stephen K. (2000), *Sustaining Affirmation. The Strengths of Weak Ontology in Political Theory*, Princeton and Oxford: Princeton University Press

Wigley, Mark (1995), *The Architecture of Deconstruction. Derrida's Haunt*, Cambridge, MA and London: MIT Press

Williams, James (2000), *Lyotard & the Political*, London and New York: Routledge

Williams, Raymond (1983), *Keywords: A Vocabulary of Culture and Society*, London: Fontana

Wolin, Richard (2001), *Heidegger's Children. Hannah Arendt, Karl Löwith, Hans Jonas, and Herbert Marcuse*, Princeton, NJ: Princeton University Press

Wolin, Sheldon (1960), *Politics and Vision. Continuity and Innovation in Western Political Thought*, Boston: Little, Brown & Co.

Wolin, Sheldon (1990), 'Hannah Arendt: Democracy and the Political', in Reuben Garner (ed.), *The Realm of Humanitas. Responses to the Writing of Hannah Arendt*, New York, Bern, Frankfurt, Paris: Peter Lang, pp. 167–86

Wolin, Sheldon (1996), 'Fugitive Democracy', in Seyla Benhabib (ed.), *Democracy and Difference. Contesting the Boundaries of the Political*, Princeton, NJ: Princeton University Press, pp. 31–45

Yar, Majid (2000), 'Arendt's Heideggerianism, Contours of a "Postmetaphysical" Political Theory?', *Cultural Values* 4/1 (January), pp. 18–39

Žižek, Slavoj (1990), 'Beyond Discourse-Analysis', in Ernesto Laclau: *New Reflections on the Revolution of Our Time*, London and New York: Verso, pp. 249–60

Žižek, Slavoj (1991), *For They Know Not What They Do. Enjoyment as a Political Factor*, London and New York: Verso

Žižek, Slavoj (1999a), *The Ticklish Subject. The Absent Centre of Political Ontology*, London and New York: Verso

Žižek, Slavoj (1999b), 'Carl Schmitt in the Age of Post-Politics', in Chantal Mouffe (ed.), *The Challenge of Carl Schmitt*, London and New York: Verso, pp. 18–37

Index